Democratic Education and the Public Sphere

This book considers John Dewey's philosophy of democratic education and his theory of public sphere from the perspective of the reconstruction and redefinition of the dominant liberalist movement. By bridging art education and the public sphere, and drawing upon contemporary mainstream philosophies, Ueno urges reconceptualization of mainstream liberalism in education and indicates innovative visions for the public sphere of education.

Focusing on Dewey's theory of aesthetic education as an origin of the construction of public sphere, this book explores his art education practices and involvement in the Barnes Foundation of Philadelphia clarifying the process of school reform based on democratic practice. Dewey searched for an alternative approach to public sphere and education by reimagining the concept of educational right from a political and ethical perspective, generating a collaborative network of learning activities and bringing imaginative meaning to human life and interaction. This book proposes educational visions for democracy and public sphere in light of pragmatism aesthetic theory and practice.

Democratic Education and the Public Sphere will be key reading for academics, researchers and postgraduate students in the fields of philosophy of education, curriculum theory, art education and educational policy and politics. The book will also be of interest to policy makers and politicians who are engaged in educational reform.

Masamichi Ueno is Associate Professor of Education at Daito Bunka University, Japan. He received his PhD in Education from the University of Tokyo. He has previously served as Visiting Associate Professor at the University of British Columbia, Visiting Scholar at the University of Luxembourg and International Scholar at Shanghai Normal University, and currently works as Visiting Professor at University of Jinan, China.

New Directions in the Philosophy of Education Series

Series Editors

Michael A. Peters, *University of Waikato, New Zealand; University of Illinois, USA*

Gert Biesta, *Brunel University London, UK*

This book series is devoted to the exploration of new directions in the philosophy of education. After the linguistic turn, the cultural turn and the historical turn, where might we go? Does the future promise a digital turn with a greater return to connectionism, biology and biopolitics based on new understandings of system theory and knowledge ecologies? Does it foreshadow a genuinely alternative radical global turn based on a new openness and inter-connectedness? Does it leave humanism behind or will it reengage with the question of the human in new and unprecedented ways? How should philosophy of education reflect new forces of globalization? How can it become less Anglocentric and develop a greater sensitivity to other traditions, languages and forms of thinking and writing, including those that are not rooted in the canon of Western philosophy but in other traditions that share the "love of wisdom" that characterizes the wide diversity within Western philosophy itself. Can this be done through a turn to intercultural philosophy? To indigenous forms of philosophy and philosophizing? Does it need a post-Wittgensteinian philosophy of education? A postpostmodern philosophy? Or should it perhaps leave the whole construction of "post"-positions behind?

In addition to the question of the intellectual resources for the future of philosophy of education, what are the issues and concerns with which philosophers of education should engage? How should they position themselves? What is their specific contribution? What kind of intellectual and strategic alliances should they pursue? Should philosophy of education become more global, and if so, what would the shape of that be? Should it become more cosmopolitan or perhaps more decentred? Perhaps most importantly in the digital age, the time of the global knowledge economy that re-profiles education as privatized human capital and simultaneously in terms of an historic openness, is there a philosophy of education that grows out of education itself, out of the concerns for new forms of teaching, studying, learning and speaking that can provide comment on ethical and epistemological configurations of economics and politics of knowledge? Can and should this imply a reconnection with questions of democracy and justice?

This series comprises texts that explore, identify and articulate new directions in the philosophy of education. It aims to build bridges, both geographically and temporally: bridges across different traditions and practices and bridges towards a different future for philosophy of education.

In this series

On Study
Giorgio Agamben and educational potentiality
Tyson E. Lewis

Education, Experience and Existence
Engaging Dewey, Peirce and Heidegger
John Quay

African Philosophy of Education Reconsidered
On being human
Yusef Waghid

Buber and Education
Dialogue as conflict resolution
W. John Morgan and Alexandre Guilherme

Henri Lefebvre and Education
Space, history, theory
Sue Middleton

Thomas Jefferson's Philosophy of Education
A utopian dream
M. Andrew Holowchak

Edusemiotics
Semiotic philosophy as educational foundation
Andrew Stables and Inna Semetsky

Childhood, Education and Philosophy
New ideas for an old relationship
Walter Kohan

Between Truth and Freedom
Rousseau and our contemporary political and educational culture
Kenneth Wain

Democratic Education and the Public Sphere
Towards John Dewey's theory of aesthetic experience
Masamichi Ueno

Democratic Education and the Public Sphere

Towards John Dewey's theory
of aesthetic experience

Masamichi Ueno

Routledge
Taylor & Francis Group

LONDON AND NEW YORK

First published 2016
by Routledge
2 Park Square, Milton Park, Abingdon, Oxon OX14 4RN

and by Routledge
711 Third Avenue, New York, NY 10017

Routledge is an imprint of the Taylor & Francis Group, an informa business

© 2016 M. Ueno

This work is an adaption and translation of a previously published work in Japanese:
学校の公共性と民主主義　デューイの美的経験論へ 2010
by University of Tokyo Press.

Translation to English by Masamichi Ueno.

British Library Cataloguing in Publication Data
A catalogue record for this book is available from the British Library

Library of Congress Cataloging in Publication Data
A catalog record for this book has been requested

ISBN: 978-1-138-83282-4 (hbk)
ISBN: 978-1-315-73576-4 (ebk)

Typeset in Bembo
by Florence Production Ltd, Stoodleigh, Devon, UK

MIX
Paper from
responsible sources
FSC® C013604
www.fsc.org

Printed and bound by CPI Group (UK) Ltd, Croydon, CR0 4YY

Contents

Foreword

Over the past decades the scholarship on John Dewey has significantly changed. Whereas in the 1970s and 1980s authors such as Richard Rorty and Richard J. Bernstein had to push hard in order for Dewey's thoughts to be taken seriously, Dewey's work is nowadays clearly "back" on the intellectual map, as is evidenced in the large number of publications that have appeared on his work from the 1980s onwards. Those who fear that the field of Dewey scholarship has become a little crowded, and that it may have become difficult to say anything new about Dewey, will be encouraged by reading Masamichi Ueno's book *Democratic Education and the Public Sphere: Towards John Dewey's theory of aesthetic experience*, as it advances Dewey scholarship in a number of ways.

One important quality of the book is that it provides a thorough account of Dewey's critique of liberalism and his democratic reconstruction of the public sphere. It does so at two levels: by carefully reconstructing Dewey's ideas and by placing them within the wider socio-political context in which these ideas emerged, particularly with regard to ongoing discussions about the role and status of the school and of education more generally. In this way Ueno not only shows how Dewey's ideas developed but also generates insights into the particular discussions in which Dewey sought to intervene, thus showing how Dewey's ideas "made sense" in relation to these discussions. A second distinctive quality of the book is the way in which Ueno shows the connections between democracy, the public sphere and the aesthetic dimension, again through a reconstruction of Dewey's ideas and a detailed discussion of Dewey's work with the Barnes Foundation. By showing the aesthetic dimension in Dewey's views about democracy and the public sphere both at the level of theory and the level of educational practice, Ueno offers a refreshingly new angle on questions about education, democracy and the public sphere and follows lines not previously pursued.

In addition to the fact that Ueno's writing is extremely well informed about the details of what happened in the United States during this period of time – which also indicates that this book is also a contribution to the historiography of Dewey – it is also important to highlight that Ueno writes about these developments as an "outsider" looking in. This quality is particularly visible in the way in which he positions the content of the book within wider discussions about democracy and the public sphere, engaging both with Western and Eastern scholarship. It is fortunate, in our view, that Ueno did not feel obliged to draw particular lessons from his explorations, particularly not lessons for "the present." Rather the book provides original insights and carefully crafted arguments that will allow readers to draw their own conclusions about the interconnections between art, democratic education and the public sphere.

Gert Biesta and Michael A. Peters
February 2015

Acknowledgements

Foremost, I would like to acknowledge that the insights presented in this volume stem from my areas of interest, including education, art, democracy and the public sphere, which I have studied throughout the past decade. This book focuses on John Dewey's theory of democratic education and the public sphere in terms of redefining the dominant liberalism of his time and associates his attempts to reconstruct traditional notions with the idea of aesthetic experience. My concerns about Dewey's educational theory were developed in my Japanese book, *The Publicness of Schools and Democracy: Toward John Dewey's Theory of Aesthetic Experience* (University of Tokyo Press, 2010), which constitutes the basis of this book.

My efforts could not have been realized without the support and assistance of my mentors, colleagues, friends and editors. I have learned a great deal from participating in conferences, seminars and meetings, and have been inspired by communication and discussions with people from around the world.

First, I would like to thank Gert Biesta and Michael A. Peters for introducing and encouraging me to join this very exciting project in the series *New Directions in the Philosophy of Education*. I am incredibly grateful to Biesta for accepting me as a Visiting Scholar at the University of Luxembourg, and for allowing me the privilege of taking part in inspiring discussions in the summer of 2013 and spring of 2014. I have gained enormous perspective through dialogue with Biesta.

I extend my deepest gratitude to Manabu Sato, my advisor during my graduate student years at the University of Tokyo, for guiding me towards researching Dewey's philosophy of education. I would like to convey my particular thanks to Larry A. Hickman, Yasuo Imai, Shigeo Kodama, Osamu Kanamori, Kensuke Goto and my colleagues at Daito Bunka University for their fruitful suggestions and cooperation. I would also like to thank the Museum of Modern Art, New York/Scala, Florence and Special Collections Research Center, Morris Library, Southern Illinois University Carbondale for providing the images of John Dewey by Henri Matisse, and John Dewey and Albert C. Barnes, respectively. Moreover, I extend my gratitude to both organizations for giving me the permission to use these images. Most of all, I appreciate the untiring support given by Routledge, particularly by editors

Clare Ashworth, Emily Bedford, Sophie Shanahan and Kristin Susser, and Annabelle Forty at Florence Production, in helping this book to reach completion. Finally, I wish to thank all of the people who, in one way or another, supported me along the path of accomplishing this book.

I dedicate this book to my family, Miki, Hanae and Mizuka, to whom I owe more than I can express.

Prologue

A Perspective to Democratic Education and the Public Sphere

Educational Reform and the Public Sphere in the Contemporary Age

The question of how democratic education and the public sphere can be developed is actively discussed in the contemporary age. Since the 1980s, the neoliberal concept of educational reform has had a dominant influence on the conceptualization of the public sphere in many countries, including the US, UK and Japan. This faction has introduced the marketization of education through an expansion of school choices and competition, inheriting the laissez-faire liberalism of the nineteenth century, which minimized government intervention in the market realm, and criticizing the welfare state of liberal democracy, the foundation of which was built from the 1930s. At the same time, this movement has strengthened the conservative movement by promoting patriotism and common culture. On the other hand, the global depression stemming from the economic crisis in 2008 has prompted the reorganization of a social and political system driven by the marketization of neoliberalism, and a reappraisal of the New Deal of President Roosevelt, who advanced governmental control during the Great Depression in the 1930s.

The neoliberalism of the 1980s accelerated the policy of small government, which aimed for balanced finances, the reduction of welfare and public services, and privatization and deregulation in response to the accumulation of a budget deficit, which had become inflated under the welfare state of liberal democracy that developed from the 1930s. In the US, Milton Friedman, who criticized New Deal liberalism and upheld laissez-faire liberalism in the nineteenth century, advocated for the introduction of the market principle of school choice and competition. Friedman argued that parents should receive school vouchers, which were state-funded tuition coupons for their children to attend private schools rather than neighbouring public schools.[1] His theory formed the basis of the economic policy of the Reagan Administration in the 1980s, and offered the theoretical foundation for the introduction of the Education Voucher in Milwaukee (1990), Cleveland (1996), Florida (1999) and other cities.

Moreover, this trend has also prompted the establishment of Charter Schools: parents, local residents and teachers manage and administer these schools by gaining public financial support. Charter Schools, also called "a new type of school," are privately administered schools built by the public sector, in which a private sector acquires special approval of a "charter," hires teachers and staff and is in charge of management. The concept was initially proposed at the conference of the American Federation of Teachers in the 1980s, and the number of schools has tended to increase over time, starting when Minnesota enacted the Charter School Law in 1991. In addition, the reform of marketization, through such changes as standardized testing, accountability and school choice, was set forth in the No Child Left Behind Act of 2001 and the Race to the Top programme in the 2010s.

Neoliberal policies also became the driving force of educational reform in Japan from the 1980s onwards. The policies proposed from 1984 to 1987 by the Ad Hoc Council on Education, an advisory body to then Prime Minister Yasuhiro Nakasone, aimed to individualize and liberalize education, and the Council set precedents in preparing for and promoting market competition through deregulation. In fact, reforms since the 1990s have promoted devolution from the state to the private sector. As seen in the promotion of the school choice system, the establishment of elite combined junior and senior high schools, the introduction of the competition principle through external evaluation of schools, moves to introduce the educational voucher system and Japanese-style Charter Schools, implementation of nationwide academic testing, reform of the Fundamental Law on Education, and reform of the Board of Education and teacher training systems, educational reform has been directed at expanding the market principle as well as reinforcing neoconservative reforms, such as the cultivation of "patriotism." Furthermore, at present a series of policies are being pushed forward with even more force, which is seen in the proposal to nurture a "zest for life" in a knowledge-based society, with focus on practice-orientated abilities, and to develop global human resources that can excel in international society. The doctrine of neoliberalism that uses market regulations such as competition and choice as its guideline has been a core principle in exercising significant influence on today's educational reforms.

Faced with this situation in education, should we advance the principles of neoliberalism, or convert to a New Deal type of governmental intervention? Or are there any alternatives to these two choices? Is democratic education truly effective in creating a public sphere in this changing society? If so, how can we open the door to providing a concrete vision of democratic education? Being in the watershed of change in various political spectrums, the answer to the question above on education and the public sphere will form the key policy issues that will be indispensable for orienting education in the near future. This question has raised the necessity of reflecting upon the political agenda that has been thrown into sharp relief by the series of educational reforms undertaken since the 1980s. At the same time, forming a reply to this question will be accompanied by a reconstruction of the relationship between liberalism and democracy, which has served for a long time as a driving force in US politics, society and education, and by the conversion of the historical and conceptual paradigm of the public and private spheres. Raymond Geuss has mentioned that we should not stick to "the public/private distinction" by separating them strictly and absolutely, but that we need to connect them to a "concrete context of human action, probably human political action." It might be worthwhile noting that his perspective offers a critical viewpoint to the premise of liberalism, that democracy can essentially be linked to the notions of human rights, the market or state without any contradictions.[2]

In this book, I will consider John Dewey's theory of democratic education and the public sphere that is connected with art education, in terms of both the criticism and reconstruction of liberalism in the 1920s and 1930s, and clarify his innovative vision of bringing about democratic processes and practices in education through the recreation of aesthetic experience. More specifically, I will explicate the deployment process of Dewey's educational theory during the above-mentioned era, when American society was experiencing the transformation of liberalism from laissez-faire to the New Deal.[3] In this period, Dewey publisheded numerous books and articles, such as *Human Nature and Conduct* (1922),[4] *Experience and Nature* (1925),[5] *The Public and Its Problems* (1927),[6] *Art as Experience* (1934)[7] and *Liberalism and Social Action* (1935).[8] I will discuss his concept of the "public sphere" as a critical realm of liberalism by extracting it from his notions of "the public," "public action," "public concern" and others, and describe a comprehensive theoretical framework and practice of education in connection with democracy and art. He attempted to emancipate the potentialities of democracy from the fetters of dominant liberalism, and was engaged in innovative school reform by defining democracy as "a way of life" and bringing "aesthetic experience" to the ground of the public sphere. The concepts of democracy and public sphere were practised in the art education project of the Barnes Foundation, in which Dewey was deeply involved.

Why, in the era of globalization in the twenty-first century, do we need to pay attention to Dewey's educational theory of the 1920s and 1930s? There exists the necessity now to open new strategies for reconstructing democratic education and the public sphere through the application of his theory, practice and policy in the historical context of the formation of liberal democracy in the 1920s and 1930s, which followed a post-war welfare state, to aid in the acquisition of a critical and expansive horizon that transcends the alternatives of current neoliberalism or New Deal liberalism. While encountering the present need for the advancement of educational reform, a re-examination of Dewey's theory of democratic education and the public sphere shows that it is a theory of significant importance for consideration in the age of globalization in the twenty-first century.

The Public Sphere as a Critique of Liberalism

It can be understood from Dewey's theory of liberalism that the root of American liberalism has been discussed from an angle centring on the influence of the concept of "rights" developed by John Locke. The interpretation of

Locke's political philosophy as one of the foundations of the country has been found in historical research on the US. As represented by Carl Lotus Becker's *The Declaration of Independence* (1922)[9] and Louis Hartz's *The Liberal Tradition in America* (1955),[10] conventional historical studies have tended to consider the consequences of Locke's philosophy on the American Revolution. According to Hartz, who was influenced by Alexis de Tocqueville's work, "the great advantage of the American" is that "he has arrived at a state of democracy without having to endure a democratic revolution." Hartz observed that the root of American liberalism lies in the fact that people had presupposed Locke's idea of "a natural law" and "a natural state," since they were seen as being born in a free and equal society.[11]

On the other hand, numerous studies that emphasize the connection between the American Revolution and republicanism were published a quarter of a century after Hartz's work. Furthermore, current research tends to pay attention to the relation between Locke's theory and the dominant political philosophy of the US, by exceeding the theoretical confrontation of whether that philosophy after the 1990s was liberal or conservative. At this point, the influence of Hartz' theory depleted, and it came to be more popular for the historians to discuss how the concepts of "rights," "consent" and "contract" stressed by Locke had an impact on the American Revolution.[12]

Another school of thought that has affected the development of liberalism in the US, along with Locke's philosophy, was nineteenth-century liberalism which promoted a laissez-faire economy and whose tradition derived from the classical economics of Adam Smith, and then Herbert Spencer's theory of social evolution. For Dewey, the theoretical genealogy that considered the market as a naturally autonomous, spontaneous and pre-established harmonious space was linked to the theory of social evolution that embraced the ideas of the "survival of the fittest" and "natural selection," which prompted the governmental deregulation and legitimization of a laissez-faire market of free competition among economic entities. As a matter of fact, Friedman supported the theories of Adam Smith and laissez-faire marketization.

The educational discourses on neoliberalism from the 1980s applied Friedman's theory and criticized the welfare state policy that was built in the progressive era of the first half of the twentieth century. For instance, Terry M. Moe of the Brookings Institute and John E. Chubb of Stanford University, who took an initiative on the topic of school choice in *Politics, Markets, and America's Schools* (1990), defended the market realm as a free and natural space, while criticizing progressive educational reforms as the cause of the national and bureaucratic control of the school. They appealed for a shift in the jurisdiction of school education to a market realm that is made into a natural space and freed from bureaucratic administration, which was seen as an artificial control. They promoted the market control of public education, in which parents and children are able to choose attractive schools according to their various needs and preferences, by introducing a school choice system and the deregulation of the school district.[13] Current neoliberalism represented by

Friedman, and Chubb and Moe, has set the welfare state of liberal democracy, ranging from progressivism and the New Deal to post-war Keynesian economics, as the object of criticism. Contrary to the liberal democratic tradition, they have developed a theory that will make nineteenth-century liberalism a model for the society. Thus, liberalism has historically provided a theoretical foundation for the discussion of education.

On the other hand, Dewey attempted to construct an alternative vision to traditional liberalism of the market and welfare states by designing an innovative form of democracy and public sphere inspired by the connection and network of trust among people. He envisioned a concept of the public sphere in sight of cooperative activity and face-to-face communication in communities through the public's participation. In his understanding, the theory of traditional liberalism, which had individualistic and naturalistic ideals in mind, led to an undermining of cooperative association and community. Meanwhile, Dewey aimed to build "democracy as a way of living together" through forming the public's interactive communication in the politics and ethics of the public sphere. In *Liberalism and Social Action*, Dewey articulated that "the first object of a renascent liberalism" that is "radical" was found in "education."[14] He was dedicated to connecting democratic education to the creation of the public sphere. His innovative vision was practised in the art education project at the Barnes Foundation in Merion, a suburb of Philadelphia. Dewey devoted a great deal of energy to developing the art education project by promoting cooperative networks with various agencies along with Albert C. Barnes, a founder of the Barnes Foundation. Dewey's theory of democratic education and the public sphere was closely related to the reconstruction of aesthetic experiences.

Conceptions of the Public Sphere

A brief overview and comparison of the conceptions of the public sphere in the present age would be effective when we discuss Dewey's public philosophy. The discussion involving the notion of the public sphere was brought into the limelight in the field of education through the introduction of the public theories of Jürgen Habermas and Hannah Arendt. An original meaning of the Latin term *res publica* is "public affair," in which *publica* derives from "populous;" and the word *publicus*, the root of the word "public," generally means "of the people" or "open for all," which constitutes the notion of the public in Western histories. But in the tradition of East Asian countries, the term "public" tended to be recognized as a realm of feudal authority or state administration associated with dominance and encompassing "the private." On the other hand, the idea of "the public" that represents human interaction and communication between different social and cultural backgrounds has not yet been fully developed. Because of these factors, the theories of Habermas and Arendt provided a new framework and prospect for discussing the concept of the public sphere.

Habermas, who succeeded the first generation of Frankfurt School figures such as Theodor Adorno and Max Horkheimer, examined the rise and decline of the "public sphere" based on liberalism, by introducing the concept of "communicative action" in the "lifeworld." In *The Structural Transformation of the Public Sphere* (1962), Habermas criticized the administrative state intervention into "civil society" under the late capitalism of the 1870s as the "colonization of lifeworld by systems," defending the notion that the "bourgeois public sphere" had been brought about by the emancipation of rational-critical discourse and communication, and had checked the arbitrary domination of administrative states or illegitimate uses of political powers. The discursive and debating political arenas, such as Britain's coffeehouses, France's salons and German's reading clubs, which emerged in the eighteenth and early nineteenth century, became models for the "bourgeois public sphere." However, they were exposed to crisis due to a degenerative transition from "a culture-debating to culture-consuming public," which took place accompanied by an expansion of the mass media and cultural industries in the middle of the nineteenth century.

The model of the "public sphere" that Habermas proposed was a discursive sphere that aimed to reach a rational consensus by citizens of the bourgeois and was founded on the theory of nineteenth-century liberalism that distinguished a "civil society" from an undercurrent state. In the second edition of *The Structural Transformation of the Public Sphere*, Habermas developed his argument of the "public sphere" by emphasizing the "civil society" as an associative space that is independent of both "a state" and "a market." What is important in his view is that "civil society" comprises "non-governmental and non-economic connections and voluntary associations" such as churches, cultural associations, academies, independent media, sports and leisure clubs, debating societies, groups of concerned citizens, grassroots petitioning drives, occupational associations, political parties, labour unions and alternative institutions.[15] Moreover, his recent theory deserves attention in that it aims to cultivate a new form of "public sphere" through building a normative arena of "a constitutional democracy" mediated by "discourse ethics."[16]

A philosophy of the public according to Hannah Arendt is also thought-provoking, considering the footprints of her experiences: she had fled to the US because of persecution by the Nazis during World War II. In *The Human Condition* (1958), Arendt defines three fundamental categories of human activities: "labour," "work" and "action." According to her distinction, whereas "labour" is the cyclical and biological process of maintaining human life and "work" is concerned with a fabricated production following the means/end rationale, wherein humans act as "what" they are rather than "who" they are, "action" is not "a space of representation," but "a space of appearance" in which individuals realize their freedom through public action. The public realm guided by human "action" and "appearance" is characterized as the "plurality" of unique individuals, and created by the constitution of "a common world." Arendt conceives of the ancient Greek polis as the prototype of the public realm, while criticizing an emergence of "the social" dominated by the private realm in contemporary life. According to her, the public realm is a space of ephemeral "in-between" of human interaction that generates "the 'web' of human relationship."[17]

Another interesting topic that Arendt raises is the concept of "the banality of evil" discussed in *Eichmann in Jerusalem* (1963). From the hearings of the trial of Adolf Eichmann (1961), who had been in charge of the persecution and execution of millions of Jews as a Nazi officer during World War II, Arendt maintained that Eichmann seemed "an average man" to observe the law of the Third Reich, contrary to the exaggerated expectation by the prosecutor and public who desired to testify his monstrous cruelty and brutality. Arendt believed that human "evil" is not something we are equipped with fundamentally, but is an ordinary and banal thing that results from the "inability to think" and "judge."[18] Her conception of "the banality of evil" was linked with a discussion on the decline of the public realm. The public realm, according to her, is not a space that encompasses the private realm as a dominant concept, but a space related to the "in-between" that activates the political and social interaction of the plurality of human beings. Yet, her theory has a limitation, since it is not sufficient in offering a concrete vision regarding an organization of public and economic policies.[19]

Richard Sennett's book *The Fall of Public Man* (1974) is a masterpiece that sketched out a decline of "the public realm" by the expansion of "the intimate society" centring on a private life in the nineteenth century. According to Sennett, who studied under David Riesman and Erik H. Erikson, the public realm was identified by the spaces of squares, streets, parks, theatres and cafes in cities in the eighteenth century. In both London and Paris, the coffee house became an "information center" where the public gained knowledge and exchanged opinions through talking, until the 1750s when parks and streets became spaces where "strangers" spoke to each other without embarrassment, and places of "sociability between classes." Sennett regarded London as "a society in which stage and streets were 'literally' intermixed" and Paris as a city where men were forced to "behave like actors in order to be sociable with each other." At that stage in the 1750s, there were not only actors but numerous spectators – young and members of upper ranks – who had seats on the stage, and these "gay bloods" paraded across the stage as the mood took them; they waved to their friends in the box; they felt no embarrassment in expressing their emotions directly when they were touched. In the market could be seen landscapes of "everyday theater in a city," wherein sellers and buyers went through "all kinds of theatrics to up or lower the price" in accordance with the change of the retail price.

On the other hand, Sennett stated that "the end of public culture" is caused by "the tyrannies of intimacy," which derive from "narcissism" and "destructive gemeinschaft." That is, while the entrance of "personality" to "the public realm" was permitted in the eighteenth century, oppression of the "personality in public" became dominant in the nineteenth century. Although "a few skilled performers" continued to express themselves actively as "professionals," a mass of people became "spectators" who did not participate in "public life," even if they were touched by the performances of great politicians or musicians. By the 1850s, "a 'respectable' audience" was "an audience that could control its feelings through silence," since "restraint of emotion in the theater became a way for middle-class audiences to mark the line between themselves and the working class." Whereas in eighteenth-century opera the audience demanded a singer to sing a particular phrase or beautiful note again immediately if they had been moved by it, it became "de rigueur" by 1870 not to applaud a singer until the end of the aria, or in between movements of a symphony, and "the house lights were dimmed too, to reinforce the silence and focus attention on the stage." Sennett also analysed a small retail store that opened in Paris in 1852 as a forerunner of the department store. There, the "rituals" and expectations of the price negotiations that the sellers and buyers theatrically transacted with each other disappeared, and the new form where buyers purchased goods at a tagged "fixed price" was established. The act of shopping changed from one that required "the public man as an actor" to his having "a personal and a passive experience" in "the public realm." Sennett's conclusion was that people lost their confidence because of the oppressive process of "personality" in the city that deprived them of theatrical factors, and fled to the "private realm" in quest of the warmth of a family and community, instead of expressing themselves actively in "the public realm." His book illuminated the theme of "the public sphere" because he overlaid it with the notions of "intimacy" and "art," yet his theory still maintains a dichotomous distinction between the public and the private.[20]

To be sure, a concept equivalent to "the public sphere" also existed in the histories of East Asian countries such as Japan and China. In this regard, the work by Yuzo Mizoguchi, which proposes the meaning of the concept "the public" as "something to do with the government," based on the linguistic origins of "the public" and "the private" in Chinese, is suggestive. A rough summary of this work is as follows: Mizoguchi first pays attention to the fact that there was a definition stating that "being public is being fair" in *Shuowen Jiezi* (100), the oldest dictionary in China. In particular, because the Chinese character for "public" (公) contains a part (厶) that means "private" (私) and another part (八) that means "to go against," he argues that "public" meant "sharing fairly and equally by going against private interest" and "removing selfishness." Drawing on *Han Feizi*, the *Shujing* (Book of History) and the *Shijing* (Book of Poems), Mizoguchi categorizes the definitions of "the public" deriving from these sources into "official affairs, the court, government and the state, which are to do with the chief (first group)," "common ownership, publication, relationships, society and collaboration, which are to do with the community (second group)" and "equality, fairness and impartiality, which are to do with sharing fairly (third group)." He further points out that while the Japanese concept of "something to do with the government" = "the public" contained the first and second groups of meaning, the third group of meaning about "fairness" and "impartiality" was not included. In the case of China, Mizoguchi argues there was a context in which "the people constituted 'the public'" and "the court and state constituted 'the private,'" due to the idea of the "fairness of heaven" in regard to "sharing equally." By contrast, in Japan, where the meanings of "fairness" and "impartiality" were missing, "the state which was supposed to occupy the largest area and the emperor who was supposed to be at the top among the court, the government, the state, relationships and society occupied a position on the border as "'something to do with the government' = 'the public,'" and this was never seen as "I" = "the private."[21]

Also, according to Takeshi Mizubayashi, a legal historian, when Chinese culture reached Japan on a large scale between the seventh and eighth centuries and the concept of "the public" was introduced, people recognized it as "ooyake" (which had existed in their native tongue, Yamato Japanese) and maintained that particular word by embedding it in a traditional concept. "Ooyake" referred to "a large yake (a house or residential building)" which was made up of the land and houses of the major local lord, and it was juxtaposed with "oyake" or the "small yake," of a minor lord. However, change in this conceptual contrast of "ooyake – oyake" was forced: Mizubayashi speculates that when Japan encountered the Chinese notion of "the public and the private," the people of the time could not find an overlap between "the private" and "oyake" and created "a new word 'watakushi' whose origin is unknown." As a consequence, the opposition of "the public (ooyake) and the private (watakushi)" was born, according to Mizubayashi.[22]

Taking this research on conceptions of the public sphere into consideration, I would describe the characteristics of Dewey's theory of democratic education and the public sphere in the following way. First, Dewey pursued the continuity of the public sphere and the private sphere by rejecting a dichotomous distinction of both notions and introducing the conception of communication. He explained communication in the public sphere in light of social action and cooperative activity in the community, in which various people seek to live together with face-to-face relationships. Second, unlike Habermas, who developed a theory of procedural and normative democracy that relied on "discourse ethics" and "communicative action," Dewey defined democracy as "a way of living together" or "a way of life, social and individual." For Dewey, democracy was connected with the processes and practices that emerge from relational networks of trust and interactive associations, not only from a fixed norm or neutralized procedure in the administrative state system.

The Renaissance of Pragmatism and Dewey Studies

Since the 1980s, with the rising movement of the "pragmatism renaissance" induced by philosophers such as Richard Rorty, Hilary Putnam, Richard Bernstein and others, reappraisals of Dewey's theory have also increased.[23] One of the features of Dewey Studies today is that the fields range from philosophy, politics and sociology to education, psychology, aesthetics and religion. Among numerous works on Dewey's theory of democracy, those of Robert B. Westbrook and Alan Ryan make outstanding suggestions since they introduce historical, theoretical and practical approaches to this theme.

According to Westbrook, Dewey was "the most important advocate of participatory democracy" in the twentieth century, due to the fact that he advocated "the belief that democracy as an ethical ideal calls upon men and women to build communities in which the necessary opportunities and resource are available for every individual to realize fully his or her particular capacities and powers through participation in political, social, and cultural life."[24] Characterizing Dewey's thoughts on "participatory democracy" as "democratic socialism," Westbrook writes that it "separate[s] the wheat from the chaff in the liberal tradition." According to him, the wheat of liberalism consists of "three values central to liberalism: liberty, individuality, and the freedom of inquiry, discussion, and expression." Meanwhile, the chaff lies in "the adventitious connection between liberalism and the legitimation of capitalism."[25]

While Westbrook embraced Dewey's "democratic socialism" and "participatory democracy" from the standpoint of expressing dissatisfaction against post-war welfare state "liberal democracy," Ryan analyses his political theory as reconciling the relationship between "liberalism" and "communitarianism." Focusing on Dewey's intention for the government to set up pension and insurance systems, and to establish a third party through engaging in political actions in the League for Independent Political Action and the People's Lobby, Ryan regards his thoughts as a welfare-state-type of "advanced liberalism."[26] Although their research includes differences in emphatic points, they have contributed to exploring a new angle of Dewey's political theory through employing historical approaches. However, research on Dewey's ideas of democratic education and the public sphere in the 1920s and 1930s connected to a concept of an aesthetic experience is incomplete, and little discussion regarding his commitment to the art education project with the Barnes Foundation has been generated in previous studies.

Aside from the historical approach taken by Westbrook and Ryan, there are educational studies that have discussed Dewey's theory of democratic education in the 1920s and 1930s. Henry A. Giroux connected education to critical democracy, termed "critical pedagogy." Affected by the public philosophy of Habermas' critical theory and Dewey's pragmatism, Giroux applied these to the pedagogical discourses of "the public sphere," which would cross the borders of differences such as race, ethnicity and so on.[27] Walter C. Parker evaluates Dewey's theory of "democratic teaching" in depth. Beyond the traditional theory of liberal democracy, which holds that "unity arises from diversity" on a "neutrality premise," Parker puts forth "'advanced' ideas of democracy" that cerebrate "enlightened political engagement" through increasing "interaction" and "deliberation" in public life. He embraces the "participatory democracy" of deliberation, which incorporates public agency, citizen action and practical politics in a plural society, in addition to "knowledge of constitutional democracy." Rather than "difference as dissolution," this model includes "social and cultural difference" and the "politics of recognition" in order to solve the "tension" between "the ends of democratic participation" and "the contest between pluralism and assimilation." Parker introduces a "Can

We Talk?" programme of deliberation on public issues, problem solving and community action that brings people of various identities together.[28] Though the theories of Giroux and Parker are oriented by Dewey's participatory idea of "democracy as a way of living," their studies position their stances as being affected by Dewey's theory of democratic education rather than concentrating on its historical context.

When we look at the historical consequences of Dewey's educational theory, a study by Ellen Condliffe Lagemann is provocative and illuminating in that she enunciates its "defeat" in the history. Analysing the theories of Stanley Hall, William James, Dewey, Edward L. Thorndike and others, Lagemann clarifies the psychological turn taken by educational studies under the guise of "science" after the late nineteenth century: "Thorndike's triumph and John Dewey's defeat was an important event in the early molding of educational scholarship." Known as the "father of the measurement movement," whose psychology was narrowly behaviourist of stimuli and responses, Thorndike's approach to the study of education was "the antithesis" of Dewey's, who formulated the concept of "behaviour" as "holistic" and "purposive." According to Lagemann, while Thorndike advocated a reliance on "specialized expertise" and promoted "educational study as a professional science," Dewey favoured "synthesis across disciplines," "open communication," "collaboration across roles" and encouraged "partnership" of various people such as teachers, administrators, parents, experts and citizens in opposition to the fostering of "professionalization" and "bureaucratization." Nevertheless, in a situation where "the study of education" spread rapidly in accordance with the nation's ever-increasing colleges and universities, and was institutionalized within "the increasingly professionalized and bureaucratic structures" of research universities, "a narrowly individualistic, behaviorally oriented, and professionalized conception of educational study" by empirical and scientific method of measurement "won," and a philosophy like Dewey's, which favoured "broader, less technocratic, more situated and developmentally oriented conceptions of education," was marginalized and "lost."[29]

Linda Darling-Hammond, inspired by Lagemann's work, also considers that "Dewey's interest in empowering teachers with knowledge for thoughtful, responsive teaching did not win out with policy makers" in the era of flourishing "behavioral learning theory" and "bureaucratic organizational theory" in the early twentieth century. According to her theory, although there were some leaders like Dewey, Ella Flagg Young, Lucy Sprague Mitchell and Lucy Wheelock who saw teachers as "intellectuals, pedagogical innovators and 'curriculum builders,'" the dominant view was that teachers were thought of as "implementers of top-down mandates and techniques specified in curriculum packages designed by others." It was this view that moved policy makers to restrict teachers" influence by limiting their autonomy and educational levels.[30] The research of Lagemann and Darling-Hammond offers important consideration by shedding light on Dewey's "defeat," in that they focus on the psychological turn of education and its influence on educational policies and institutionalizations in the early twentieth century.

Dewey's ideas that were developed in the 1930s were introduced to Japan soon after. Shunsuke Tsurumi, who worked to introduce the philosophy of pragmatism to Japan, which he encountered while studying at Harvard University, takes the view that Dewey's ideas and the philosophy of pragmatism attracted attention as the theoretical basis of the New Deal policies introduced by the Roosevelt Administration, a development that was almost concurrent with the establishment in Japan of the national mobilization and the Imperial Rule Assistance Association regime after the outbreak of the Sino-Japanese war, which was foreshadowed by the Manchurian Incident of 1931. According to Tsurumi, it was principally a movement by Japanese Marxists resisting "nationalism" as the "last barricade."[31] The active members included Ikutaro Shimizu, Kiyoshi Miki, Masamichi Shinmei and Yasujiro Oomichi. Also, in reference to the educational context of Dewey's philosophy, not only was a perspective linking education and the public sphere established by the post-war press, including Shunsuke, Kazuko Tsurumi and others, but a perspective on Dewey's ideas developed since the 1930s was also contained in the new praxis of education that included problem-solving education and life-unit education. In fact, a number of translations of Dewey's books on ideas for schools, originally published in the 1930s and 1940s, were published in the period immediately after the war through to the end of the 1970s. For instance, *Experience and Education* (1938)[32] was translated by Minoru Harada and published by Shunju-sha in 1950.[33] Following that, Dewey's *Education Today* (1940)[34] was translated by Hiroshi Sugiura and Satoru Ishida and published by Meiji Tosho Shuuppan in 1974,[35] and *Problems of Men* (1946)[36] was translated by Hiroshi Sugiura and Takeo Taura and published in 1976.[37]

Nevertheless, the theme of Dewey's ideas on democratic education and the public sphere tied to aesthetic experience in the 1920s and 1930s has not yet been fully discussed as comprehensive research. This is primarily because of the tendency for educational studies on Dewey's school policy, curriculum and teacher education to focus mainly on either his practices of the University of Chicago Laboratory School in the late 1890s and early 1900s, or his works *School and Society* in 1899[38] or *Democracy and Education* in 1916.[39] As a matter of fact, aside from *Experience and Education* in 1938, Dewey's writings regarding school reform and educational policy were distributed and dispersed in various short articles in magazines, newspapers, lectures, correspondence and political and educational practices, and were not published as a comprehensive work in the 1920s and 1930s. However, when we look at his school theory in light of the conceptions of democracy and the public sphere, it is possible to clarify his educational vision that was connected with processes and practices of democratic politics. What is especially important is to investigate this in the context of democratic politics and art education. This book will advance an approach that allows us to look at his concept of public education by connecting ideas of democracy and the public sphere to aesthetic experience.

Democracy and the Public Sphere in Dewey's Theory of Art Education

My overall interest in this book is to describe Dewey's theory and practice of democratic education and the public sphere as tied to aesthetic experience, by analysing the deployment process of liberalism in the 1920s and 1930s. In particular, I will look at his educational vision of democratic politics of a dialogical community in terms of extracting the public sphere as a critical realm of liberalism. Dewey's concept of democracy as "a way of living together" underscores his philosophy of democratic education, which would be formed through building interactive, dialogical and cooperative face-to-face communication in the public sphere. Then, I will explicate Dewey's engagement in the reconstruction of art education, which is in connection with the democratic ideals of aesthetic experience in the Barnes Foundation. This is important not only because it was an era in which various thoughts on liberalism, represented by the shift from laissez-faire to the New Deal, were competing with each other, but also because it formed a serious and transformative crossroads of democracy in which the real and authentic value of the public sphere was questioned. This book highlights democratic education that exceeds the principles of traditional liberalism, such as laissez-faire marketization and the New Deal welfare state, by bridging the distance between aesthetic experience and the public sphere.

This book is organized in the following way. In Chapter 1, I discuss Dewey's concepts of democracy and the public sphere along with his critique of liberalism in the 1920s. I then turn to his reconceptualization of market, nature and politics as defined by John Locke and laissez-faire in *Human Nature and Conduct* and *The Public and Its Problems*. Dewey's conception of "nature" can be characterized not as the depoliticized individualism of nineteenth-century liberalism, but as interactive and cooperative community and association. He rejected the dichotomy between the public realm and the private realm, and captured it in a relational and continuous way from a functional point of view, defining the public sphere as a political and ethical space that is created and recreated through human action.

In Chapter 2, I set out my argument for Dewey's attempts at teaching democracy with his concrete commitment to the democratic politics of progressivism in the 1920s. He was involved in educating citizens in dialogical communities in the face of narrow nationalism, characterized by the hostile, intolerant and exclusive movements that had spread throughout society. I will clarify Dewey's commitment to political issues with regard to democratic processes and practices. I will also examine his theory of educational science in an era in which the quantitative research of educational measurement had a dominant influence on educational studies. Against this background, Dewey defended educational studies led by qualitative research, a project closely linked with fostering school reform based on dialogical communities.

In Chapter 3, I pursue Dewey's theory and practice of democratic education in the 1930s, analysing his assertion in *Liberalism and Social Action* that "the first object of a renascent liberalism" consists of "education." During the transitory period from laissez-faire to the New Deal, Dewey took up the contentious relationship between liberalism and democracy with respect to education and the public sphere. He criticized the mainstream liberalism of laissez-faire and the New Deal through political involvement in the League for Independent Political Action and the People's Lobby, and attempted to theorize democratic education by organizing social action and intelligence. I will discuss his definition of democracy as "a way of living together" along with a philosophy of the "common man."

Chapter 4 focuses on Dewey's theory of education for a changing society from the standpoint of seeing schools as agencies of public action. Social changes that were brought about by the Great Depression and the New Deal prompted progressive educators to tackle the issue of the relation between schools and social reconstruction. The Teachers College of Columbia University played a central role in the study of this field. I will compare Dewey's educational theory with those of William Heard Kilpatrick, George Counts, John Lawrence Childs and others who contributed to the study in the journal *The Social Frontier*. I look at Dewey's conception of democratic education by investigating his ideas regarding individualism and culture in education, reflective thinking, the teaching profession and educational freedom and equality.

In Chapter 5, I outline Dewey's theory of art, which was the foundation of his creation of democracy and the public sphere. Although Dewey's *Art as Experience* is widely known, there was little discussion in it that bridged his notions of aesthetics and public theory. However, it should be noted that he related notions of "the public" and "communication" with "art" in *The Public and Its Problems* and *Experience and Nature*. I begin this chapter by setting Dewey's aesthetics in historical context through comparing his thoughts to contemporary theorists such as Herbert Read, Benedetto Croce, Adorno and Walter Benjamin, who had all, more or less, contributed to connecting art with politics. Then, I will explore how Dewey theorized the democratic education of art during the periods of urbanization, industrialization, mechanization and the development of popular culture and mass society.

In Chapter 6, I will clarify Dewey's involvement in the art education project in the Barnes Foundation. The Barnes Foundation was established by Albert C. Barnes in Merion, Pennsylvania in December 1922. The aim of the Barnes Foundation was the "Advancement of education and the appreciation of the fine arts."[40] Barnes was greatly inspired by Dewey's educational theory and their friendship deepened. Dewey was inaugurated as a director of the art education project in the Barnes Foundation. Through this project, Dewey and Barnes aimed to build a new and innovative art education research centre through promoting cooperation with the University of Pennsylvania, Columbia University, the Philadelphia Museum of Art, the Pennsylvania Academy of the Fine Arts and public schools in Philadelphia (prior to other institutions in the US). Dewey and Barnes were also engaged in educational reform centring on art education by establishing the group Friends of Art and Education in the

1930s. However, achieving their goals was not an easy task and they faced various difficulties in the process. I will sketch out Dewey's innovative attempts to foster art education in the Barnes Foundation by connecting art education with democratic processes and practices.

Chapter 7 will discuss Dewey's idea of democratic education and the public sphere from the perspective of the criticism and reconstruction of liberalism. He was devoted to tackling the issue in various articles such as "Future of Liberalism" (1935), "The Meaning of Liberalism" (1935), "Liberalism and Equality" (1936), "Liberalism and Civil Liberties" (1936), "A Liberal Speaks Out for Liberalism" (1936) and others.[41] I will focus on his assertion that the relation between democracy and education is mutual and reciprocal, in the sense that democracy itself is an educational principle, measure and policy, and is also constantly and continually explored, rediscovered, remade and reorganized. Then, I clarify the concrete footprints he made in democratic politics, in line with his philosophy of "a way of living together," to face educational crises.

Notes

1 Milton & Rose Friedman, *Free to Choose: A Personal Statement*, New York: Harcourt Brace Jovanovich, 1980.
2 Raymond Geuss, *Public Goods, Private Goods*, Princeton, NJ: Princeton University Press, 2001.
3 John Dewey, *The Early Works of John Dewey, 1882–1898*, 5 vols, Jo Ann Boydston (ed.), Carbondale: Southern Illinois University Press, 1967–1972; *The Middle Works of John Dewey, 1899–1924*, 15 vols, Jo Ann Boydston (ed.), Carbondale: Southern Illinois University Press, 1976–1983; *The Later Works of John Dewey, 1925–1953*, 17 vols, Jo Ann Boydston (ed.), Carbondale: Southern Illinois University Press, 1981–1991; *The Correspondence of John Dewey, 1871–1952*, Larry A. Hickman (ed.), InteLex Corporation, 2005.
4 John Dewey, *Human Nature and Conduct, The Middle Works*, vol.14, pp.1–230.
5 John Dewey, *Experience and Nature, The Later Works*, vol.1, 1988, pp.1–326.
6 John Dewey, *The Public and Its Problems, The Later Works*, vol.2, pp.235–372.
7 John Dewey, *Art as Experience, The Later Works*, vol.10, pp.1–352.
8 John Dewey, *Liberalism and Social Action, The Later Works*, vol.11, pp.1–65.
9 Carl L. Becker, *The Declaration of Independence: A Study in the History of Political Ideas*, New York: Alfred A. Knopf, 1942.
10 Louis Hartz, *The Liberal Tradition in America: An Interpretation of American Political Thought Since the Revolution*, New York: Harcourt, Brace, 1955.
11 Ibid.
12 See, for example, Joyce Appleby, *Liberalism and Republicanism in the Historical Imagination*, Cambridge, MA.: Harvard University Press, 1992; Nancy Cohen, *The Reconstruction of American Liberalism, 1865–1914*, Chapel Hill, NC; London: The University of North Carolina Press, 2002.
13 John E. Chubb and Terry M. Moe, *Politics, Markets, and America's Schools*, Washington, DC: The Brookings Institution, 1990.
14 John Dewey, *Liberalism and Social Action*, op. cit., pp.41–44.
15 Jürgen Habermas, *Strukturwandel der Öffentlichkeit*, Frankfurt am Main: Suhrkamp, 1990.

16 Jürgen Habermas, *Theorie des kommunikativen Handelns*, Frankfurt am Main: Suhrkamp, 1981; *Erläuterungen zur Diskursethik*, Frankfurt am Main: Suhrkamp, 1991; *Faktizität und Geltung: Beiträge zur Diskurstheorie des Rechts und des demokratischen Rechts*taats, Frankfurt am Main: Suhrkamp, 1998.

17 Hannah Arendt, *The Human Condition*, Chicago, IL: The University of Chicago Press, 1958.

18 Hannah Arendt, *Eichmann in Jerusalem: A Report on the Banality of Evil*, New York: The Viking Press, 1963.

19 See Naoshi Yamawaki, *Glocal Public Philosophy: A Vision of Good Societies in the 21st Century*, Tokyo: University of Tokyo Press, 2008, pp.12–14.

20 Richard Sennett, *The Fall of Public Man*, Cambridge: Cambridge University Press, 1977.

21 Yuzo Mizoguchi, "The Public and Private in Chinese History of Thought," Takeshi Sasaki and Tea-Chang Kim (eds), *The History of Thought of the Public and Private: Public Philosophy*, vol.I, Tokyo: University of Tokyo Press, 2001, pp.35–58.

22 Takeshi Mizubayashi, "The Prototype and Development of the Japanese 'Public-Private' Distinction," Takeshi Sasaki and Tea-Chang Kim (eds), *The Public and Private in Japan: Public Philosophy*, vol.III, Tokyo: University of Tokyo Press, 2002, pp.1–19.

23 See Richard Rorty, *Philosophy and the Mirror of Nature*, Princeton: Princeton University Press, 1979; *Contingency, Irony, and Solidarity*, Cambridge; New York: Cambridge University Press, 1989; *Objectivity, Relativism, and Truth*, Cambridge; New York: Cambridge University Press, 1991; *Philosophy and Social Hope*, London: Penguin Books, 1999; Hilary Putnam, *Reason, Truth and History*, Cambridge, MA: Cambridge University Press, 1981; *Realism and Reason*, Cambridge, MA: Cambridge University Press, 1983; *The Collapse of the Fact/Value Dichotomy and Other Essays*, Cambridge, MA; London: Harvard University Press, 2002; *Ethics without Ontology*, Cambridge, MA: Harvard University Press, 2004; Richard J. Bernstein, *The Restructuring of Social and Political Theory*, Philadelphia: University of Pennsylvania Press, 1978; *Beyond Objectivism and Relativism: Science, Hermeneutics, and Praxis*, Oxford: B. Blackwell, 1983; *The New Constellation: The Ethical-Political Horizons of Modernity/Postmodernity*, Cambridge, UK: Polity Press, 1991.

24 Robert B. Westbrook, *John Dewey and American Democracy*, Ithaca: Cornell University Press, 1991, pp.xiv–xv.

25 Ibid., pp.430–431.

26 Alan Ryan, *John Dewey and the High Tide of American Liberalism*, New York: W. W. Norton, 1995.

27 Henry A. Giroux, *Border Crossings, Cultural Workers and the Politics of Education*, New York; London: Routledge, 1993, pp.12–13.

28 Walter C., Parker, *Teaching Democracy: Unity and Diversity in Public Life*, New York: Teachers College Press, 2003.

29 Ellen C. Lagemann, *An Elusive Science: The Troubling History of Education Research*, Chicago: The University of Chicago Press, 2000.

30 Linda Darling-Hammond, *Powerful Teacher Education: Lessons from Exemplary Programs*, San Francisco, CA: Jossey-Bass, 2006, pp.77–78.

31 Shunsuke, Tsurumi, "The Outline of the Development of Pragmatism," *Iwanami Lectures on Modern Thought vol.6: People and Freedom*, Tokyo: Iwanami Shoten, 1952, pp.1–49.

32 John Dewey, *Experience and Education, The Later Works*, vol.13, pp.1–62.

33 John Dewey, *Experience and Education*, translated by Minoru Harada, Tokyo: Shunju-sha, 1950.

34 John Dewey, *Education Today*, New York: G. P. Putnam's Sons, 1940.

35 John Dewey, *Education Today*, translated by Hiroshi Sugiura and Satoru Ishida, Tokyo: Meiji Tokyo Shuppan, 1974.

36 John Dewey, *Problems of Men*, New York: Philosophical Library, 1946.
37 John Dewey, *Problems of Men*, translated by Hiroshi Sugiura, Takeo Taura, Tokyo: Meiji Tokyo Shuppan, 1976.
38 John Dewey, *The School and Society, The Middle Works*, vol.1, pp.1–109.
39 John Dewey, *Democracy and Education, The Middle Works*, vol.9, pp.1–375.
40 Albert C. Barnes, "The Barnes Foundation," *The New Republic*, vol.34, no.432, 14 March 1923, p.65.
41 John Dewey, "Future of Liberalism," *The Later Works*, vol.11, pp.258–260; "The Meaning of Liberalism," *The Later Works*, vol.11, pp.364–367; "Liberalism and Equality," *The Later Works*, vol.11, pp.368–371; "Liberalism and Civil Liberties," *The Later Works*, vol.11, pp.372–375; "A Liberal Speaks Out for Liberalism." *The Later Works*, vol.11, pp.282–288.

1 Democracy and the Public Sphere

A Critique of Liberalism and Its Politics

In the 1920s, Dewey considered education from the perspective of democracy and the public sphere, and tackled school reform as a central issue. He attempted to reconstruct the civil society of traditional liberalism, and searched for ways to rebuild democratic education and the public sphere. During the periods between progressivism and the Great Depression, and the two World Wars, the US encountered societal changes such as industrialization, urbanization, technological advances and the progress of mass society. Those factors made changes to people's lives and sets of values unavoidable. Moreover, the huge industrial organizations that appeared against the background of the expansion of mass production and consumption led to the unprecedented development of capitalism, which contributed to bringing the US towards the centre of the world economy and to the enjoyment of glorifying prosperity.

However, the huge growth of the organization and systemization of business enveloped society, and eroded people's daily lives. Lewis Mumford analysed critically that man himself becomes "goods" and "the machine" with the birth of huge organizations by mechanization.[1] Instead of communication with people of visible individuality, depersonalized relations with the anonymous constituted interpersonal relations in society, and social adaptation to an efficiency-driven system that concentrated on the production and consumption of goods came to form the dominant lifestyle. The concept of Dewey's public philosophy was prepared to face such societal changes. Dewey regarded the decline of face-to-face relations as "the eclipse of the public," and was engaged in reconstructing an "articulate public" through democratic education.[2]

Conventionally, Dewey's public education theory tends to be interpreted within the framework of liberalism and it is subject to attack, especially his concept of nature and naturalism, from the following three directions. The first is opposition from neoconservatism. According to E. D. Hirsch, Dewey emphasizes as the cornerstone of his theory the educational view of Jean-Jacques Rousseau, who made children's "natural growth" the ultimate goal, and therefore did not fully recognize the public mission of an adult who conveys "cultural literacy" to children.[3] The second is criticism by neoliberalism. John E. Chubb and Terry M. Moe pay attention to Dewey's theory in the form of the rejection of progressive education. Their opposition to progressive education focuses on the bureaucratic control of educational systems that this movement has built in an artificial way. They position the marketization of nineteenth-century liberalism as a natural control system of opposite poles, and advocate the advancement of educational reform that maximizes competition among schools and the role of choices.[4] The third is criticism from Marxism of the extension of revisionist approaches. According to William A. Paringer, the naturalism that forms the basis of Dewey's liberal educational thought is unable to meet the challenge of fitting into the existing industrial structure, since it would conceal and melt various ideological confrontations that lurk in reality.[5] While the first and third schools reject Dewey's naturalism, the second positions progressivism opposite naturalism. These criticisms have thrown light onto the fact that Dewey's educational theory has been at issue for several decades now, and the concept of nature constitutes one of the key and controversial factors under discussion.

On the other hand, there has been an innovative movement to reappraise and reinterpret Dewey's theory of democratic education and the public sphere reflecting the trend of the pragmatism renaissance since the 1980s. For instance, Westbrook strongly supports Dewey's "democratic ideals" of "participatory democracy," emphasizing the contrast with Walter Lippmann's "realism" that affirms bureaucratic control by the social elite.[6] And, according to Ryan, Dewey's commitment to the task of building "advanced liberalism" was wedded to the idea of "communitarian strain;" in other words, "individuals need communities, and liberal communities consist of associated individuals."[7] However, there remains no comprehensive research on the relation between Dewey's theory of democratic education and the public sphere that looks at the concept of nature. It is hard to say whether sufficient research on concrete school reforms in the 1920s and 1930s has accumulated, since his theory of school reform for that period was distributed throughout many papers and articles.

Dewey advocated the importance of public participation and communication by criticizing the market control or welfare state control of education, and developed innovative school reforms with democracy and the public sphere as underlying principles. The school was regarded as a central agency that fostered social change and created culture, and he investigated educational methods of democracy for creating "a way of living together." This chapter will outline Dewey's vision of school education in the 1920s in accordance with the principle of democracy and the public sphere. I will reinterpret his naturalism, which tended to be grasped within a framework of traditional liberalism, and reconstruct a conception of the public sphere through envisioning the conflicts and confrontations between liberalism and democracy.

Political and Ethical Naturalism

Human Nature and Conduct was published in 1922, based on Dewey's lectures at Leland Stanford Junior University in the spring of that year. In the introduction of the book, he raised the question: "Why did morality set up rules so foreign to human nature?" He criticized the traditional notion of morality concerned with controlling human nature from a transcendental position, saying that "moral principles that exalt themselves by degrading human nature are in effect committing suicide," or else "they involve human nature in unending civil war, and treat it as a hopeless mess of contradictory forces."[8] After its publication, Dewey's ethical theory was interpreted as explaining morality from the standpoint of "naturalistic empiricism." However, it is important to examine the notion of nature, since Dewey has been consistently criticized as defining naturalism by traditional liberalism.

Much of what is called the "individualism" of the early nineteenth century has in truth little to do with the nature of individuals. It goes back to a metaphysics which held that harmony between man and nature can be taken for granted, if certain artificial restrictions upon man are removed. Hence it neglected the necessity of studying and regulating industrial conditions so that a nominal freedom can be made an actuality. Find a man who believes that all men need is freedom from oppressive legal and political measures, and you have found a man who, unless he is merely obstinately maintaining his own private privileges, carries at the back of his head some heritage of the metaphysical doctrine of free will, plus an optimistic confidence in natural harmony.[9]

Dewey rejected the metaphysical notion of nature as the harmony between humans and nature without politics. In terms of moral philosophy, his concept of naturalism was not founded on the standpoint of classical liberalism exemplified in Locke's theory, which assumes that "the natural state" is the one deprived of "political society," but on the idea that "nature" is closely related to political, economic and social activity. Namely, Dewey did not share the assumption that the foundation of "human nature" is based on individuals and individual rights and freedoms, and that the concept of nature could be reduced to a state without political and social relationships. For Dewey, Locke's moral philosophy was founded not on human communicative interaction, but rather on the concept of control in an individualistically interpreted pre-political state of nature.

Dewey sought to bring "morals to earth" by refusing to accept "the separation of morals from human nature." For him, "the cost of confining moral freedom to an inner region" was "the almost complete severance of ethics from politics and economics," and it reflected the "separation of moral activity from nature and the public life of men." While a whole school of morals has flourished by "restricting morals to character" and "separating character from conduct, motives from actual deeds," the recognition of "moral action" in analogy with "functions and arts" would eliminate the causes that understand morals from a subjective and individual viewpoint.[10] Terry Hoy argues that Dewey's notion of "a reflective morality," which was derived from "naturalistic humanism," grows out of "conflict between ends, responsibility, rights and duties where the task of a reflective morality is to clarify problems." According to Hoy, the keynote of Dewey's approach to moral inquiry was his emphasis on "the practical meaning of a situation" and "intelligence" that can avoid "the inadequacies of fixed ends and final goals."[11]

An effort to bring "morals to earth" was concerned with constructing ethics in view of a variety of people's experiences and pluralistic values in the lifeworld through the denial of the metaphysical concept of nature. Hilary Putnam, who regards Dewey "as just one member of my list of 'heroes'" and appraises *Human Nature and Conduct*, enthusiastically proposes the idea of "pragmatic pluralism," also called "ethics without ontology" or "ethics without metaphysics." One reason why Putnam sees Dewey as belonging to his "list of 'heroes'" is because Dewey emphasized that "the function of ethics" is not to "arrive at 'universal principles,'" nor to "produce 'system,'" but to "contribute to the solution of practical problems." For Putnam, Dewey's ethics rested not on "a single interest or aim" deriving from "a system of principles," but rather on "a system of interrelated concerns" that would be mutually supported, but with the potential for tension: he calls it "motley," following Ludwig Wittgenstein's term.[12]

Dewey reconstructed concepts relating to the ethics of rights, freedom and morality not from the idea of "natural harmony," but from political and social processes and practices of the creation of pluralistic values that emerge from interactive experiences in the world. Destroying the "fixed distinction" between the human and the physical, as well as that between the moral and the political, was seen as a measure to accomplish this. He claimed that one needed to turn from moral theories to the "human struggle for political, economic and religious liberty, for freedom of thought, speech, assemblage and creed," and that through these processes, one would find himself "out of the stiflingly close atmosphere of an inner consciousness and in the open-air world."[13] In the face of the industrialization, urbanization and realization of mass society in the 1920s, it was not appropriate to call on primitive naturalism; rather, there was a demand to propose a new concept of politics and ethics.

The Reconstruction of the Public Sphere: Market, Nature and Democracy

The Public and Its Problems was written from the standpoint of embodying the concepts of democracy and the public sphere. It was Dewey's consistent insistence in the 1920s that the assumption of an ultimately harmonious state between humans and nature without political society was not adequate, and that Locke's liberal idea of a natural state had to be reconstructed with public theory in line with human communicative interaction and activity:

> Freedom presented itself as an end in itself, though it signified in fact liberation from oppression and tradition. Since it was necessary, upon the intellectual side, to find justification for the movements of revolt, and since established authority was upon the side of institutional life, the natural recourse was appeal to some inalienable sacred authority resident in the

protesting individuals. Thus "individualism" was born, a theory which endowed singular persons in isolation from any associations, except those which they deliberately formed for their own ends, with native or natural rights. The revolt against old and limiting associations was converted, intellectually, into the doctrine of independence of any and all associations. Thus the practical movement for the limitation of the powers of government became associated, as in the influential philosophy of John Locke, with the doctrine that the ground and justification of the restriction was prior non-political rights inherent in the very structure of the individual.[14]

Here, we can understand Dewey's opposition to the liberal theories exemplified by Locke's naturalism, which assumed that a natural state was an individual state and understood man's desires or actions as being from a naturalistic point of view. For Dewey, the concept of the natural state premised by classical liberalism meant that the individual was a human isolated from the community and excluded from the political and ethical spaces constructed through human interaction. He called this state the "naked individual," which indicated the "sweep[ing] away [of] all associations as foreign to his nature and rights save as they proceeded from his own voluntary choice, and guaranteed his own private ends."[15]

Dewey was especially critical of nineteenth-century liberalism that bowed to the classical liberal concept of naturalism. That is to say, nineteenth-century liberalism expanded the concept of nature to include the market economy, and then placed emphasis on this market-oriented concept of nature. He interpreted the nineteenth century's laissez-faire liberalism as an ideology that functioned according to the metaphysical concept of market-driven nature:

> The economic movement was perhaps the more influential because it operated, not in the name of the individual and his inherent rights, but in the name of Nature. Economic "laws," that of labour springing from natural wants and leading to the creation of wealth, of present abstinence in behalf of future enjoyment leading to creation of capital effective in piling up still more wealth, the free play of competitive exchange, designated the law of supply and demand, were "natural" laws. They were set in opposition to political laws as artificial, man-made affairs. The inherited tradition which remained least questioned was a conception of Nature which made Nature something to conjure with. The older metaphysical conception of Natural Law was, however, changed into an economic conception; laws of nature, implanted in human nature, regulated the production and exchange of goods and services, and in such a way that when they were kept free from artificial, that is political, meddling, they resulted in the maximum possible social prosperity and progress. Popular opinion is little troubled by questions of logical consistency. The economic theory of laissez-faire, based upon belief in beneficent natural laws which brought

about harmony of personal profit and social benefit, was readily fused with the doctrine of natural rights.[16]

What we can infer from this citation is that the metaphysical interpretation of nature that expanded the concept of "natural law" to include economic activity was followed by the legitimacy of this laissez-faire liberal ideology. In opposition to classical liberalism that placed the notion of nature as transcendent from society, laissez-faire liberalism aimed to function in the real society mediated by the market economy. The idea of "natural law" was in nature a transcendental concept. However, it had a major influence on society, mainly because the notion of nature was associated with economic activity. In laissez-faire liberalism, the market was assumed to be a space where people interacted naturally with each other and constructed natural relationships directed by human activity. It was assumed that human relationships in the market economy were independent of political space and that humanity could thus achieve ultimate harmony with nature. Besides, the market was also premised to be an individual space, since it was defined as a space unrestricted by social and political intervention and association. In the era of nineteenth-century liberalism, the notion of the market was thought to encompass the natural and individualistic relationships forming out of human activity.

Dewey criticized the traditional liberal definition of the public. According to him, the assumption of nineteenth-century liberalism was in itself a fallacy and deviation from democracy, made clear in the passage below.

> It would be a great mistake, however, to regard the idea of the isolated individual possessed of inherent rights "by nature" apart from association, and the idea of economic laws as natural, in comparison with which political laws being artificial are injurious (save when carefully subordinated), as idle and impotent.[17]

Dewey put an emphasis on the fallacy of the liberal idea of a natural state separate from human interaction and association. He insisted that the result of perpetuating such a fallacy was "a skew, a deflection and distortion, in democratic forms." For him, putting such individualistic matter in such a broad statement was a "process of complete submergence," an opinion undertaken, in fact, "at the very time in which he was being elevated in theory."[18] Dewey regarded a deflection in democracy as being provoked by market-oriented liberalism. He felt that such an individualistic way of thinking would lead to a disintegration of the individual in reality, even though such a theory assumes emancipation of the individual.

Now a few questions arise. Why was market-centred naturalism seen as a deflection and distortion of the democratic state? What needed to be done to conquer this issue? What were Dewey's vision and idea about the notion of the public? For Dewey, the laissez-faire liberal hypothesis, which stated that the natural state united with market individualism is separate from the political state, was in itself a fallacy. Plus, he considered it a mistake to assume that people think in rationally economic terms in a market society. In reality, people's decisions follow the customs and institutions constructed through human interaction. And these kinds of customs and institutions premise the existence of communities that are constructed and recognized through common activities. Dewey believed that there existed a fiction of laissez-faire liberalism, as discussed below.

> Incidentally we have trenched upon the other doctrine, the idea that there is something inherently "natural" and amenable to "natural law" in the working of economic forces, in contrast with the man-made artificiality of political institutions. The idea of a natural individual in his isolation possessed of full-fledged wants, of energies to be expended according to his own volition, and of a ready-made faculty of foresight and prudent calculation is as much a fiction in psychology as the doctrine of the individual in possession of antecedent political rights is one in politics.[19]

Dewey's rejection was directed towards the nineteenth-century liberalism's assumption that even though mankind is located in the natural state apart from political society, he is thought to possess the power of economic judgement. To the liberal school, "desire was a conscious matter deliberately directed upon a known goal of pleasures," and "the mind was seen as if always in the bright sunlight, having no hidden recesses, no unexplorable nooks, nothing underground."[20] Although laissez-faire liberalism worked on the premise that a man in a natural state is deprived of political and social interaction, he was seen to have economic knowledge and desires. For Dewey, the liberal hypothesis stating that the individual is endowed with the rational power to foresee and make calculations about a market society without social conditions was a fiction. He explained this idea using a concrete image, saying that such a liberal hypothesis is like the moves in a fair chess game. Namely, this kind of economic man is embodied by the chess player who knows all the moves in advance.

Consequently, the liberal view of a clear and transparent individual was a fiction for Dewey: "the desires, aims and standards of satisfaction which the dogma of 'natural' economic processes and laws assumes" are "socially conditioned phenomena" and "reflections into the singular human being of customs and institutions." Thus, the market realm is not a genuine system organized autonomously by rational individuals, "an original possession of persons in their own structure."[21] Nor is it a natural space that exists outside of customs and institutions. Dewey thought that a man in the market space follows the political and social activities and institutions that are associated with human interaction. In other words, the values of liberalism should not be individualistically naturalized in a pre-political state, but have to be reinterpreted in relation to political and social interactions in communities.

Politics and Ethics of the Public Sphere

The key point in Dewey's public theory was that his notion of the public sphere was constructed on the basis of a democratic community mediated by communicative interaction. He recognized the public sphere in the light of human interaction, rejecting the idea of a directive or causative power that controlled the public. He felt that people should not look for "state-forming forces" or "the origin of the state," because to explain the state by saying that man is a political animal was to travel in a proverbial circle. That kind of process would be similar to the explanatory method of attributing religion to a religious instinct, the family to marital and parental affection, and language to a natural endowment. He acknowledged that such theories reduplicated the effects to be accounted for in a causal force. He went on to say that people have looked in "the wrong place," in that they have sought "the nature of the state in the field of agencies, in that of doers of deeds, or in some will or purpose back of the deeds." They have tried to explain the state in light of "authorship."[22] Dewey tried to reconstruct the relationship between the public and the private as follows.

> We then take our point of departure from the objective fact that human acts have consequences upon others, that some of these consequences are perceived, and that their perception leads to subsequent effort to control action so as to secure some consequences and avoid others. Following this clew, we are led to remark that the consequences are of two kinds, those which affect the persons directly engaged in a transaction, and those which affect others beyond those immediately concerned. In this distinction we find the germ of the distinction between the private and the public. When indirect consequences are recognized and there is effort to regulate them, something having the traits of a state comes into existence. When the consequences of an action are confined, or are thought to be confined, mainly to the persons directly engaged in it, the transaction is a private one.[23]

Dewey placed an emphasis on his insistence that one must start from "acts which are performed," not from "hypothetical causes for those acts, and consider their consequences." One must introduce "intelligence," or "the observation of consequences as consequences, that is, in connection with the acts." He explained the concept of the public and the private in the following way. When A and B communicate with each other, the action is "a transaction;" both are involved and concerned and one or both may be helped or harmed. The results of any advantage or injury do not extend beyond A and B; the communication exists between these two and is defined as "private." However, "if it is found that the consequences of the conversation extend beyond the two directly concerned, that they affect the welfare of many others, the act acquires a public capacity."[24] In that way, the division of the private and the public was designed according to the consequences of human interaction. The public was interpreted as an active realm that went beyond the direct human relationship, while the private was thought of as the realm that was involved with only those people who shared a direct transaction.

Concerning the conceptual distinction between the public and private spheres, Dewey's theory encouraged the redefinition of the public by traditional liberalism, especially the concept as it was premised by the nineteenth century's laissez-faire market-centred liberalism. This strategy can be summed up in the following three points.

First, Dewey's idea of the public sphere avoided setting up the public and the private as fixed and established spaces partitioned out by a priori divisions. Traditional liberalism was founded on a priori segmentation of the public and the private, such as the state or market realms. According to Dewey, civil society advocated by traditional liberalism worked from the hypothesis that ongoing individualism would be consummated through the emancipation of private market spaces from the state defined as the public. Yet, neither public nor private spheres were determined realms of the state or free market separate from human actions, but were pluralistic spaces constructed and reconstructed through the organizing of communicative interactions between people.

Second, the relationship between the public and private spheres was reinterpreted by Dewey as a continuous realm. His theory deconstructed the dualism of the public and the private by suggesting that the private is involved with the quality of the public. This meant parting from the theory of civil society of traditional liberalism. The premise of two confrontations between the public and private spheres is seen in the nineteenth-century liberal attitude of laissez-faire. That is, although the economic theory of laissez-faire promoted the liberation of the private individual from governmental authority, it was an idea that protected the coordinative and corrective market as a realm independent of a state, and made obvious the confrontation of the public and private spheres. While traditional liberalism maximized the social realm of the private sphere as a natural space, it minimized the responsibility of the state system identified with the public sphere.

Third, the distinction between the private and public spheres was not equivalent to the distinction between the individual and the social. "Many private acts are social; their consequences contribute to the welfare of the community or affect its status and prospects."[25] The concept of the public sphere was emerging and reconstructing processes and practices that were to be determined critically, continuously and experimentally, which was common to the concept of pluralism. An emphatic point would shift from a substantial and established realm, where it bore normative value, to the direction of the mutual action process of the human being who would generate the public sphere. According to Dewey, the relation between the public and private spheres was not necessarily at odds and conflicting, but was reciprocal.

The idea that the public sphere was designed by human interaction enlightened for Dewey a way to build community and associations through face-to-face communication. Dewey attempted to reconstruct the market-centred social realm into the political and ethical realm of the public sphere.

In imagining an "articulate public" through face-to-face communication, he opposed the market-centred liberal notion that encouraged "the eclipse of the public." He insisted that "men have always been associated together in living, and association in conjoint behaviour has affected their relations to one another as individuals."[26] It was essential to achieve a democratic community inspired by face-to-face associations, for he felt that this would transform impersonal and mechanical relationships into active and expressive interactions.

Dewey, Lippmann and Wallace

The Public and Its Problems was published in response to Lippmann's book *The Phantom Public* (1925). Lippmann was a prominent journalist who, in the early twentieth century, was engaged in releasing a journal *The New Republic* and publishing many books: *Liberty and the News* (1920), *Public Opinion* (1922) and many more. When Thomas Woodrow Wilson was inaugurated as US President, Lippmann was involved in the creation of the "Fourteen Points" about peace (1918) for World War I, for an American delegation of the Paris Peace Conference.

Lippmann's thoughts were influenced by Graham Wallace, a political scientist who taught Lippmann when he was a student at Harvard University. In *Human Nature in Politics* (1908), Wallace turned his attention to the "irrationality" of the human being who constitutes democracy. He insisted that various political judgements, such as elections, votes and opinion manifestations, are not results of "an intellectual process" of human action, but "irrational conclusions" that are formed by prejudice, intuition, custom and instinct. Those elements are led by stimulus from the environment that surrounds people in their everyday lives. For Wallace, "political entities" are likely to be determined by the irrational factors of social customs and the instincts with which people become familiar and grow used to accepting in everyday life.[27]

Lippmann developed and applied the theory of the "irrationality" of human nature by Wallace to the theory about "public opinion." Lippmann's concepts of "pseudo-environment" and "stereotype," which constitute the central ideas of "public opinion," were known to the public. According to him, since "true environment" is too vast and complicated, and will change easily, one is not able to grasp and recognize that external world directly. Therefore, when looking at the environment, people will recognize beforehand certain things in a person they see that are based on the simplified "image" and "pictures in the head" cultivated through previous experiences, education, culture and so on.

Man also looks at the external world according to certain "stereotypes" formed by culture. Since the external world is too confusing and elusive to see and perceive directly, "stereotypes" are formed that give framework and perspective to the thoughts. A stereotype automatically determines the object that captures one's interest and the angle from which it is looked at, and offers a sense of security and stability. Therefore, people's political judgements are regulated by the stereotypes. Even newspapers and reports are not free from stereotypes; rather, they will strengthen the image of a stereotype. Thus,

Lippmann directed criticism towards a theoretical premise of democracy, the premise of the self-fulfilling individual owning knowledge and information in advance of political action and activity. He regarded this as "the democratic fallacy."[28]

Lippmann's *The Phantom Public* developed the argument put forth in *Public Opinion*. In it, the democratic ideals of citizens participating in and judging political issues were challenged. Lippmann rejected the notion of "the omnicompetent, sovereign citizen" as a false and unattainable ideal. He thought that the individual man does not have opinions on all public affairs or knows how to direct the ones he has. So he believed people must abandon the ideals of democracy. He illustrated this by taking up concrete figures from the Chicago mayoral election of 1923. That is, out of 1,400,000 eligible electors, there were only 900,000 registered to vote, and only 723,000 who actually voted in the election. Besides this, about 70 per cent of abstainers did not even pretend to have a reason for not voting, meaning they did not have the consciousness of not caring about voting, and about a quarter of those said honestly that they were completely uninterested. Moreover, while the number of eligible voters tripled between 1896 and 1920, the percentage of the popular vote cast at presidential elections declined from 80.75 to 52.36. From these figures, Lippmann considered it a "fallacy" to assume that all people want to participate actively in government. He concluded that the public is a "phantom public," and that public affairs should be directed and controlled by experts.[29]

Dewey praised Lippmann's work. In particular, Dewey supported the idea of "the fallacy of the omnicompetent citizen." However, Dewey's prescription was in contrast to Lippmann's. Dewey was not able to consent to elitism as the solution for the issue. Although Dewey admitted that the "eclipse of the public" was a serious problem, he attempted to get over it by the revival of an "articulate public," instead of solving it in the form of control by the social elite. Dewey tried to reconstruct the anonymized space created by industrial capital into a community flourishing through the dialogical interaction of "face-to-face relationships." He promoted the conversion from "the Great Society" to "a Great Community."[30]

> Till the Great Society is converted into a Great Community, the Public will remain in eclipse. Communication can alone create a great community.[31]

Dewey's idea of "the Great Community" was adopted from Graham Wallace's book, *The Great Society* (1914).[32] "The Great Society" refers to an industrial and market-centred society organized by impersonal and anonymous beings. It is founded by a "naked individual" isolated from shared experiences who deconstructs both the individual and the public sphere. In contrast, "the Great Community" is constructed on the basis of face-to-face association, empowered by "the highest and most difficult kind of inquiry and a subtle, delicate, vivid and responsive art of communication." This community will be consummated when "free social inquiry" is wedded to "the art of full and moving communication."[33]

Dewey was a strong advocate of the significance of association and community, defining association as physical and organic, and communal life as moral: that is, emotionally, intellectually, consciously sustained.[34] He suggested that the idea of democracy would take on "a veridical and directive meaning" only when it was construed as the "marks and traits of an association which realizes the defining characteristics of a community." "Fraternity," "liberty" and "equality" isolated from "communal life" lead to "hopeless abstractions." "mushy sentimentalism" or "extravagant and fanatical violence."[35]

Democratic Community and the Public Sphere

In the 1920s, Dewey aimed at the emergence of democracy and the public sphere in line with the reconstruction of traditional liberalism. The changes to liberalism from Locke to laissez-faire had built a civil society that assumed the natural state is separate from the political state harmonically. It was characteristic for traditional liberalism to naturalize the political and define the nature in the individual dimension.

This premise has been taken over by current critics of Dewey's educational theory. Hirsch and Paringer criticized Dewey's educational thought as being an extension of Rousseau's naturalism. Neoliberalism, which takes its genealogy from nineteenth-century liberalism, has positioned political and artificial controls of progressive bureaucratization at opposite poles of the natural market. Current neoliberalism promotes marketization by minimizing the political intervention of the state and naturalizing the market realm as free, and by emancipating spaces that can maximize competition and the efforts of individuals to make rational choices. Dewey redefined the notion of naturalism that formed the roots of traditional liberalism.

The central theme of Dewey's public theory consisted of the reconstruction of the Great Society into the Great Community, in which "an organized, articulate public" comes into being. He investigated the formation of a community in which people have face-to-face communication. He adopted a strategy that cancels two clause confrontations of the public and private spheres. The distinction between the public and private spheres was not an a priori confrontation concept. Instead, Dewey emphasized the continuity of both concepts from the functional viewpoint of human interaction. He placed a community and an association at the base of the public sphere. Man's rights and freedom, he believed, are dependent on the relation and context of communication with others wherein people live cooperatively, as opposed to being dependent on ideas that could be reduced to a pre-political state of nature. Dewey's rejection was directed against traditional liberal thought that rights and freedom are individualistically naturalized outside of human interaction. Those values should be interpreted not only from the concept of nature but also from politics and the ethics of the public sphere.

Soon after the publication of *The Public and Its Problems*, book reviews were published in various journals and newspapers. In the *New York Herald Tribune*

Books of 27 November 1927, Sterling P. Lamprecht, a philosopher, commented that Dewey is "more responsible than any other man of our day for bringing philosophy into touch with the practical affairs of the world." According to his review, *The Public and Its Problems* sought to give "philosophical status" to "some ideas which are at present of vague import" by embodying "intelligence in institutions and methods," which would be of relevance to everyday life. It has been said that Dewey proposed conditions that would contribute to making the public effectively aware of its own existence and functions in life.[36]

Robert E. Park wrote a book review in *The American Journal of Sociology* in 1928, in which he characterized Dewey's book as being "less a discussion of the public and public opinion than actually an oblique attack on the problem of the state." For Park, Dewey described "the state realistically as a going concern" rather than "a philosophical abstraction defined in legal and normative terms" – meaning that while the state is, in part, an idea, it should also be regarded as a part of nature.[37]

Stephen Pepper's book review made a critical analysis of Dewey's work, since in the book "the theory" comes first and "the plea" afterwards, but in thought, "the plea" to save democracy is certainly first and the "theory" afterwards. Moreover, Pepper criticized the fact that Dewey avoided suggesting a concise definition of the state, and that his thoughts were oriented by "causes," not by "consequences" as he supposed. For him, Dewey's theory referred not to the states in which we live but to the ideal democratic state in which we wish to live; furthermore, he stated that it was "only a normative and not a descriptive theory."[38] Likewise, O. de Selincourt was critical about Dewey's book in that while Dewey insisted that things should not be explained in terms of "causes" but of "consequences," he did not explain how these concepts differ. For Selincourt, Dewey had little to say about "the proper organization of states and publics" because the Great Community he sought was worldwide, yet the only way to discover publics would appear to be through small local communities.[39]

Generally speaking, book reviews of *The Public and Its Problems* tended to analyse Dewey's theory of the state, and they were not necessarily positive and favourable comments. On the other hand, Robert Morss Lovett's review paid attention to the idea of association. He claimed that Dewey seemed to "warn us" not to exaggerate "the authority of the state" by furnishing it "mystical or supernatural sanction." He drew the following six points form Dewey's volume: "freedom of social inquiry and of distribution of its conclusions;" "belief in the power of communication to unite men in the realization of this good;" "faith" in "intelligence as an element in the human experiment with a power to affect results;" "belief in the power of art to release man from inhibitions;" "belief in elementary education as a means to the formation of habits of associated action" and "in adult education, the improvement of the methods of debate, discussion, and persuasion;" and the "restoration of local communal life." For Lovett, "Dewey's faith in democracy is the fact that man is by nature associative, prone to common action."[40]

Thus, Dewey attempted to construct the public sphere by reinterpreting the naturalism of traditional liberalism and restoring the ideas of democratic community and association. It was after the pragmatism renaissance of the 1980s, represented by the research of Westbrook, Ryan and others, that Dewey's political philosophy was reappraised. However, even when the reference to Dewey's naturalism was made, that research tended to be limited to philosophical and psychological considerations consisting mainly of *Experience and Nature* (1925), and not focused on his thoughts regarding the relationship between the marketization of the economy and naturalism, which Dewey had investigated deeply.

However, criticism that focused on Dewey's educational theory raised the necessity of re-examining his political philosophy from the perspective of naturalism. Liberalism and democracy are not essentially harmonized. Both concepts produce disagreement and tense relations. The public sphere is built through a democratic community of interactive, face-to-face communication. The notion of the public is not limited to a procedural and neutralized realm of democracy. The public sphere is involved with political and ethical spaces. Dewey stressed that the relationship between the public and the private is not a fixed and existent realm, such as the state or market, but is always constructed and reconstructed by the communicative participation of democratic politics and ethics.

Notes

1 Lewis Mumford, *The Myth of the Machine: Technics and Human Development*, New York: Harcourt, 1967, p.188.
2 John Dewey, *The Public and Its Problems*, op. cit., pp.304–324.
3 E. D. Hirsch Jr., *Cultural Literacy: What Every American Needs to Know*, Boston, MA: Houghton Mifflin, 1987, pp.9–14.
4 John E. Chubb and Terry M. Moe, *Politics, Markets, and America's Schools*, op. cit.
5 William A. Paringer, *The Paradox of Liberal Reform: A Critique of Deweyan Praxis*, Ann Arbor, MI: UMI, 1989.
6 Robert B. Westbrook, *John Dewey and American Democracy*, op. cit.
7 Alan Ryan, *John Dewey and the High Tide of American Liberalism*, op. cit., p.359.
8 John Dewey, *Human Nature and Conduct*, op. cit., p.4.
9 Ibid., p.210.
10 Ibid., pp.8–16.
11 Terry Hoy, *The Political Philosophy of John Dewey: Towards a Constructive Renewal*, Westport, CT: Praeger Publishers, 1998, pp.44–45.
12 Hilary Putnam, *Ethics without Ontology*, op. cit., pp.4–22.
13 John Dewey, *Human Nature and Conduct*, op. cit., pp.9–11.
14 John Dewey, *The Public and Its Problems*, op. cit., p.289.
15 Ibid., p.290.
16 Ibid., pp.291–292.
17 Ibid., p.294.
18 Ibid., p.294.
19 Ibid., p.299.
20 Ibid., p.299.
21 Ibid., p.299.

22 Ibid., pp.242–247.
23 Ibid., pp.243–244.
24 Ibid., pp.243–244.
25 Ibid., p.244.
26 Ibid., pp.304–324.
27 Graham Wallace, *Human Nature in Politics*, New Brunswick, NJ: Transaction Books, 1981.
28 Walter Lippmann, *Public Opinion*, New York: Macmillan, 1922.
29 Walter Lippmann, *The Phantom Public*, New Brunswick, NJ: Transaction Publishers, 1993.
30 John Dewey, *The Public and Its Problems*, op. cit., pp.304–350.
31 Ibid., pp.323–324.
32 Graham Wallace, *The Great Society*, New York; Macmillan, 1914.
33 John Dewey, *The Public and Its Problems*, op. cit., p.351.
34 Ibid., p.330.
35 Ibid., p.329.
36 Sterling P. Lamprecht, "Philosophy Put in Touch With Affairs," *New York Herald Tribune* Books, 27 November 1927, p.4.
37 Robert E. Park, "Book Reviews: The Public and Its Problems," *The American Journal of Sociology*, vol.34, 1928, pp.1192–1194.
38 Stephen Pepper, "Book Reviews: The Public and Its Problems," *The International Journal of Ethics: A Quarterly Devoted to the Advancement of Ethical Knowledge and Practice*, vol.38, 1927–1928, pp.478–480.
39 O. de Selincourt, "New Books: The Public and Its Problems," *Mind: A Quarterly Review of Psychology and Philosophy*, vol.37, 1928, pp.368–370.
40 Robert Morss Lovett, "A Real Public," *The New Republic*, vol.52, no.664, 24 August 1927, pp.22–23.

2 Creating Dialogical Communities in Schools

Education and Politics

In Chapter 1, I outlined a framework of Dewey's concepts of democracy and the public sphere that underlies visions of educational reforms in the 1920s. The discussion entailed the re-distinction between the public and the private as set by traditional liberalism. I characterized the theory of liberalism as a school that assumes an individualistically interpreted pre-political state of nature. In this chapter, I will explicate how Dewey connected his public philosophy with the concrete practices of democratic education. The crucial point of my argument in this chapter is to clarify how Dewey was engaged in educational practices as a matter of politics. Dewey's theory of democracy exhibits his commitment to restoring dialogical communities characterized by face-to-face relationships in education. For him, educational issues were clearly concerned with democratic politics.

Democratic Politics of Progressivism

Dewey's public philosophy was developed in the form of educational reforms in the 1920s. He was heavily engaged in democratic politics through actual educational events. During the presidential election of 1924 following the death of Warren Gamaliel Harding, while John Calvin Coolidge Jr of the Republican Party and John W. Davis of the Democratic Party stood as candidates, Dewey strongly supported Robert M. La Follette of the Progressive Party. La Follette was known for realizing open government for the people: as Governor of the state of Wisconsin, he introduced workers" compensation and a minimum wage, as well as the direct election of senators and female suffrage.

Dewey appealed for support of La Follette at a meeting in New York. Dewey highly evaluated La Follette's policy of understanding the reality of public problems by getting to the bottom of all the facts, and making these known to the people. He also supported La Follette's platform on international affairs that demanded a revision of the 1919 Versailles Treaty of World War I, since it criticized the outlawry of war and approached international problems from an economic perspective.[1] La Follette and the Progressive Party earned the support of farmers, labour activists and socialists by proposing government ownership of railroads and electric utilities, support for farmers, the deregulation of labour action, illegalization of child labour and protection of civil liberties. Although La Follette gained 17 per cent of the popular vote, he was defeated in the election. Coolidge became the 30th President on 3 August 1923. During the Coolidge Administration, the US experienced prosperous economic growth through the promotion of full-scale marketization by tax cuts and reductions in federal expenditures and debt.

In the next presidential election of 1928, Herbert Hoover of the Republican Party, Alfred E. Smith of the Democratic Party, Norman Thomas of the Socialist Party and several others stood as candidates. Dewey believed the policies of Thomas and the Socialist Party to be the most appropriate for proposing fundamental solutions to the political and social issues of unemployment, unequal redistribution and low living standards for people of low income, issues which were all heightened during the Coolidge Administration. Thomas, who was a pacifist, succeeded Eugene Debs for leadership of the Socialist Party and then ran for the presidential election. Thomas was inaugurated as Director of the League for Industrial Democracy in 1922. The League for Industrial Democracy was founded in 1905 as a socialist group of the Intercollegiate Socialist Society. The League rejected laissez-faire liberalism and urged the establishment of socialism by educating students about labour action and industrial democracy. Dewey expressed his support for, and cooperation with, the League. Dewey also served as the President of the League in 1939.[2]

Although Dewey showed his approval for Thomas' policies, he ultimately decided to vote for Smith instead of Thomas. Dewey admitted that, ideally, he should have supported Thomas and the Socialist Party considering the solutions to the political, economic and social problems initiated by Thomas, but he decided to cast his vote for Smith of the Democratic Party in order to prevent the establishment of the Hoover Administration (since the political situation at the time dictated that the election was basically between Hoover and Smith). Dewey's concerns were directed at conservative and oppressive political movements that began following the enforcement of the Prohibition Law, and the fact that religious and racial "bigotry and intolerance" had spread throughout society. Dewey held Smith in high regard since the latter had tackled these issues with "a humane and sympathetic sprit" as Governor of New York.[3] However, Hoover won the election by gaining a total of 58.20 per cent of the total votes cast, while Smith gained 40.77 per cent and Thomas 0.72 per cent.

With regard to the results, Dewey pointed out that presidential elections in the 1920s were "upon the whole determined by fear." According to his explanation, hundreds of thousands of citizens who voted independently or for Democratic candidates at local elections voted for the Republican Party at the federal elections every four years, and did so because of "a vague but influential dread lest a monkey-wrench be thrown into the economic and financial machine." It seemed "definitely better" for citizens to "endure the ills" they already suffered rather than "take the chance of disturbing industry." It was the majority of voters" "fear" and "dread" that constituted "the determining factor" to keep the ruling party in office in the 1928 election.[4]

Thus, Hoover was inaugurated as the 31st President in 1929 and Charles Curtis was elected as Vice-President. Hoover's governance continued a laissez-faire practice through its minimal intervention into social affairs.

Education for Citizenship: Community and Tolerance

During the 1920s, the US experienced urbanization and the expansion of a consumer society through the development of the auto, steel, railroad and oil industries and, as a result, achieved economical and material prosperity. Enterprise integration was activated and monopolistic rule by oligopoly began.

However, contrary to this economic prosperity, conservative and oppressive values permeated society. Discrimination against immigrants and minorities spread, and incidents of intolerance occurred frequently; among these were the expansion of the Ku Klux Klan, who asserted white Protestant superiority and appealed for the exclusion of black people and immigrants from the Emergency Quota Act (Johnson Quota Act, 1921); the Immigration Act (1924), which restricted the immigration of people from Southern and Eastern Europe and forbade Japanese immigration; the Scopes trial (1925), in which high school biology teacher John Thomas Scopes was found guilty of violating Tennessee's Butler Act (prohibiting the teaching of the theory of evolution in public schools); and the execution of anarchists Nicola Sacco and Bartolomeo Vanzetti (1927).

As a political and ethical philosopher, Dewey reacted to the issues sensitively, making critical utterances against them. In his lecture at the National Conference of Social Work held in Washington, D.C. in May 1923, Dewey expressed his concerns about the prevailing phenomena of "social intolerance" and "the growth of religious and racial intolerance" of "Americanization," which are "causes of divisions, of separation, and of mutual distrust." He stated that it would undermine "the community" of "feeling of respect for one another" and "trust in one another."[5] The Ku Klux Klan expanded its influence in the 1920s. Although there were fewer than 5,000 members in the early 1920s, it had gained the support of millions of people within a few years. It was hard for Dewey to accept the spread of unjustness and intolerance that arose from racial, ethnic and religious differences. He saw it as a lack of justice that immigrant children experienced discrimination in schools.

The enactment of the Immigration Act increased the pressure on domestic as well as newly arrived immigrants. According to David Tyack, "the restriction of immigration did not solve the problem of what to do with the people already here." Exclusive anti-immigration movements had spread and the frenzy for nationalism became the pillar of public education policies. There was strong pressure from various lobbying groups such as the American Legion, the American Bar Association and the Daughters of the American Revolution to pass laws stipulating the teaching of American history and the Constitution, and promoting "super-patriotic instruction" by banning the teaching of German in public schools. Thus, by 1923, 39 states required the teaching of "citizenship,"

33 states mandated that all teachers pass a test on the Constitution in order to obtain a teaching licence and 35 states enacted legislation making English the only language of instruction in public schools. While promoting the assimilation of immigrants, discrimination against minorities prevailed.[6]

In Dewey's view, when looking at the composition of the population, society is forced to face diversity and heterogeneous elements in everyday life. This was a reason why he felt that public schools should protect student diversity by "bringing children of different religions, of different traditions, of different races, and of different languages together" and "hav[e] them in contact with each other in common play, study and work" in the community as a whole. Even though there was a great danger of developing "a very narrow nationalistic spirit" and "patriotism," he believed that society needed to realize that whatever breeds "hostility and division without" is bound to produce "hostility and division within." Dewey stressed that the chief role of the school was "the shuttle which has carried the threads across and woven the otherwise separate threads into a coherent pattern" by providing students of different backgrounds "an opportunity to travel the road to learning," and which should continue to bring together "exceedingly heterogeneous elements of our population" through developing a social consciousness and ideals in children.[7]

In an address entitled "Social Purpose in Education" given at the State Conference of Normal School Instructors at Bridgewater, MA on 5 September 1922, Dewey emphasized that schools have a responsibility to educate students to be "good citizens." Students must be prepared to be members of communities by recognizing "the ties that bind them to all the other members of the community" and "the responsibility they have to contribute to the upbuilding of the life of the community." There are three phases for realizing this. First, it was not sufficient for Dewey to think of "good citizenship" in terms of "the political relations, duties and responsibilities of the person," or especially in terms of "the relation to the government." "Good political citizenship" should be grasped not only based on information about the nature of the government, but also from "a more concrete and vital knowledge" in every aspect of social life and relationships in the community. The second aspect of the social aim of education is concerned with industry. Dewey stressed that schools are supported by the community and have social purposes in training individuals to take care of themselves, industrially and economically, and to take care of those who are dependent on them. This suggests that it is important to create cooperative activities in social relationships with others. Third, "good citizenship" is related to people who can enjoy their life and leisure in a socially profitable way – in other words, the appreciation of art, science, history and literature should be encouraged.[8]

Even more important than these three points, in "What Is a School For?" published in *The New York Times* on 18 March 1923, Dewey insisted that public schools should exist to serve "the purposes of the community as a whole" and to develop "good citizens in the most comprehensive sense of that term." In order to do so, it would be necessary for schools to broaden the course of study to encompass a curriculum that goes beyond routine repetitions. "A narrow curriculum" is the one that "was taught mainly on the basis of routine, of following precedents – ways of instruction as restricted as were the subjects taught." The role of the school should not be restricted to instructing knowledge about the subject matter; rather, it is important that it teach "good citizenship" that serves to enrich community experiences.[9] In "Individuality in Education" (1923), Dewey defined "individuality" from the perspective of the "social individual," stating that individuality does not mean "a sort of isolation or separation of one person from another" that is opposed to "the community spirit." Teaching individuality is concerned with "a matter of spirit, of soul, of mind and the way in which one enters into cooperative relations with others."[10]

Education and Politics

In "Education as Politics" published in The New Republic in 1922, Dewey began his discussion with the theory of Matthew Arnold, that the "chief advantage of education is the assurance it gives of not being duped." Dewey added to this by saying that education gives the ability to discriminate and make distinctions that penetrate below the surface. He refused to teach "an undiscriminating gulping mental habit" that consisted of "avoidance of the spirit of criticism in dealing with history, politics and economics." For, although there is an implicit belief that this avoidance is the way to educate "good citizens," Dewey believed that it would merely produce "a loyal patriot."

It is crucial to think about the influence on the public by newspapers, printings, magazines and other news sources, since these new types of mass media in the 1920s were developing rapidly. Dewey was cautious of the fact that the media might function as "propaganda" that served to blind and mislead the public and guide the intellectual into confusion and ignorance. The point is, he was wary about whether the media evoked the spirit of criticism or fed into an undiscriminating gulping mental habit. By referring to Lippmann's idea of "stereotype," which might be created from the propaganda of mass media, Dewey highlighted the importance of educating "the public mind" on the basis of critical thinking and insightful judgement in schools. Dewey felt that teachers had a responsibility to cultivate "the habit of suspended judgment, of skepticism, of desire for evidence, of appeal to observation rather than sentiment, discussion rather than bias, inquiry rather than conventional idealizations." In fostering these qualities, schools would be "the dangerous outposts of humane civilization" but would also become "supremely interesting places." Then, it would transpire that "education and politics are one and the same thing," since "politics" for Dewey meant "the intelligent management of social affairs."[11]

One of the incidents in which Dewey was deeply involved in the 1920s was the trial of Sacco and Vanzetti. On the afternoon of 5 April 1920, a paymaster and security guard of a shoe company in South Braintree, MA were murdered by two men as they were carrying a factory payroll of $15,776. On May 5, Sacco and Vanzetti, Italian anarchists believing that social justice could be achieved by the abolition of government, and who worked as a shoemaker and a fish peddler in the factory, were arrested for the crime of murder. They were found guilty by the jury, even though there was insufficient physical evidence of murder. Protests over the convictions of the men were held in cities throughout the world, including New York, London, Paris, Berlin, Milan and Geneva. Socialists and radicals protested their innocence; since fears surrounding communism and radicals were prevalent in society, it seemed that anti-radical and anti-immigrant hysteria had led to the arrest and trial of Sacco and Vanzetti. However, they were executed on 23 August 1927.

Dewey also protested the trial, along with Lippmann and other prominent intellectuals. He was apprehensive about the trend permeating within society of threatening individuals" freedom of thought and beliefs. In "Psychology and Justice" (1927) in *The New Republic*, Dewey opposed the execution of Sacco and Vanzetti and stated that no discussion of their innocence or guilt could restore them to life. For Dewey, it was an issue of ensuring social justice, in a comprehensive sense, in the tone and temper of public opinion where racial division and class interests were involved, and one that raised the significance of developing and professing "respect for justice and devotion to equality and fraternity."[12]

In "The Fruits of Nationalism" (1927), Dewey analysed the origin of nationalism. Historically, nationalism emerged from the idea of "loyalty to a nation," which became a substitute for "the decay of personal absolutism and dynastic rule." While referring to the idea of Carlton Hayes, that nationalism had become "the religion of multitudes," Dewey pointed out that "nationalistic religions and [their] rationalization" produce "intolerant disregard of all other nations." In this regard, "patriotism" degenerated into "a power for evil" and "a hateful conviction of intrinsic superiority." According to him, "the rabies" that sent Sacco and Vanzetti to execution was "proof of how deeply such patriotism may canker."[13]

What disappointed Dewey were the societal tendencies that violated social justice and the rights of immigrants and people who did not share mainstream political, social and religious values. The congestion of people's suspicion and anger grew ceaselessly, while prejudices and discrimination against minorities spread throughout society. These situations might have blocked Dewey's attempts to restore democracy and the public sphere. Nationalistic practices gave rise to the formation of firm boundaries, and intercepted any exterior activity by the others. The trial of Sacco and Vanzetti contributed to dissolving people's lifestyles into homogeneous spaces under the disguise of patriotism, and led to the vagueness of their critical thinking and discernment. For Dewey, it was a matter of reviving the public sphere, to protect rights and justice and encourage a spirit of insightful and discriminating criticism in school students.

Furthermore, Dewey was eager to support the teachers' union, encouraging school teachers to be involved in organizing social action. He delivered lectures to the Teachers' Union of the City of New York in 1927 and 1928. This union was established by Henry Richardson Linville and Abraham Lefkowitz in 1916, in cooperation with the American Federation of Teachers. In the intolerant era of the 1920s, radicals led by Red Scare gathered in New York, which was the central base of US Bolshevism. The administration of New York City vigorously worked to expel the radicals of socialism and communism and sweep away their educational projects. The Lusk Laws, legislated in the 1920s, required teachers to show a loyal, obedient and patriotic attitude by enabling the revocation of teachers' licences in the event that they were considered disqualified or inept. The Teachers' Union of the City of New York protested the laws, since through them teachers became the target of thorough suppression. They appealed by pointing out the necessity of class size reduction, an increase in teachers' wages, improvement in their living standards and reform of the pension system.[14]

At the heart of Dewey's criticism of the legislation of the Lusk Laws was that it put teachers under "suspicion." He remarked, "personally, I feel resentful at this."[15] In light of promoting a close connection between teachers' and other labour unions, Dewey announced that the time had come to build "the principle of organization and cooperation and the recognition of common interests of all of those who work in any way."[16] The cooperative organization of the teachers' and labour unions was demanded in the 1920s, since in spite of the expansion of the economic gap and inequality between the rich and the poor, there was hardly any diminution in the disparity between income and wealth.

According to Paul Krugman, the US was "a vastly unequal society" in the 1900s, but "the level of inequality" remained almost unchanged through the 1920s. He was of the opinion that it reflected "the weak bargaining position of labor;" despite the fact that unionization rates and the influence of the unions gradually rose after 1900, by the late 1920s union membership, which comprised more than 17 per cent of the labour force in 1924, was back below 11 per cent due to counteraction by employers. Under this situation, large employers were free to set wages and working conditions without fear of organized opposition. Krugman concluded that "cultural and racial divisions among those with shared common economic interests prevented the emergence of an effective political challenge to extreme economic inequality."[17]

On 12 January 1928, Linville sent a letter to Dewey describing how he had heard from Gertrude Hartman that Dewey told her he would like to talk with Linville about establishing connections with the public school system. Hartman, who was the editor of the journal *Progressive Education* and the principal of Merion Country Day School in Pennsylvania, was also a keen supporter of Dewey. In *The Child and His World* (1922), Hartman proposed key ideas of progressive education by introducing Dewey's works.[18] In a letter to Dewey, Linville mentioned that it was a "serious mistake" for the progressive education movement to leave teachers' unions out of it, and that it was their pleasure to build cooperation between the two.[19] In response to Linville, Dewey gave a lecture at a meeting of the Teachers' Union of the City of New York in 1928. He declared his support for the teachers' union, while criticizing the oppressive and conservative decision taken by the council of the American Federation of Labor.[20]

Dewey strongly criticized the exclusive trend of suppression against people or groups that did not necessarily share the so-called mainstream thoughts and ideologies of society. He showed his opposition against prejudice that was especially directed at teachers. All of Dewey's oppositions and criticisms were because he felt a sense of crisis in that era of exclusion and suppression, triggered by the Lusk Laws.

Progressive Education and Qualitative Research in the Era of the Educational Measurement Movement

In his "Progressive Education and the Science of Education" address at the Eighth Annual Conference of the Progressive Education Association on 8 March 1928, Dewey focused on the topic of the relationship between progressive education and educational science. At that time the educational measurement movement, represented by the development of behavioural psychology and the professional bureaucratization of school systems, had expanded its influence throughout the education system by means of educational reforms. Standardized testing, the quantitative measurement of intelligence and quantitative research into education came under the umbrella of "science."

With regard to the concept of "educational science," the meaning of "science" itself was re-examined by Dewey in his address. Contrary to the idea that defined "science" as "a single and universal system of truths," "a rigid orthodoxy" and "a standardized set of beliefs accepted by all," Dewey interpreted it as "a body of verified facts and tested principles which may give intellectual guidance to the practical operating of schools." He believed that "educational science" should not be "a dead monotonous uniformity" that saw the aim of education as a fixed and absolute truth that restrained the practices of the school, but was something related to "facts" and "principles" that had been verified as functioning in democratic processes and practices.[21]

Notwithstanding strong opposition to it, Dewey upheld the progressive education movement by reviving its theories. One criticism arose from the "quantitative measurement" and "behavioral psychology" that swept over "educational research" from the 1890s to the 1920s. According to Lagemann, "educational research" emerged as "an empirical, professional science, built primarily around behaviorist psychology and the techniques and ideology of quantitative measurement." The quantitative measurement and behavioural psychology to which Lagemann referred had spread rapidly throughout the nation under the conditions of "professionalization" and "bureaucratization" during the era of ever-increasing numbers of colleges and universities.[22] Edward Thorndike's research, which introduced the behavioural perspective in psychology through his research on the outcomes of behaviour, specifically in relation to the stimulus–response theory of learning, had a huge impact on the educational measurement movement. John Broadus Watson, author of

Psychology: From the Standpoint of a Behaviorist (1919), contributed to popularizing the concept of "behaviorism,"[23] while Burrhus Frederic Skinner is known for inventing the new approach of "radical behaviorism" of the "operant conditioning chamber."

In addition, the introduction of a new system of testing called the IQ test, led by Lewis Madison Terman, soon spread widely. Terman, who had studied the intelligence test of Alfred Binet in France, published the "Stanford–Binet Intelligence Scales" in 1916 in order to measure students' abilities and intelligence by efficiently diagnosing their cognitive or developmental deficiencies, and differentiated school curricula that would best suit them. This took into consideration the fact that teachers faced difficulties teaching immigrants, due to the inflow of this population to urban areas. The IQ test was widely accepted as "scientific" and "objective," since its characteristics consisted of measuring the scores by computing the ratio of "mental age" to "chronological age." After receiving a request from Robert Mearns Yerkes, President of the American Psychological Association, Terman ended up playing a major role in developing an intelligence test for the US Army. The Army Intelligence Test was used on about two million people to measure the intelligence of recruits during World War I. The quantitative research and measurement of intelligence that advocated reliance on the test as "a professional science" were welcomed broadly in both schools and society.

Lagemann stated that, unlike philosophy, which was guided by "abstract values" and "theological beliefs," psychology involved "empirical research" and this lent it an aura of "objective science" that philosophy lacked. While these approaches were in great demand in the era of "professionalization" and "bureaucratization," other approaches to the study of education, specifically developed by Dewey, were pushed to "the margins." However, "Thorndike's triumph was not complete" and Dewey's philosophical approach was never totally eclipsed. In this regard, Dewey's theory reappeared from time to time in spite of his "defeat" in the twentieth century.[24]

Dewey's lecture on "Progressive Education and the Science of Education" was a response to the above situations. He highlighted that a progressive educator does not need to be unduly scared by the idea that science is constituted by quantitative results. The practices of traditional schools promoted the introduction of IQ tests and measurements that reflected modes of school administration wherein marks, grading, classes and promotions played key roles. The purpose of measurement was to set up a "norm," and this made possible the establishment of a more precise classification system. Contrary to imposing external subject matter and standards, Dewey praised progressive schools since they shared a common emphasis on respect for individuality, freedom, genuine mental activity, sincere emotional expression, growth and social relations such as communication and social intercourse.

The difference between the quantitative research of measurement and the qualitative research of education was related to the viewpoint of individuality and society: progressive schools grasped "individuality" from the viewpoint of "something developing and to be continuously attained," not "something given all at once and ready-made." Progressive schools also conceived education as a way to build a social order different in quality and direction from the existing one. The central point of Dewey's discussion lay in the idea that qualitative processes and results would not spoil the development of "science," since the quality of activity and its consequences were more important than the quantitative element.[25]

Dewey further investigated the theme of educational science in *The Sources of a Science of Education* in 1929. He drew two conclusions regarding the relationship between "educational practices" and "sciences." First, "educational practices" provide "the material that sets the problems" of "educational science," while "sciences" are "the sources from which material is derived to deal intellectually with these problems." The second is linked with the idea of "the objection to arm-chair science." This does not deny that thinking may be done in an armchair: rather, Dewey's objection was directed at "the remoteness of the thinking which is done from the original source of intellectual supplies." He attempted to restore the "vital connection between field-work practice and the research work." Concrete educational experience, he believed, was "the primary source of all inquiry and reflection;" it sets the problems and tests, modifies, confirms or refutes the conclusions of intellectual inquiries.[26]

Lagemann indicated that *The Source of a Science of Education* had not received the attention it deserved in spite of its incisive and illuminating contents. Dewey's commitment to integrating theory and practice was oriented towards pleading for more reliance on the philosophy of educational study than on quantification, since neglecting the philosophy of it would blind scholars to the wider meanings of education.[27] According to Linda Darling-Hammond, contrary to the confluence of behavioural learning theory and the bureaucratic organizational theory that led to the deskilling and controlling of teaching by limiting teaching autonomy, Dewey saw teachers as intellectuals, pedagogical innovators and "curriculum builders."[28] In the final paragraph of *The Source of a Science of Education*, Dewey wrote that "education is by its nature an endless circle or spiral" and "it is an activity which includes science within itself."[29]

Schools as Dialogical Communities: Education and Democratic Politics

The democratic politics that Dewey had in mind historically was "the town meeting" of a community, because communication in a town meeting made it possible for people to exchange their thoughts and ideas concerning the building of schools, roads and the peace of the community. Having developed arguments and discussions through face-to-face relationships, people could sustain their lives, culture and the environment. With regard to public school, a "school district" was formed by the township of "self-governing communities." More specifically, people built a schoolhouse, hired teachers and paid salaries to the teacher from the taxes in the school district. It was the political decision making by communicative interaction that set the school curriculum, administrative organization and educational methods. Through responding to public opinion and thoughts, the school committee contributed to educational reform in the community by democratic politics.[30]

The concept of communication was investigated by Dewey more deeply in terms of the distinction between "soliloquy" and "dialogue." For him, "logic" recurs to the primitive sense of the word: "dialogue." Contrary to "dialogue," "soliloquy" is a broken and imperfect thought in which ideas are not communicated, shared or reborn in expression. It is striking that Dewey paid attention to the role of "hearing" in dialogue. Dewey believed that "the connections of the ear with vital and out-going thought and emotion are immensely closer and more varied than those of the eye." He continued to opine that "vision is spectator, hearing is a participator." "Hearing" would furnish "social intelligence" for the public, when what was heard circulated by word of mouth from one to another through communication. The point that Dewey used to distinguish between soliloquy and dialogue was to explain that the latter generates intelligent activities through hearing others' voices, while the former constructs a world that lacks the existence of the other in human interactions. According to Dewey, dialogical communities of hearing therefore go beyond the ignorance and prejudice of the masses.[31]

It is undoubtedly true that opening a way to realize democratic processes and practices was not an easy task. However, it is also important to bear in mind that a new concept of democratic politics and the public sphere would be generated through acquiring the insightful habit of critical thinking, and promoting social justice and dialogical communities of face-to-face relationships. For Dewey, the distinctive feature of educational science was its focus on qualitative processes and the results of an endless circle or spiral, rather than fostering quantitative approaches to something given all at once and ready-made. Thus, the encouragement of educational reforms was connected to the participation of the public in democratic politics.

Notes

1 John Dewey, "Dewey Aids La Follette," *The Middle Works*, vol.15, p.317.
2 John Dewey, "Address of Welcome to the League for Industrial Democracy," *The Later Works*, vol.14, pp.262–265.
3 John Dewey, "Why I am for Smith," *The Later Works*, vol.3, pp.184–185.
4 John Dewey, "Individualism, Old and New," *The Later Works*, vol.5, pp.91–92.
5 John Dewey, "The School as a Means of Developing a Social Consciousness and Social Ideals in Children," *The Middle Works*, vol.15, pp.150–157.
6 David Tyack, *Seeking Common Ground: Public Schools in a Diverse Society*, Cambridge, MA: Harvard University Press, 2003, pp.74–77.
7 John Dewey, "The School as a Means of Developing a Social Consciousness and Social Ideals in Children," op. cit., pp.150–157.
8 John Dewey, "Social Purpose in Education," *The Middle Works*, vol.15, pp.158–169.
9 John Dewey, "What Is School For?," *The Middle Works*, vol.15, pp.190–192.
10 John Dewey, "Individuality in Education," *The Middle Works*, vol.15, pp.170–179.

11 John Dewey, "Education as Politics," *The Middle Works*, vol.13, pp.329–334.
12 John Dewey, "Psychology and Justice," *The Later Works*, vol.3, pp.186–195.
13 John Dewey, "The Fruits of Nationalism," *The Later Works*, vol.3, pp.152–154.
14 See Sol Cohen, *Progressives and Urban School Reform: The Public Education Association of New York City 1895–1954*, New York: Bureau of Publications, 1964, pp.103–104.
15 John Dewey, "The School as a Means of Developing a Social Consciousness and Social Ideals in Children," op. cit., p.153.
16 John Dewey, "Why I Am a Member of the Teachers Union," *The Later Works*, vol.3, pp.269–275.
17 Paul Krugman, *The Conscience of a Liberal*, New York: W. W. Norton & Co., 2007, pp.17–27.
18 Gertrude Hartman, *The Child and His World: An Interpretation of Elementary Education as a Social Process*, New York: E. P. Dutton, 1922.
19 Henry R. Linville to John Dewey, 12 January 1928, Special Collections Research Center, Morris Library, Southern Illinois University Carbondale, IL; *The Correspondence of John Dewey*, vol.2.
20 John Dewey, "Labor politics and Labor Education," *The Later Works*, vol.5, pp.338–345.
21 John Dewey, "Progressive Education and the Science of Education," *The Later Works*, vol.3, pp.257–259.
22 Ellen C. Lagemann, *An Elusive Science: The Troubling History of Education Research*, op. cit., pp.16–22.
23 John B. Watson, *Psychology: From the Standpoint of a Behaviorist*, Philadelphia, PA: Lippincott, 1919.
24 Ellen C. Lagemann, *An Elusive Science: The Troubling History of Education Research*, op. cit., pp.1–63.
25 John Dewey, "Progressive Education and the Science of Education," op. cit., pp.257–268.
26 John Dewey, "The Sources of a Science of Education," *The Later Works*, vol.5, pp.1–40.
27 Ellen C. Lagemann, *An Elusive Science: The Troubling History of Education Research*, op. cit, pp.231–232.
28 Linda Darling-Hammond, *Powerful Teacher Education: Lessons from Exemplary Programs*, op. cit., pp.77–78.
29 John Dewey, *The Sources of a Science of Education*, op. cit, p.40.
30 John Dewey, *The Public and Its Problems*, op. cit., pp.304–307.
31 Ibid., pp.371–372.

3 Education, Democracy and the Public Sphere

The Transformation of Liberalism

The past 30 years have seen a remarkable rise in interest in the reconstruction of the public sphere in education. Perhaps one of the most prominent movements to dominate educational reform during this period was the ideology of neoliberalism. While criticizing the welfare state liberalism that started with the New Deal of the 1930s, the proponents of neoliberalism attempted to expand the market principle of schools by promoting privatization, liberalization and the deregulation of choice and competition. On the other hand, the global economic depression stemming from the monetary crisis in 2008 exposed the limitations of neoliberalism, and prompted a renewed interest in New Deal liberalism which pledged to restore prosperity through large-scale government intervention in the economy. In this era of the transformation of liberalism, designing a new vision of democratic education and the public sphere was called for.

The increased interest in a public philosophy that was distinct from traditional liberalism and that reflected the changing post-1980s world focused attention on the philosophy of Habermas and Arendt. Habermas convincingly insisted on the need for establishing "civil society" and a "public sphere" by "communicative action" in the "lifeworld." For him, it was obvious that democracy was in crisis because of the "colonization of [the] lifeworld by systems." The model of the public sphere that Habermas advocated was derived from the civil society of nineteenth-century liberalism: that is, criticizing a post-war welfare state and reviving democracy on the basis of the ideal procedure of deliberation and decision making. Whereas Habermas' work was directed at restoring the civil society of liberalism, Arendt's approach, which saw "the polis" of ancient Greece as a prototype, tended to reflect a republican interpretation of the public sphere in which political activity was performed. Or, to put it another way, for Arendt an expansion of "the social" entailed an eclipse of "the public" and "political action," which was distinct from the activities of "labour" and "work" and would bring about and preserve the public realm.

Dewey criticized two social forms that symbolized traditional US liberalism (i.e. the market principle of laissez-faire and the welfare state of the New Deal in the 1930s). He observed that, historically, liberalism had corrupted the ideals of democracy and community. At the centre of his project was the development of democracy and the public sphere in education. By calling his position "renascent liberalism," he embarked on the reconstruction of the public sphere by defining democracy as "a way of living together." In *Liberalism and Social Action* (1935), Dewey stated that "the first object of a renascent liberalism is education;, after asserting the necessity for liberalism to become radical.[1] Education was thought to have a positive role in the transformation of liberalism.

However, in *Liberalism and Social Action*, education was not concretely discussed. Dewey's educational theories in the 1930s were instead developed through numerous short pieces published in various articles. He advocated the importance of public participation and communication by criticizing the market control or the welfare state control of education, and developed innovative school reforms with democracy and the public sphere as underlying principles. The school was regarded as an educational agency that was connected with social and cultural changes, and he investigated educational methods of democratic politics for creating "a way of living together." In this chapter, I will look at Dewey's educational theories and practices of the 1930s, taking the concepts of democracy and the public sphere into consideration.

The Transformation of Liberalism and Education in the 1930s

In the 1930s, Dewey searched for ways to invent democracy and the public sphere that were distinct from the principles of traditional liberalism. His suggestions for the restoration of the public sphere can be seen in the following statement.

> Liberalism must now become radical, meaning by radical perception of the necessity of thorough-going changes in the set-up of institutions and corresponding activity to bring changes to pass.[2]

> When, then, I say that the first object of a renascent liberalism is education, I mean that its task is to aid in producing the habits of mind and character, the intellectual and moral patterns, that are somewhere near even with the actual movements of events.[3]

For Dewey, it was not enough to develop just "piecemeal policies" for solving the problem of the large "gulf" between what "the actual situation ma[de] possible" and "state itself" – there was a fundamental difference between "reform," which temporarily relieved social evils without social ideas and action and resulted in comprehensive plans, and "re-formation," which changed the systematic institutionalization of a phenomenon from its essence. The process by which change was produced was considered to be radical.[4]

However, what was the actual state to which Dewey referred? And in what sense did it need re-formation? Dewey stressed that when traditional liberalism first led to laissez-faire-type market principles, it caused a weakening of democracy and the community. He understood it to be a state that entrapped the public sphere during crisis. That is, logic that emphasized the predominance of economic objectives over political objectives was interpreted (at that time) as being the present state of liberalism. Its history and changes to its interpretation could be traced from Locke's definition of it, to classical economics, to welfare state liberalism.

Dewey claimed that the ideological groundwork that invited the principles of market liberalism was initially prepared by the liberalism of Locke. Locke's thoughts on the liberalism of governments were that it was "instituted to protect the rights that belong to individuals prior to political organization of social relations," and those rights were summed up in the American Declaration of Independence: the rights of life, liberty and the pursuit of happiness. Dewey took up the "rights of property" in Locke's philosophy, stating that it originated "in the fact that an individual has mixed himself, through his labour, with some natural hitherto unappropriated object." According to Dewey's interpretation of this initial liberalism, the government was considered to have a duty to protect the "rights of property" as the "natural rights" with which an individual was endowed.[5]

The whole temper of this philosophy is individualistic in the sense in which individualism is opposed to organized social action. It held to the primacy of the individual over the state not only in time but in moral authority.[6]

Here, it needs to be pointed out that the confrontational view that juxtaposed the individual and society was according to the ideals set out by traditional liberalism. For Dewey, this led to the idea that two different domains, termed the spheres of "political society" and the "individual," existed, and through this idea he came to the understanding that "in the interest of the latter the former must be as contracted as possible." This thought was tied to market individualism, which explains its economic predominance in politics.[7]

What is more important is the fact that not only economic individualism, but also moral individualism materialized in liberalism in its initial phase. Initial liberalism stood by the position of considering that a natural law was "the counterpart of reason, being disclosed by the natural right with which man is endowed," and because of this, the assumption of moral individualism, where an individual can use reason, existed autonomously. Dewey acknowledged that the problem lay in the theory that reason was considered as "an inherent endowment of the individual," not as a thing developed and maintained by "men's moral relations to one another." He believed that an individual will keep away from political and ethical domains by assuming that individual freedom is opposed to social action or cooperative activity.[8]

This tendency was promoted by the appearance of classical economics in the late eighteenth and the nineteenth century. Adam Smith, David Ricardo, Thomas Robert Malthus and John Stuart Mill had at that time developed the study of economics that denied mercantilism and claimed the primacy of individual freedom of economic activity through minimal government intervention. Dewey argued that although classical economists respected the principle of the free economic activity of individuals, "this freedom was identified with absence of governmental action, conceived as an interference with natural liberty," and led to "the formation of laissez-faire liberalism." He also described how the concept of the "rights of property," which initial liberalism assumed, brought about the economical formation of laissez-faire.[9]

Dewey regarded Adam Smith as a typical proponent of the market principle. Though limitations were attached to this understanding, as Smith did not necessarily stick to the idea of marketization unconditionally, Dewey paid attention to the fact that Smith claimed "the activity of individuals, freed as far as possible from political restriction, is the chief source of social welfare and the ultimate spring of social progress." For Dewey, Smith emphasized that "there is a natural or native tendency in every individual to each better his own estate through putting forth effort (labour) to satisfy his natural wants." The history of nineteenth-century liberalism consisted of "the guidance of an invisible hand" and, as explained by Smith, "the efforts of individuals for personal advancement and personal gain accrue[d] to the benefit of society, and create[d] a continuously closer knit interdependence of interests." Dewey made it clear that its ultimate purpose was to "subordinate political to economic activity."[10]

Social Organization of Actions and Intelligence

The Republican Administrations of the 1920s and early 1930s, of Harding, Coolidge and Hoover, promoted laissez-faire liberalism enlightened by the theory of classical economics. The Coolidge Administration adhered to the legitimacy of the free market principle that would leave the business cycles to natural processes. In that era of unprecedented economic growth, Coolidge believed in small government of the laissez-faire theory, in which the chief role of the government was to support business and serve economic sectors as a whole. At that time, mega-industries and holding companies appeared one after another, GNP showed a 45.6 per cent rise from 1921 to 1929, and people's standards of living improved dramatically.

Coolidge was eager for deregulation and enforced cuts to income and sales taxes. Whereas inland revenue declined from $5,400 million in 1920 to $2,600 million in 1925, the federal budget continued to have a return of $700 million to $1 billion every year, due to the increase in tariff revenues caused by a huge trade surplus and capital export. Under the Coolidge Administration, the laissez-faire system, or classical economics, was promoted, and the policy was inherited by the Hoover Administration. A definite upsurge in economic prosperity during these administrations made it difficult to doubt laissez-faire policies of marketization.

On the other hand, this was also a time when economic gaps and inequalities greatly expanded. According to Paul Krugman, pre-New Deal America was "a land of vast inequality in wealth and power, in which a nominally democratic political system failed to represent the economic interests of the majority." The share belonging to the high-income group of the total income in the 1920s showed that 10 per cent of the highest earners gained 43.6 per cent of the income, and 1% of the highest-earners group earned 17.3 per cent of the income. In spite of the great disparities in income, increasing number of poorly paid workers and minimally taxed elites, the demand for the American government to play an important role in the mitigation of inequalities was not strong. This was not because the concepts of public aid and welfare state had yet to be invented in the world, since old-age pensions, unemployment insurance and national health insurance had been introduced in Germany in the 1880s. Rather, the absence of strong demand was the outcome of the decline in organized labour and the weakness of employees. Krugman concludes that "cultural and racial divisions among those with shared common economic interests prevented the emergence of an effective political challenge to extreme economic inequality."[11]

Dewey made an issue of the ideology of such market principles in society as representing "the actual state" of liberalism. Since society was seen to be opposed to individuals and set upon removing the social restrictions imposed on them, it would be "ineffective" to solve the problems of social organization and integration.[12] For him, "it is in organization for action that liberals are weak," and without the organization of social action and intelligence, there was a danger that "democratic ideals may go by default." The translation of ideas and faith into social action and cooperative intelligence signified that "vital and courageous democratic liberalism" was the one force that could avoid a disastrous confusion.[13]

The recognition of connecting democracy to education requires the opening of dialogical spaces of communication organized by social actions and cooperative intelligence. It indicates that democratic politics involve the social organization of interactive communication; it aims to contribute to the solution of various issues that would be forgotten if neglected by market-centred liberalism. In this sense, the public sphere is not the space that emerges naturally. In order to promote social justice and equality, the public sphere should be organized by democratic politics in accordance with public action and intelligence. Dewey thought that without the recreation of society and culture organized by social and cooperative actions, democratic politics could not be accomplished. Democratic politics, for him, had their foundation in the design of his democratic education and public sphere, steeped in the politics and ethics of "renascent liberalism."

Democracy as a Way of Living Together: Philosophy of the Common Man

In "Democracy Is Radical," published in *Common Sense* in 1937, Dewey highlighted the point that democracy is radical because it requires great changes, economic, legal and cultural, to existing social institutions.[14] He expressed this as "cooperative democracy" and "creative democracy." In *Education and Social Change* (1937), he stated:

> Democracy also means voluntary choice, based on an intelligence that is
> the outcome of free association and communication with others. It means
> a way of living together in which mutual and free consultation rule instead
> of force, and in which cooperation instead of brutal competition is the
> law of life; a social order in which all the forces that makes for friendship,
> beauty, and knowledge are cherished in order that each individual may
> become what he, and he alone, is capable of becoming.[15]

Democracy was defined as "a way of living together" through free association
with others, communication and mutual consultation. Democracy was far larger
than "a special political form" or "a method of conducting government, of
making laws and carrying on governmental administration." According to his
thought, "the political and governmental phase of democracy" was a means
to achieve the ends that lay in the wide domain of human relationships and
the development of human personality: namely the best means to realize "a
way of life, social and individual."[16]

> The key-note of democracy as a way of life may be expressed, it seems to
> me, as the necessity for the participation of every mature human being in
> formation of the values that regulate the living of men together – which
> is necessary from the standpoint of both the general social welfare and the
> full development of human beings as individuals.[17]

Axel Honneth, who regards Habermas' "proceduralism" and Arendt's
"republicanism" as prevalent notions in the contemporary age seeking the
"democratic public sphere" after the "criticism of liberalism," highly appreciates
Dewey's theory of "democracy as a reflective cooperation" in light of pursuing
a "third way," which constitutes an alternative to their movements. According
to Honneth, Dewey began his discussion of democracy from a "model of social
cooperation" in line with "a reflective form of community cooperation"
instead of a "model of communicative deliberation" through "intersubjective
speech." Honneth calls Dewey's theory "expanded democracy," which is
different from "republicanism" and "democratic proceduralism."[18] Bernstein
also comments positively on Dewey, pointing out that his "vision of radical
communal democracy" is not "a set of formal procedures" but a "moral ideal."
For Bernstein, the theme that runs throughout Dewey's social and educational
writings was "the need to reconstruct democratic communal life – a form of
life that requires and cultivates civic virtue."[19]

Although Honneth and Bernstein share a common approach that aims
to exceed "procedural democracy" from the standpoint of "a criticism of
liberalism," their visions differ in that, while Honneth places an emphasis
on "a reflective form of community cooperation," Bernstein pursues a "moral
ideal" of democracy. Dewey's focus on democracy was one that would become
"part of the bone and blood of the people."[20] "Democracy as a way of life"
cleared the ground for interpreting the idea of the public sphere within the

dimensions of the participation of every human being in the formation of a political and ethical life of free association, which constitutes values through social action and intelligence.

In Dewey's democratic theory there existed "faith in the possibilities of human nature" and "belief in the Common Man." In an article titled "Creative Democracy: The Task Before Us" (1939), he claimed that "belief in the Common Man" was "without basis and significance," save as a means for "faith in the potentialities of human nature" as that nature was exhibited in every human being irrespective of race, colour, sex, birth, family or material or cultural wealth. His theory signified that "democracy is a way of life controlled by a working faith in the possibilities of human nature."[21] Dewey extended the theories of traditional liberalism, which had its roots in the individualistic idea of naturalism of "democracy as a way of life," and this opened up the possibility of participation in cooperative action and intelligence. Dewey's idea of the public sphere was not founded on the concept of natural rights and a law of nature, but consistently showed faith in the potentialities of human nature and the Common Man.

Dewey announced the necessity for building democracy through "the method of mutual consultation and voluntary agreement" after saying, "the very fact of exclusion from participation is a subtle form of suppression."[22] Here, the ideas of participation and suppression are important since suppression is not only the thing resulting from the visible use of power by specific members of the government, but also a subtle form of executing exclusion from participation. It indicates that exclusion might occur in communities where the majority of the members reach agreement, as minorities are likely to be governed by them indirectly as a result. This is a reason why Dewey interpreted exclusion from participation as a form of suppression, and searched for a way for people to live together with dialogical and interactive communication. The ideas of creative democracy, cooperative democracy and the democratic community were set forth to prevent exclusion from participation.

Liberal journals and newspapers took up book reviews of *Liberalism and Social Action* after its publication. Alfred M. Bingham's review in *Common Sense* in 1935 evaluated Dewey's volume in depth, mentioning that it was a book that "lifts one out of one's seat with intellectual enthusiasm." For him, contrary to Hoover's policy, the New Deal, communism and fascism, Dewey's book aimed to "restore one's faith in the role of intelligence" and represented "a pinnacle of the human mind and spirit." Bingham added that Dewey's idea of "renascent liberalism" was "the synthesis between liberalism and radicalism" in which "cooperative intelligence followed up in action that has made possible social progress, not brute force or dogmatism."[23]

According to Edwin T. Buehrer, who published a review in *The Christian Century* in September 1935, Dewey identified liberalism with "applied social intelligence" and perceived that "human beings have, in the last analysis, no other effective method to which they can resort." On the other hand, Buehrer raised questions with regard to current social tensions: "What is the efficacy of the profit motive?" "What is the nature of freedom under a state of economic regimentation?" "To what extent is the socialization of industry desirable and possible?" "What, in lieu of violence, are the techniques of revolution to which intelligence can and must resort?" Buehrer remarked that it is "a matter of regret" that Dewey did not extend his book to include those topics, and expressed hope that "further analysis will yet come from Professor Dewey's pen."[24]

John Chamberlain's review, published in *Current History* in 1935, regarded Dewey's liberalism as socialism. He commented that *Liberalism and Social Action* is "in part, a clarification of the confusion surrounding the word 'liberal,' and in part an obfuscation of the word." By Chamberlain's assertion, "to be truly liberal today, says Dewey, one must be a Socialist." He also pointed out that, historically speaking, "the adjective 'liberal' was first used substantively to mean an adherent of the Manchester school of free-trade capitalism," but that it had come to "resort to illiberal means to perpetuate itself, must suppress civil liberties, habeas corpus, integrity of the personality and so on." Based on these changes he identified, Chamberlain asked "why does not Dewey call himself a libertarian Socialist, or a democratic Socialist?"[25]

Reinhold Niebuhr, a Protestant theologian, published a review of Dewey's work in *The Nation* on 11 September 1935. For Niebuhr, the ultimate end towards which Dewey strived was "socialistic," though he also believed that Dewey had been not only "the leading philosophical exponent of liberal doctrine" but also "the fountain and source of liberal pedagogical theory and method." In Niebuhr's understanding of Dewey's philosophy, "the great contribution of historic liberalism" was its emphasis on "liberty and intelligence." However, Niebuhr criticized Dewey's "faith" in "intellectual liberalism," since it did not recognize "the relation of social and economic interest to the lay of intelligence upon social problems." Additionally, in spite of the fact that Dewey wanted to "resolve social difficulties without violence," his discussion lacked "realism" because he saw violence only as "a consequence of a social ignorance" which could only be eliminated by a more perfect intelligence. In Niebuhr's conclusion, he stated that "whatever the possibilities and necessities of social intelligence in social action, that thesis is a hopeless one," and, so far as renascent liberalism rested on it, would "confuse the political problem." Niebuhr called it "the pathos of liberalism."[26]

Horace M. Kallen's review, entitled "Salvation by Intelligence," was published in *Saturday Review of Literature* on 13 December 1935. According to Kallen, Dewey sought the "new birth of liberalism," rejecting both laissez-faire and collectivism, and believing that the task of liberalism was to "keep the ways to the good life wide open for every man" by organizing a "cooperative intelligence." However, Kallen claimed that Dewey did not suggest a concrete "program to implement the principle."[27] Book reviews of Dewey's *Liberalism and Social Action* were also published in the *New York Times Book Review* (1935),[28] *The New Republic* (1936),[29] *People's Lobby Bulletin* (1936),[30] *The International Journal of Ethics* (1936),[31] *The American Journal of Sociology* (1938)[32] and others.

All of this suggests that Dewey tried to overcome traditional liberalism by regarding democracy as "a way of living together." Teaching democracy was a project that for him would go beyond the tradition of liberalism, which was developed on the basis of individualism and centring on the freedom of individual economic activity, investigations into industrial efficiency, and security about the neutrality of political and institutional procedures. Thus, through dialogical communication and participation, in connection with cooperative actions and intelligence, democratic education would promote "a way of life, social and individual" that would protect the politics and ethics of the public sphere.

Politics of a Third Party: Democratic Processes and Practices

In his attempts to create democratic processes and practices, Dewey encountered various difficulties, specifically during the era of the Great Depression and the New Deal in the 1930s. The vision of educational reform that Dewey had sketched required significant changes to democratic politics.

The Great Depression, which arose from the crash of the New York Stock Exchange on 24 October 1929, triggered a catastrophic depression worldwide and promoted policy shifts on political, economic and social affairs. In the US around 1924, the capital inflow centred on speculation activated by the stock market and the Dow Jones Industrial Average soared five times in five years, reaching a peak average stock price of $381.17 on 3 September 1929. However, the stock market began to fall on 24 October that year and on 29 October, known as "Black Tuesday," the stock market price of General Motors that had led the prosperity of the 1920s suddenly dropped. The banks in Arkansas, Illinois, North Carolina, Indiana and Mississippi, and the Bank of the United States in New York State, went bankrupt. The amount of gross investment in domestic residence, equipment and stock fell to no more than 35% between 1929 and 1930. Consequently, production control, deflation, an increase in the unemployment rate and income reduction all accelerated.

The instability of the financial system stemming from a fluctuation in the stock price on Wall Street massively affected the world economy, which resulted in the breakdown of the largest bank in Austria, Creditanstalt, in 1931. During the period between 1929 and 1932, the US experienced the large-scale fall in its GNP from $101,300 to $50,800 million, which resulted from the sudden drop in industrial production to 46%, national income to 51 per cent, company sales to 50 per cent and export returns to 36 per cent, of initial levels.[33]

Political and social changes that occurred during this period encouraged Dewey to engage in democratic practices. He was deeply involved in political and social activities through the League for Independent Political Action and the People's Lobby. On December 15, 1928, around 50 scholars, writers, editors and civil activists gathered at the International House on the Upper West Side of New York in order to prepare for the establishment of the League for

Independent Political Action. Dewey, William Edward Burghardt Du Bois, Reinhold Niebuhr, Zona Gale, James Maurer, Oswald Garrison Villard, Paul Howard Douglas, Norman Thomas and others participated in the meeting.

These attendees had not necessarily had active exchanges with each other beforehand, and their interests were not necessarily completely complementary. For instance, although Dewey and Du Bois had interacted with each other at the National Negro Conference held in New York in May 1909 (held in preparation for the inauguration of the National Association for the Advancement of Colored People (NAACP)), little exchange had occurred between them otherwise.[34] Du Bois, who in 1895 was the first African American to receive a PhD from Harvard University, contributed to commanding the Niagara Movement in 1905 and created the National Association for the Advancement of Colored People. Du Bois was a prominent activist for Pan-Africanism through tackling racial discrimination and inequalities, and by writing many books, including *The Souls of Black Folk* (1903) and *Darkwater: Voices from within the Veil* (1920).[35]

The members of the League for Independent Political Action came to share their interests gradually through their correspondence. The League looked up to the Labour Party and the Fabian Society in Britain as models for their organization. Dewey, Du Bois and others agreed to prepare for the establishment of a third political party that was inspired by these British societies' political actions. Dewey was elected as the first President of the League for Independent Political Action in September 1929. On 13 October 11 days before the stock market crash, Dewey was a guest on the radio programme *World of Radio*. In that programme, Dewey criticized the old parties that showed off "old phrases" and "old slogan[s]" for surrendering "abjectly to domination by big business interests." For him, leaders of the League for Independent Political Action believed that American society needed "reorganization" based on a sense of the realities of human life.[36]

In an article titled "What Do Liberals Want?," published in *Outlook and Independent* on 16 October 1929, Dewey pointed out that liberals were hard to organize because of "a natural bond of cohesion among conservatives and reactionaries." For him, if liberals were "tired," it was because they lacked the support and invigoration of a unified common movement. In that sense, the League for Independent Political Action intended to cooperate with liberal groups and individuals to bring them into "conscious contact" and promote "solidarity" among them, which would form "the condition of further effective political action."

After accepting a request by Benjamin C. Marsh, Dewey was also inaugurated as the President of the People's Lobby in 1929. As President of the People's Lobby, he turned his criticism against the Hoover Administration's post-Depression policy. According to the article "Attacks Wage Disparity" in *The New York Times* on 26 December 1929, the People's Lobby issued a statement that there should be "a fairer distribution of the national income" because the income of millions of American families was far below the requirements of decent living. By indicating figures from 1927, that 11,112 persons received an aggregate annual income of close to $3 billion, and that in the same year 866,581 wage earners received an average annual wage of $1,073, Dewey showed his concern about this inequality and the expansion of the economic gap. He appealed to the federal government to spend billions of dollars towards federal child relief, unemployment and old-age pensions by taxing incomes over $10,000.[37] Dewey also urged members of Congress to support the Wheeler–La Guardia Bill to establish the Federal Child Relief Board that would appropriate $25 million for child relief for the balance of the fiscal year 1930. The People's Lobby asserted that the bill was relief for children in distress due to problems faced by their parents that included prolonged strikes, unemployment and extreme poverty.[38]

Dewey also asked the Hoover Administration to provide relief to low-income families, and insurance for the unemployed and elderly people, since 3,000,000 to 5,000,000 individuals had experienced unemployment for a period of at least three months (and some for up to over a year), with little prospect of substantial improvement for employment. In a letter he asked President Hoover to make a request of the Congress that, before suspending the appropriation of at least $250 million for the subvention of a state unemployment insurance system, the federal government first pay half of the benefits.

Demanding federal aid for a state unemployment insurance system was not because the aid would prevent unemployment itself, but because economic conditions were so dire. Dewey stated at that time that "mechanization has proceeded so far and so fast that our past policy of laissez faire with respect to other industries is as fatal as it was with respect to agriculture," and that the federal government had an obligation to overcome the difficulties of mechanization (resulting in profits for the few through cheaper production costs) not only for the sake of "human welfare," but also for "national prosperity."[39] Dewey made a public statement asking President Hoover to call Congress to a special session in order to take measures for creating a system of unemployment insurance.[40] Referring to the fact that unemployed individuals and their dependents amounted to 12,000,000 people, or one tenth of the population, Dewey mentioned that it was not "an accident" but "the inevitable result of economic policies fostered by both major parties," requiring Congress to urgently appropriate $500 million for relief operations, though it needed $2 billion to actually change the situation.[41]

It was his strong belief that there was a need to establish a third political party through the League for Independent Political Action, facing the situation that President Hoover had not taken fundamental measures to address the economic depression and dramatic increase in the number of people unemployed. Dewey and other members complained about the policies of the Republican and Democratic Parties, and in the Representative election of 1930, Dewey voted for the Socialist Party. He showed his support for Baruch Charney Vladeck, socialist candidate for Representative in the Eighth

Congressional District, Brooklyn, Samuel Orr, socialist candidate for Congress in the Twenty-third District, and Abraham Isaac Shiplacoff in the Twelfth District.[42] However, the elections in those three districts resulted in victory for the Democratic Party.

It was not easy for the League to create a new political party, though League members were in agreement about the intention to create a third party. The crucial point was: who would be suitable to lead the party? Norman Thomas, who ran for presidential election in 1928, and his supporters had the idea that the Socialist Party was suitable for playing the leading role of a third party. Meanwhile, the liberal and progressive groups tended to share the thought that the Socialist Party would not attract the attention of the middle class, which had gained political influence with the development of mass society in the 1920s.

Finally, the League decided to support George William Norris, who was the senator of Nebraska. Although Norris belonged to the Republican Party, he voted against the Republican candidates and declared that his policy was influenced by progressive ideals. For instance, Norris attacked Henry Ford's project in the Tennessee Valley that produced electricity and fertilizer for profit, and proposed that the government should lead the project instead. In the Seventy-first Congress in 1930, Norris put forth the Anti-Injunction Bill which prohibited employers from preventing the formation of unions or taking legal action against union organizers in active labour disputes.

In December 1930, Dewey sent a letter to Norris asking him to become a representative of a third party and command the new political movement. For Dewey, Norris stood for "social planning and social control," despite the fact that the Republican Party stood for "rugged individualism" by giving "free rein to private competition." He also noted that, contrary to the Republican Party, which placed "property rights" first, Norris placed "human rights" first. It was important for Dewey that notice be taken of the fact that people were suffering from an unemployment crisis, the increasing fear of insecurity, unjust distribution of wealth and the nationalism and militarism which led to World War I. For Dewey, a new party with a "philosophy of life" could stop "these evils." He asked Norris to "participate in the thrill and enthusiasm of a great movement which is our own and which will realize for common men their rightful heritage," since millions of progressives were longing for the establishment of a new political alignment.[43] However, Norris did not accept the offer to lead a third party, though he welcomed the new political actions and movements generated by the League for Independent Political Action. Norris considered himself "a good Republican" and chose to realize progressive policies by belonging to the Republican Party.[44]

The project that encouraged Norris to lead a new political party ended in failure. Nevertheless, the League for Independent Political Action did not throw away the hope of building a new political party. Dewey criticized President Hoover's policy in articles published in the *People's Lobby Bulletin*. He highlighted the fact that the government should be responsible for unemployment and that voters needed to demand congress to tax wealth instead of want.[45] In the article "Prospects for a Third Party" in *The New Republic* of 27 July 1932, Dewey admitted that "there was no expectation of immediate success in forming a united mass party, much less of its victory in any proximate presidential election," and made a statement that the League would support Thomas and the Socialist Party in the presidential election in 1932.[46] According to the editorial of *The New York Times* on 4 November 1932, Dewey believed that people who were not satisfied with the policies of the established parties needed to vote for the socialist candidates, since they were intelligent enough to develop political and social actions.[47]

In a letter to President Hoover, Dewey requested that the US support disarmament at the World Disarmament Conference in Geneva, along with John Nevin Sayre, Chairman of the Emergency Peace Committee, John Haynes Holmes, Chairman of the War Registers League, Devere Allen, Chairman of the Pacifist Action Committee, Dorothy Detzer, Executive Secretary of the Women's International League for Peace & Freedom, Norman Thomas, Director of the League for Industrial Democracy, and others. They urged President Hoover to instruct the American delegates of the Geneva Conference to propose a 50 per cent reduction in global armaments levels to take effect in 1933, with the prospect of complete and universal disarmament in the near future.[48]

Dewey voted for Thomas in the presidential elections of 1932 and 1936. However, the election on 8 November 1932 resulted in a landslide victory for Franklin Roosevelt of the Democratic Party. In "The Future of Radical Political Action" published in *The Nation* in January 1931, Dewey issued a statement that the League for Independent Political Action aimed to promote "education and organization" and agreed to set forth "philosophy" as a basis for an effective political movement. He remarked that the League would invite "cooperation," in order to encourage "the need for political action to bring about radical changes in our present economic and financial system."[49] Even after Roosevelt was inaugurated as the 32nd President in March 1933, Dewey's belief in creating a new political party did not change. In the "Imperative Need: A New Radical Party" in *Common Sense* 2, September 1933, he asserted that "the need is imperative for the immediate formation of a strong united radical third party."[50] It should be noted that Dewey put forward radical policies from the standpoint of building a fair and equal society where economic gaps and inequalities had largely expanded. It was a reaction to those concrete political issues that urged him to form the concept of democratic education and the public sphere.

Dewey's Challenges to the New Deal

As I have shown in the previous chapters, one of the significant features of Dewey's theory of democracy was his striving for a reconstruction of liberalism. However, the ideal society that he had in mind was not the welfare state liberalism of the New Deal that President Roosevelt promoted in the 1930s after the Great Depression. The New Deal started in 1933 and developed a welfare state policy for finance, agriculture and industry, as well as an unemployment policy and social security programme. Through public works by the Public Works Administration, the Tennessee Valley Authority, Works Progress Administration relief programme, enactments of National Industrial Recovery Act, Agricultural Adjustment Act, National Labor Relations Act and Wagner Act, the New Deal urged the promotion of relief for the unemployed and low-income families and recovery from the economic downturn. It was this transformation that prompted the doctrine of liberalism to abandon the beliefs of classical economics in a small government, and change to active government intervention.

Dewey sent letters to President Roosevelt in 1933. In a letter dated 8 March, Dewey appealed for the reconstruction of the banking system, insisting that it should function as "a social institution" rather than as "an instrument in the hands of private promoters." He proposed that the government should take initiatives in outlawing holding companies, abolishing affiliates, recasting the Federal Reserve System, reorganizing postal savings through the increase of interest rates, and fully publicizing all essential factors of the corporate financial management system.[51] He also urged President Roosevelt to revise the Revenue Act.[52] Dewey cooperated with teachers, social workers and editors of liberal journals to send a telegram to the White House requesting President Roosevelt to hold a half-hour meeting with them in April 1934.[53] Marvin H. McIntyre, Assistant Secretary of the President, responded that the President would be glad to meet with them on 27 April.[54] Although Dewey was not able to attend the meeting, and sent a letter again suggesting that it was necessary to plan and carry out a project by means of protecting the organization of labour, Villard and other members met President Roosevelt.[55] President Roosevelt also responded to Dewey, informing him that "I was sorry that you could not be here with the rest of the group," but "we had a very satisfactory talk."[56]

Dewey made critical comments about the New Deal in the following articles: "Unemployed and Underpaid Consumers Should Not Pay Billion Dollars Subsidy to Speculators," "Relief Is Vital," "The Banking Crisis," "Congress Faces Its Test on Taxation," "The Real Test of the New Deal," "Superficial Treatment Must Fail" and others published in the *People's Lobby Bulletin* in 1933.[57] According to Westbrook, Dewey argued that "voluntary corporatism of the sort Roosevelt was fostering without a prior removal of the prerogatives of capital was destined not to evolve into democratic socialism but into a state capitalism or even fascism." Westbrook's view was that "such state capitalism" might weather "the immediate economic crisis" but was not able to contribute to "industrial democracy or long-term economic security."[58]

Contrary to Westbrook's analysis, Ryan is critical about Dewey's involvements in the League for Independent Political Action and the People's Lobby, in the sense that Dewey did not have a "sense of the positive value of party systems" in democracy and not much "feel" for the realities of political life. Namely, the People's Lobby is "an interesting symptom of center-left dissatisfaction with Roosevelt but no more," since it "made no difference to the history of the New Deal," and that what they did instead was "a very minor sideshow." For Ryan, though Dewey's attempts to seek a "planning society" instead of a "planned society" were tied to "his emphasis on participatory democracy," it was unilluminating because he did not touch the central question of "what does participatory democracy look like?"[59]

In "Future of Liberalism" published in 1935, Dewey discussed the limitations of traditional liberalism: that is, "the kind of freedom" was restricted to "the question of governmental intervention" and was discussed with reference to "the freedom of individuals in the conduct of business enterprise." Meanwhile, he indicated that the New Deal involved the "rejection of laissez-faire individualism" and "modification of one form of liberalism."[60] Dewey criticized the New Deal type of liberalism as follows.

> But the policy advanced, that of the governmental intervention to redress the imbalances brought about by freedom of business entrepreneurs is not connected with any idea of extending the scope of freedom and expanding its meaning. The action recommended is rather thought of as a restriction of liberty in behalf of greater social security. No reference is made to the regimentation and lack of freedom now suffered by the great mass of workers. Nothing is said about the larger phases of liberty that have to do with freedom of the many to participate in the culture that is now possessed by society but not distributed. But the former point is not outside; it belongs in any discussion of freedom that is limited to the economic phase. Moreover, it appears when a socially planned economy is adversely considered. But as far as workers are concerned the only things taken up is security, and that not as a prerequisite of freedom, as a necessary condition of social stability. If this is as far as liberalism can go, I fear it is bankrupt and doomed.[61]

From Dewey's perspective, a New Deal-type of welfare state was not considered to extend the opportunity to citizens to participate in creating culture or forming society. The concepts of freedom and equality should not have been interpreted from only an economic viewpoint, since those concepts were concerned with the greater phases of liberty that were concerned with the freedom of citizens to participate in democratic processes and practices. Dewey's concepts of democracy and the public sphere not only denied the principles of a laissez-faire market, but also maintained a distance from the welfare state liberalism of the New Deal.

From this perspective, Dewey wrote a letter to President Roosevelt on 22 October 1936 since he had information that Roosevelt had accepted an invitation to attend the exercises commemorating the 50th anniversary of the Statue of Liberty, to be held on 28 October. Dewey expressed his concern that, though the Statue of Liberty had been "a symbol of special significance" to the millions of immigrants who sought "freedom from oppression and equality of opportunity," this tradition was "in danger of being completely discarded" in the 1930s. He urged President Roosevelt to declare that the American people are opposed to "the present widespread alien-baiting and persecution of the foreign-born" and that this country would promise "equal opportunity for the immigrants" through re-establishing "the proud principle it once maintained as an asylum for political and religious refugees."[62]

On 23 February 1937, *The New York Times* unveiled a contradiction in Dewey's thoughts concerning the relationship between his demand to the federal government and his persistence in terms of school education. According to the article, Dewey attended an education meeting in New Orleans on 22 February 1937. At this meeting was discussed the fact that he had sent a telegram to President Roosevelt asking him to submit "an outline of diverse national interests" for a Supreme Court programme, and appoint the person who would represent diverse interests at the Supreme Court. Meanwhile, at the same meeting, Dewey complained that "there is a great deal of indoctrination now going on in the schools, especially with reference to narrow nationalism, under the name of patriotism, and to the dominant existing economic regime." Putting these elements together, *The New York Times* was of the opinion that Dewey was wrong in his ideas to impose doctrines on children, but right to impose them on the Supreme Court; in other words, "schools should be free, but courts should not."[63]

When Lippmann published a new book titled *An Inquiry into the Principles of the Good Society* in 1937, Dewey wrote a review of it in *Common Sense* called "Liberalism in a Vacuum: A Critique of Walter Lippmann's Social Philosophy." Lippmann repeatedly changed his opinions about the Great Depression and the New Deal: although Lippmann initially criticized President Roosevelt, he announced that he would support the New Deal in the early stages. However, Lippmann changed his position again to criticize the New Deal, saying that it was a socialistic "planned economy."[64]

To be sure, it is true that Dewey admitted there were important suggestions in Lippmann's book, but he criticized the solution that Lippmann proposed as "an idealistic Utopia," since it rested upon "an extremely abstract simplification" of the choice between liberalism and a totalitarian state. For Dewey, Lippmann assumed that "the good society" was one governed by the "legal system" which institutionalized "equal and reciprocal rights and duties of individuals." The central point of Dewey's rejection of Lippmann's idea can be summed up by the belief that there was "a law higher than that of any positive legal system" – namely "the supremacy of the ties, relations and interdependence among human beings over the desires, activities and institutions which foster and support activities for purely individual profits." Dewey explained that "the problem of translating this moral supremacy into concrete economic and legal terms is the ultimate problem of politics."[65]

The theoretical consequences of his view indicated that Lippmann's interpretation of liberalism was individualistic, which Dewey criticized as

"Liberalism in a Vacuum." Dewey attempted to restore a relational and reciprocal domain of human interaction that would create a system of politics and ethics of the public sphere, rejecting the society governed only by the "legal system."

The Case of Leon Trotsky

Dewey reacted not only to domestic issues but also to international problems occurring in that era that saw an increasing range of political strains on global society. One of his criticisms was directed at Joseph Stalin, who had enacted the Soviet Constitution in 1936 and had strengthened an autocratic rule by adopting the Great Purge. Stalin became leader of the Communist Party in 1922 and gained power by winning the intra-party struggle after the death of Vladimir Ilyich Lenin in 1924. Stalin implemented the first Five Year Plan, which fostered the collectivization of agriculture and the industrialization of economic systems in 1928.

At the time this plan started, Dewey visited Leningrad and Moscow. He made favourable comments about his impressions of Russia from these visits, and especially praised the school education system. Dewey's thoughts about Russia were revealed in "Impressions of Soviet Russia" in 1928, which comprised "Leningrad Gives the Clue," "A Country in a State of Flux," "A New World in the Making," "What Are the Russian Schools Doing?," "New Schools for a New Era" and "The Great Experiment and the Future."[66] Dewey's affirmative stance on Russia was reported by the mass media in the US: on 6 December 1928, *The New York Times* published an article titled "Dr. Dewey Praises Russia's Schools," introducing his opinion that the "Soviet is making great strides in its experimental work."[67]

But Dewey changed his attitude to Russia in the mid-1930s, since he had become sceptical about communism when Stalin rose to absolute power as the supreme ruler of the Soviet Union. After the incident in which Sergei Mironovich Kirov, an early Bolshevik leader, was assassinated by a gunman at his office in 1934, Stalin escalated the suppression of opposite factions and dissident elements in the Communist Party, culminating in the Great Purge. In April 1934, Dewey published the article "Why I Am Not a Communist" with Bertrand Arthur William Russell and Morris Raphael Cohen.[68] In "Class Struggle and the Democratic Way," published in 1936, Dewey announced that he could not share the communists" concept of the "class struggle" between the capitalist bourgeoisie and the proletariat, because their premise was that "class struggle" was and always had been "the source of social change," and this conditioned "the nature, the rise, and the fall of all social and cultural institutions." He claimed that "the democratic frame of reference" would make it possible to energize "action" and direct "critical reflection and educational thought," and that it must be accomplished by "the social, rather than a class interest."[69]

The case of Leon Trotsky strengthened Dewey's criticism against Russia. Although Trotsky exercised leadership in the October Revolution, being second in rank to Lenin in 1917, he was dismissed by the party after his defeat in the power struggle with Stalin and was obliged to become an expatriate after the death of Lenin. In the Moscow trials in August 1936 and January 1937, many of the members of the Bolsheviks, including Trotsky, were prosecuted and found guilty. Trotsky and his son Sedov were suspected of conspiring with Adolf Hitler and the Japanese emperor to implement a confidential agreement that they would cede Ukraine to the Third Reich, after Germany and Japan had helped Trotsky in his anti-Stalinist struggle and successfully disassembled the Soviet Union. Trotsky defected to Mexico and appealed his innocence in an unjust trial. In the US, the American Committee for the Defense of Leon Trotsky was set up to inquire into the truth about Trotsky's trial. Dewey signed an appeal calling for the investigation in October 1936. He agreed to head its committee in response to a request by George Novack of the Trotskyist Communist League of America in February 1937.

In a meeting of the New School for Social Research held in New York on 1 March, Dewey delivered an address titled "Declaration of Purposes by the American Committee for the Defense of Leon Trotsky." He said that he heartily agreed with Novack's idea that the Trotsky trial would rank in historic issues with the case of Sacco and Vanzetti of the 1920s. On behalf of the committee, Dewey announced that "the very possibility of human progress" was inseparable from "the establishment and dissemination of social truths," and that when the truth was "obscure and contested" it was essential to "let the truth be known." It was obvious, he stated, that society should maintain and protect "the immemorial right of asylum for political refugees of all shades of opinion" in spite of the differences in political opinions. No man accused of crime must be found guilty and excluded from society until "a full and fair opportunity to present his answer to his accusers and to argue his innocence" was given to him.[70]

Furthermore, the committee members organized the Commission of the Inquiry into the Charges against Leon Trotsky in the Moscow Trials with the aim of an investigation and hearing while Trotsky was in political exile in Mexico. Dewey, who was elected as Chairman of the Commission, arrived in Mexico City on 5 April. The commission conducted the hearing at the home of Diego Rivera in Coyoacan. Rivera, known for leading the Mexican Muralism Movement under the influence of cubism in the era of the Mexican Revolution, was sympathetic to Trotsky's ideas. The commission's hearing for Trotsky continued for eight days. At the beginning of the public session held on 10 April, Dewey said that they were there "neither to defend nor to prosecute" Trotsky, but that their function was to "bring to the light the objective facts" and "ascertain the truth" humanely, by hearing whatever testimony.[71]

The Commission of Inquiry published a report, *The Case of Leon Trotsky: Report of Hearings on the Charges Made against Him in the Moscow Trials*, in 1937. From the testimony of the public hearing, they asserted that the Moscow trials were completely unjust and unfair, and that Trotsky was innocent.[72]

The conclusion of the report was that "no effort was made to ascertain the truth" in the Moscow trials and "they do not represent the truth." The Commission found Trotsky and Sedov "not guilty."[73]

However, the court in Moscow continued the Great Purge, not having accepted the report of the commission. Dewey was disillusioned with the Russian situation. Through this, Dewey came to be seen as hostile to the communists in the US. On 19 December 1937, the *Washington Post* wrote of Dewey's denouncement of "Russian dictatorship."[74]

A Criticism of a Totalitarian State

Dewey was opposed to the political situations of Germany, Italy and Japan; in November 1937 these three countries signed the Anti-Comintern Pact, which was ostensibly directed against the ideologies of the Comintern of the Communist International. Nazi leader Hitler had cancelled the Treaty of Versailles in March 1935 by rejecting the armed forces conditions, and Austria was annexed to Germany in March 1938.

On 6 December 1937, Dewey sent a telegram to Albert Einstein, the physicist who had defected from Germany and taken a post at the Institute for Advanced Study in Princeton. After the outbreak of the Japan–China War, Dewey proposed to Einstein that people of all countries organize a voluntary boycott against Japanese goods, refuse to sell and load war materials to Japan and cease any cooperation with Japan that would help their policy of conquest, all measures proposed for the sake of protecting humanity, peace and democracy.[75] Japan had spearheaded the invasion of China after the Kwantung Army engineered the Mukden Incident in September 1931, withdrew from the League of Nations in March 1933 (as did Germany, Italy, Spain and others), began the Japan–China War, ignited by the Lukow-kiao Incident in July 1937, and concluded the Anti-Comintern Pact in November of the same year.

In the US, President Roosevelt gave priority to the revival of the domestic economy after the Great Depression, and maintained a neutral position on the expansion of invasion by fascist countries so as not to be involved in any prolonged dispute. The US Congress enacted the Neutrality Act in August 1935, forbidding exports of arms, munitions and implements of war to belligerent countries. Public opinion was largely negative in regard to participation in the war. According to an opinion poll in 1937, more than 90 per cent of citizens replied that the US should not participate in any war, even if it broke out again in Europe.

Dewey was opposed to the idea of participating in warfare and mentioned that the US should explore other ways to contribute to building peace and democracy for human beings. He sent telegrams to Mahatma Gandhi and Romain Rolland that contained the same idea as the one he had proposed to Einstein. Einstein approved of Dewey's project, mainly because it would bring about progress in areas of reason and justice.[76] In May 1939, the Committee for Cultural Freedom, on which Dewey served as Chairman, was launched with the support of Sydney Hook.[77] On 27 May, *The Nation* published a "manifesto" of the committee, stating that their intention was to protect freedom of culture and art against the totalitarian movements in Germany, Italy, the Soviet Union, Japan and Spain.[78] The editorial of *The New Republic* on 31 May also took up the topic of the establishment of the Committee for Cultural Freedom.[79]

What annoyed the editors of *The Nation* and *The New Republic*, which were known as liberal journals, was that the Committee for Cultural Freedom had included the Soviet Union in the current list of totalitarian states. Three months later, Hitler and Stalin concluded the German–Soviet Nonaggression Pact. While condemning the totalitarianism of Germany, American liberal intellectuals expressed their support for the Soviet Union. The fact that this committee had suggested the totalitarianism of the Soviet Union provoked anger from liberal intellectuals.

Having encountered the rage of liberal intellectuals, Dewey sent a letter on 26 May 1939 to the editors of *The New Republic* objecting to their identity as a journal. The reason that Dewey objected was because liberal journals assumed that the commission perceived that "entire liberty" was present in the US but not in Germany, Italy and Russia. In protest against the journal, Dewey made it clear that "the dangers existing here and now in America are the reason for the formation of the committee," and that it would not be sufficient just to denounce the rising tide of fascism and totalitarianism, but to also develop "a positive and aggressive campaign" against them.[80] Dewey enclosed this purport in a letter sent to Hook on the same day.[81] What was needed, he conceived, was a realization of "democratic ends," which required "democratic methods" to maintain an "ever-increasing release of the powers of human nature" and that secured and widened cultural freedoms of cooperative action and intelligence.[82] Thus, Dewey's stance against fascism and Stalinism differed from that of typical liberal journals such as *The Nation* and *The New Republic*.

The point that can be drawn from this discussion is that Dewey was fully cognizant of the necessity of taking democratic processes and practices of education into action. In "Democracy Is Radical," he asserted that "the end of democracy is a radical end" since "the fundamental principle of democracy is that the ends of freedom and individuality for all can be attained only by means that accord with those ends;" he continued to assert that in the US, values consisted of an "insistence upon freedom of belief, of inquiry, of discussion, of assembly, of education: upon the method of public intelligence in opposition to even a coercion that claims to be exercised in behalf of the ultimate freedom of all individuals."[83] Dewey criticized laissez-faire liberalism, the New Deal, Stalinism and fascism by seeking ways to regenerate democracy and the public sphere in education in the 1930s. As noted earlier, Dewey's statement that "the first object of a renascent liberalism is education" should be interpreted from the viewpoint of his attempts to reconstruct politics and education in democratic processes and practices.

Notes

1 John Dewey, *Liberalism and Social Action*, op. cit., pp.41–44.
2 Ibid., p.45.
3 Ibid., p.44.
4 Ibid., p.45.
5 Ibid., pp.6–7.
6 Ibid., p.7.
7 Ibid., p.8.
8 Ibid., pp.7–8.
9 Ibid., p.11.
10 Ibid., pp.9–11.
11 Paul Krugman, *The Conscience of a Liberal*, op. cit., pp.17–19.
12 Ibid., pp.20–23.
13 John Dewey, *Liberalism and Social Action*, op. cit., p.64
14 John Dewey, "Democracy Is Radical," *The Later Works*, vol.11, pp.297–299.
15 John Dewey, "Education and Social Change," *The Later Works*, vol.11, p.417.
16 John Dewey, "Democracy and Educational Administration," *The Later Works*, vol.11, pp.217–218.
17 Ibid., p.217.
18 Axel Honneth, *Das Andere der Gerechtigkeit: Aufsätze zur praktischen Philosophie*, Frankfurt am Main: Suhrkamp, 2000, pp.282–305.
19 Richard J. Bernstein, *The New Constellation: The Ethical-Political Horizons of Modernity/Postmodernity*, op. cit., pp.232–233.
20 Ibid., p.225.
21 John Dewey, "Creative Democracy: The Task Before Us," *The Later Works,* vol.14, p.226.
22 John Dewey, "Democracy and Educational Administration," op. cit., p.218.
23 Alfred M. Bingham, "Books," *Common Sense*, vol.4, 1935, p.28.
24 Edwin T. Buehrer, "In Defense of Liberalism," *The Christian Century*, vol.52, no.1210, 25 September 1935, p.35.
25 John Chamberlain, "The World in Books," *Current History*, vol.43, 1935, pp.v–vi.
26 Reinhold Niebuhr, "The Pathos of Liberalism," *The Nation*, vol.141, no.3662, 11 September 1935, pp.303–304.
27 Horace M. Kallen, "Salvation by Intelligence," *Saturday Review of Literature*, 13 December 1935, p.7.
28 Henry Hazlitt, "John Dewey's History and Analysis of 'Liberalism,'" *New York Times Book Review*, 1 September 1935, p.9.
29 Kenneth Burke, "Liberalism's Family Tree," *The New Republic*, vol.86, no.1109, 4 March 1936, pp.115–116.
30 "Liberalism and Social Action," *People's Lobby Bulletin*, vol.5, no.10, February, 1936, pp.1–2.
31 Frank H. Knight, "Pragmatism and Social Action," *The International Journal of Ethics: A Quarterly Devoted to the Advancement of Ethical Knowledge and Practices*, vol.46, January, 1936, pp.229–236.
32 Melchior Palyi, "Book Reviews," *The American Journal of Sociology*, vol.44, no.3, November, 1938, pp.480–481.
33 See, for example, Peter Temin, *Lessons from the Great Depression: The Lionel Robbins Lectures for 1989*, Cambridge, MA: MIT Press, 1989; and John Kenneth Galbraith, *The Great Crash 1929*, Boston; New York: Houghton Mifflin, 1997.
34 David Levering Lewis, *W. E. B. Du Bois: The Fight for Equality and the American Century 1919–1963*, New York: Henry Holt, 2000, pp.252–253.
35 W. E. B. Du Bois, *The Souls of Black Folk*, Oxford: Oxford University Press, 2007. *Darkwater: Voices from within the Veil*, Oxford: Oxford University Press, 2007.

36 John Dewey, "John Dewey Assails the Major Parties," *The Later Works,* vol.5, p.442.

37 John Dewey, "Attacks Wage Disparity," *The Later Works,* vol.5, p.431.

38 John Dewey, "Child Relief Steps Urged on Congress," *The Later Works,* vol.5, pp.432–433.

39 John Dewey, "Asks Federal Fund to Aid Unemployed," *The Later Works,* vol.5, pp.434–435.

40 John Dewey, "Asks Hoover to Act on Unemployment," *The Later Works,* vol.5, pp.436–438.

41 John Dewey, "Puts Needs of Idle at Two Billions," *The Later Works,* vol.5, p.439.

42 John Dewey, "Dewey Supports Vladeck," *The Later Works,* vol.5, p.443.

43 John Dewey, "Dewey Asks Norris to Lead New Party." *The Later Works,* vol.5, pp.444–446.

44 John Dewey, "Insurgents Back Norris in Refusing to Quit Republicans," *The Later Works,* vol.5, pp.504–505.

45 John Dewey, "The Key to Hoover's Keynote Speech," *The Later Works,* vol.6, pp.357–363; "President Dewey Calls on Hoover to Recognize Government Responsibility for Unemployment," *The Later Works,* vol.6, pp.372–373; "The Federal Government and Unemployment," *The Later Works,* vol.6, pp.377–378; "Voters Must Demand Congress Tax Wealth Instead of Want," *The Later Works,* vol.6, p.392.

46 John Dewey, "Prospects for a Third Party," *The Later Works,* vol.6, pp.246–252.

47 "Socialist Candidates," *New York Times,* 4 November 1932, p.8.

48 John Dewey *et al.* to Herbert Hoover, 15 January 1932, Jane Addams Collection, Swarthmore College Peace Collection, Swarthmore, PA; *The Correspondence of John Dewey,* vol.2.

49 John Dewey, "The Future of Radical Political Action," *The Later Works,* vol.9, pp.66–70.

50 John Dewey, "Imperative Need: A New Radical Party," *The Later Works,* vol.9, pp.76–80.

51 John Dewey to Franklin D. Roosevelt, 8 March 1933, Research Center, Minnesota Historical Society, St. Paul, MN; *The Correspondence of John Dewey,* vol.2.

52 John Dewey to Franklin D. Roosevelt, 6 April 1933, John Dewey Papers, Special Collections Research Center, Morris Library; *The Correspondence of John Dewey,* vol.2.

53 John Dewey *et al.* to Louis McHenry Howe, 13 April 1934, Franklin D. Roosevelt Library, Hyde Park, NY; *The Correspondence of John Dewey,* vol.2.

54 Marvin H. McIntyre to Oswald Garrison Villard, 19 April 1934, Franklin D. Roosevelt Library; *The Correspondence of John Dewey,* vol.2.

55 John Dewey to Franklin D. Roosevelt, 26 April 1934, Franklin D. Roosevelt Library; *The Correspondence of John Dewey,* vol.2.

56 Franklin D. Roosevelt to John Dewey, 30 April 1934, Franklin D. Roosevelt Library; *The Correspondence of John Dewey,* vol.2.

57 John Dewey, "People's Lobby Bulletin," *The Later Works,* vol.9, pp.249–290.

58 Robert B. Westbrook, *John Dewey and American Democracy,* op. cit., p.440.

59 Alan Ryan, *John Dewey and the High Tide of American Liberalism,* op. cit., pp.245–314.

60 John Dewey, "Future of Liberalism," op. cit., p.258.

61 Ibid., p.258.

62 John Dewey to Franklin D. Roosevelt, 22 October 1936, John Dewey Papers; *The Correspondence of John Dewey,* vol.2.

63 "Dr. Dewey Regulates Judges. But Not Children," *New York Times,* 23 February 1937, p.26.

64 Walter Lippmann, *An Inquiry into the Principles of the Good Society,* Westport, CT: Greenwood Press, 1973.

65 John Dewey, "Liberalism in a Vacuum: A Critique of Walter Lippmann's Social Philosophy: An Inquiry into the Principles of the Good Society, by Walter Lippmann. Boston: Little, Brown and Co., 1937," *The Later Works,* vol.11, pp.489–495.

66 John Dewey, "Impressions of Soviet Russia," *The Later Works,* vol.3, pp.203–250.

67 "Dr. Dewey Praises Russia's Schools," *New York Times,* 6 December 1928, p.3.

68 John Dewey, "Why I Am Not a Communist," *The Later Works,* vol.9, pp.91–95.

69 John Dewey, "Class Struggle and the Democratic Way," *The Later Works,* vol.11, pp.382–386.

70 John Dewey, "Declaration of Purposes by the American Committee for the Defense of Leon Trotsky," *The Later Works,* vol.11, pp.303–305.

71 John Dewey, "Introductory of the Statement of the Commission of Inquiry," *The Later Works,* vol.11, p.306.

72 The Preliminary Commission of Inquiry, The Case of Leon Trotsky: Report of Hearings on the Charges Made against Him in the Moscow Trials, New York; London: Harper & Brothers, 1937.

73 John Dewey, "Summary of Findings," *The Later Works,* vol.11, pp.321–323.

74 "John Dewey, Great American Liberal, Denounces Russian Dictatorship," *Washington Post,* 19 December 1937.

75 John Dewey to Albert Einstein, 6 December 1937, John Dewey Papers; *The Correspondence of John Dewey,* vol.2.

76 Albert Einstein to John Dewey, 7 December 1937, Special Collections Research Center, Morris Library; *The Correspondence of John Dewey,* vol.2.

77 "New Group Fights Any Freedom Curb," *New York Times,* 15 May 1939, p.13.

78 The Committee for Cultural Freedom"Manifesto," *The Nation,* vol.148, no.22, 27 May 1939, p.626.

79 "Liberty and Common Sense," *The New Republic,* vol.99, no.1278, 31 May 1939, pp.89–90.

80 John Dewey to *New Republic,* 26 May 1939, John Dewey Papers; *The Correspondence of John Dewey,* vol.2.

81 John Dewey to Sidney Hook, 26 May 1939, John Dewey Papers; *The Correspondence of John Dewey,* vol.2.

82 John Dewey, "Democratic Ends Need Democratic Methods for Their Realization," *The Later Works,* vol.14, pp.367–368.

83 John Dewey, "Democracy Is Radical," op. cit., pp.298–299.

4   Education for a Changing Society

Schools as Agencies of Public Action

How did Dewey try to build democratic education? Why did he aim to create democracy and the public sphere in schools? What made it difficult for him to construct democratic processes and practices in the field of education? In this chapter, I will clarify and expound on Dewey's commitments to democratic education and the public sphere for a changing society in the 1930s.

Education and Social Change

The rapid social changes that began after the Great Depression raised fundamental questions for educators with respect to the social function of schools. The Teachers College of Columbia University took an initiative in this research. Even after Dewey had retired and became Professor Emeritus of Columbia University in 1930, other staff influenced by his educational ideas developed their ideas in the studies of education, psychology and sociology. During this period, Teachers College was constituted of prominent professors such as David Eugene Smith, Frank Morton McMurry, Paul Monroe, Edward L. Thorndike, George Drayton Strayer, Nickolaus Louis Engelhardt, Jesse Homer Newlon, Harold Rugg, Robert Bruce Raup, Childs, Kilpatrick, Counts, Edmund de Schweinitz Bruner, William Fletcher Russell, Goodwin Barbour Watson and others.

Around 1930, many professors who were engaged in educational research at Teachers College shifted their position from child-centred education to the social reconstructionist approach of progressive education. Kilpatrick, Rugg, Counts, Childs, Raup, Watson, Bruner and Newlon started to hold regular meetings in order to exchange their thoughts on the prospects for education. These members played a significant role in the Progressive Education Association in the 1920s, and speculatively advanced a concept for social reconstruction by means of education in the face of social and economic changes in the 1930s. According to C. A. Bowers, who studied the history of progressive education during the Great Depression, despite the fact that progressive educators displayed "an ingenious ability for devising new teaching methods," they were not successful in articulating "their educational objectives" clearly. In his view, they were "almost totally silent" when they were asked to answer the question of what should be the social responsibilities of the school.[1] By the autumn of 1933, it was obvious that social reconstructionists were not satisfied with the Progressive Education Association, mainly because it was too weak to provide effective solutions in that period of struggle. Kilpatrick and his colleagues began to find it difficult to develop their theories in the Progressive Education Association.[2] Therefore they came to discuss the issue in cooperation with the Educational Policies Commission, the American Historical Association of the Commission on Social Studies and the American Council on Education of the American Youth Commission.

One of the lines of thinking that gave a direction to combining schools with social reconstruction was Counts' work, *Dare the School Build a New Social Order?* (1932), which was derived from three lectures given in February 1932; one was addressed to the Progressive Education Association in Baltimore, the second to a division of the Department of Superintendence in Washington, DC and the third to the National Council of Education, also in Washington, DC. Counts pointed out that "progressive education cannot place its trust in a child-centred school" in that it had come to reflect "the viewpoint of the members of the liberal-minded upper middle class" and had not elaborated a "theory of social welfare." The new direction of the school in which progressive educators should move forward could be summarized in his suggestion that, "if Progressive Education is to be genuinely progressive, it must emancipate itself from the influence of this class, face squarely and courageously every social issue, come to grips with life in all of its stark reality, establish an organic relation with the community, develop a realistic and comprehensive theory of welfare, fashion, a compelling and challenging vision of human destiny, and become less frightened than it is today at the bogies of imposition and indoctrination."[3]

While Counts started studying education as a graduate student under the guidance of Charles Judd at the University of Chicago, his theory was quite different from Judd's theory; unlike Judd, who fostered the professionalization and bureaucratization of schools through psychological approaches, Counts turned his interests to sociological issues. He then got a job at the Teachers College and was influenced by the education in the Soviet Union through his visits there in 1927, 1929 and 1936. For him, the situation at that time in the US was far from one of democracy, since the "rugged individualism" of laissez-faire liberalism formed the dominant ideologies. He stressed that the "choice" was no longer between "individualism" and "collectivism," but rather between "two forms of collectivism" – the one "democratic" that is devoted to the people, and the other "feudal in spirit" for the benefit of the privileged class. Schools played a role in leading social changes towards realizing "collectivism" in democracy.[4]

In 1933, the Committee of the Progressive Education Association on Social and Economic Problems, which was led by Counts, published *A Call to the Teachers of the Nation*. The Committee's intention was to promote social reconstruction through education during the Depression. They aimed to abandon "the doctrine of laissez-faire" and its idea of economical individualism and instead adopt a highly integrated and organized social order by gearing education towards "collectivism." What teachers needed to bear in mind was that they were responsible for the construction of a better social order by reorganizing a democratic tradition.[5]

These movements evoked a concern for social reconstruction through education. Kilpatrick, Dewey, Childs, Raup, Boyd Henry Bode, H. Gordon Hullfish and V. T. Thayer published a book titled *The Educational Frontier* in 1933.[6] Dewey and Childs wrote the chapters "The Social-Economic Situation and Education" and "The Underlying Philosophy of Education." According to Dewey and Childs, though the aim of education had been couched as "the individual," that is, "the complete and harmonious development of all the powers of the individual, physical, intellectual, moral" until about the turn of the twentieth century, there had occurred a significant shift that put an emphasis on "social aims" and "social forces and factors." As a result, education had come to be thought of as "a process of transmission and reconstruction of culture," in which the encouragement of individuals to participate in the task of "a constantly changing society" was highlighted. Schools should be "a form of community life."[7]

Dewey and Childs showed that "the process of social change and of education" were "correlative and interactive." They remarked that education might be improved when people aim at "a better, a more just, a more open and straightforward, a more public, society, in which free and all-round communication and participation occur," and that education should assume "an increasing responsibility for participation in projecting ideas of social change."[8] According to their theory, it was obvious that a school itself should nurture a "community life" concerned with creating a better and more just society, through encouraging communication and participatory processes for the transmission and reconstruction of culture.

Principles of Social Reconstruction

In 1933, Norman Woelfel and Mordecai Grossman, who were graduate students at the Teachers College of Columbia University, proposed to Kilpatrick that he publish a new journal dealing with the topic of social reconstruction and education. Accepting the proposal, Kilpatrick talked about it with Childs, Newlon, Rugg and others. Shortly after, Kilpatrick was inaugurated as the Chairman of the Editorial Board. There were 27 researchers on the Board of Directors, including Dewey, Sydney Hook, Bruner, Childs, Newlon, Raup, Rugg, Watson and others, and three editorial staff members headed by Counts. The journal's Board of Directors pledged to donate financial support, and two foundations donated $900. *The Social Frontier* was published as a monthly journal in October 1934; each copy cost 25 cents and a subscription for one year was $2. While the journal had more than 2,000 subscribers for the first issue, this had increased to 5,000 by 1937.[9]

The editors of *The Social Frontier* proclaimed that the age of "individualism" in the economy was closing and that the age of "collectivism" was emerging. The individualistic interpretation of economy and ethics that urged progress through market competition became impossible. They urged that educators should take an active part in "social reconstruction," in which schools were seen as the centre of the "educational agencies" that would function as the frontiers of social change. The editors aimed at the innovation of a society that could be characterized as an integration of social life, in order to encourage all possibilities regarding the affluence and refinement of human experience. They aimed to criticize laissez-faire individualism and to realize, socially, an improvement on collectivism through education.[10]

However, there were some limitations to their attempts. Bowers convincingly observed that the editors of *The Social Frontier* "never thoroughly and systematically examined the New Deal's social philosophy as embodied in legislative enactments." Bowers indicated that even though some editors took up the issues of the New Deal of the Roosevelt Administration, the systematic evaluation of the social philosophy came from the same ideological persuasion of the social reconstructionists. He added that even if the importance of their criticism against capitalism was admitted, it was surprising that there had not been a single dissenting voice to discuss "its positive aspects" or "the possibility of its social usefulness." The editors did not consider that economic collectivism might impose "restrictions" on certain freedoms cherished by traditional liberals, much less analyse the social, political or psychological problems involved in the reconstruction.[11]

As a matter of fact, the vision of social reconstruction suggested in *The Social Frontier* was not significantly different from the New Deal policies of the Roosevelt Administration. In 1929 during the Hoover Administration, the President's Research Committee on Social Trends was established with the aim of preparing for the construction of a planned economy. Wesley Clair Mitchell, who served as Professor of Economics at Columbia University, was inaugurated as the Chairman of the Committee. Dewey knew Mitchell well, not only because the latter had studied at the University of Chicago and had taken Dewey's course, but also because Mitchell was the husband of Lucy Sprague Mitchell, who, having been influenced by Dewey's educational theory, had set up the Bureau of Educational Experiments in New York City.[12] Charles Edward Merriam, a Professor at the University of Chicago, served as the Vice-Chairman of the Committee. The Committee announced in 1933 that the government would provide the basis for the formation of national policies in *Recent Social Trends in the United States*.[13] President Roosevelt then started the planned economy of the New Deal in the fields of industry, commerce, agriculture, finance and so on. The members of *The Social Frontier* could not envision concrete policies and processes of social reconstruction through education, and that was a reason why the social reconstructionists lost their critical and influential power in politics.

The ways in which we can interpret Dewey's philosophy in *The Social Frontier* group form a controversial issue. According to Lawrence A. Cremin, "all of the authors were of the Deweyan persuasion; four of the seven were members of the Kilpatrick group." Cremin realized that the major formation of this new "frontier" position was directed at urging "a restatement of Dewey's philosophy appropriate to depression America."[14] Diane Ravitch discusses the fact that, though the members of *The Social Frontier* group were not communists, they admired the Soviet Union. In Ravitch's framework, Dewey was also heartened to learn that Soviet educators were committed to the project method, and had successfully broken down the barriers between school and society by adopting an entire educational system that drew links between the two.[15]

It was not without reason that Dewey had a central position in this group. Considering the fact that there was "John Dewey's Page" included in the monthly paper in the journal, it might well have been the case that he played an important part in their theorization. However, the direction that Dewey envisioned was not necessarily in agreement with the philosophy of *The Social Frontier*. Westbrook made it clear that the intention of the group was to criticize "the individualism of child-centered progressivism" and to seek to develop "radical politics:" that is, to criticize "American capitalism and the New Deal" and urge teachers to join "the democratic left." Dewey devoted his energy to distinguishing his position from that of child-centred progressivism and social reconstructionism.[16]

In the 1930s, the John Dewey Society for the Study of Education and Culture formed a radical wing along with *The Social Frontier* group. The John Dewey Society began to publish a yearbook in 1937, arguing energetically about the relation between school and society. The committee comprised Dewey, Kilpatrick, Newlon, Watson, George W. Hartmann, Ernest O. Melby, George D. Stoddard, Hilda Taba and Laura Zirbes.

"A Teacher and Society" (1937) was adopted as the theme of the First Yearbook of the John Dewey Society. Dewey and Watson contributed by submitting an article titled "The Forward View: A Free Teacher in a Free Society." According to Dewey and Watson, "the ideal of democracy demands the fullest possible development of personality in all – irrespective of birth, wealth, creed, or race – through cooperative association with others, and mutual understanding and consent." They added that "the teachers of a free society will be continuous curriculum-builders."[17] The themes of the other yearbooks included *Educational Freedom and Democracy* (1938),[18] *Democracy and the Curriculum* (1939)[19] and *Teachers for Democracy* (1940).[20] In these yearbooks, the authors argued various topics about education that had an impact on democratic politics.

Education and Changing Social Order

The relation between education and social reconstruction was a theme of great importance in Dewey's philosophy of education. Bowers clarified that progressive educators in the 1930s were divided by their conflicting views concerning measures to rescue the nation from the ravages of the Depression. For Bowers, one faction argued that "the social and moral condition of man could not be improved until his social environment had been radically overhauled," believing that the educators needed to identify the prevailing social ills and that the schools needed to deliberately contribute to correcting them. The other faction, according to Bowers, thought social reconstruction could be accomplished only by indirect means. Though both factions shared an interest in creating a better society, their concern was to "release the creative energies of the child." Bowers pointed out that both factions claimed to be "the true custodians" of Dewey's philosophy.[21]

Dewey gave a lecture at the annual meeting of the National Education Association held in Washington, DC on 22 February 1932. The article, titled "The Economic Situation: A Challenge to Education," was published in the *Journal of Home Economics* in June of the same year. Motivated by the discussion of the social function of the school, he advocated that "the present economic collapse" was "a challenge to every institution," including schools. He went on to say that "the primary social duty of education" was not to "perpetuate the existing social order — economic, legal, and political," but to "contribute to its betterment" in a constructive and positive way. What disappointed him was that the majority of school students went forth unprepared to meet the realities of the world in which they lived, due to the fact that "the split between their generous beliefs and liberal hopes and what they get into is often tragic." This, he believed, was because of "the policy of concealment and laudation" formed by the ruling economic elements where everything was "fixed and settled." Dewey urged the need for teachers to unite in order to inform the public of "economic and social realities" more adequately and to combine to impress upon them "the right and duty of intellectual freedom" as they encountered changes of "acquiescent complacency" to "honest critical intelligence," and of "the fiction of a static and finished political and industrial society" to "the reality of a constantly shifting, altering, unstable society."[22]

On 1 March 1933, Dewey delivered an address titled "Education and Our Present Social Problems" at the meeting of the Department of Supervisors and Directors of Instruction at Minneapolis. He urged educators to think about methods of approaching social problems instead of considering them in a hurried and thoughtless way, which he felt was characteristic of "reactionaries," since the growing interest in social reconstruction reminded him of a similar stirring at the time of World War I. However, although Dewey agreed that schools had close ties with political and social changes, he maintained a prudent stance as to the assertion that education was an immediate solution to social problems and social reconstruction. For teachers, what brought about closer ties between education and actual social responsibilities was to discuss "educational affairs" and "the organization and conduct of the schools." In other words, introducing a large degree of responsibility for teachers should be encouraged in the school and community. Dewey objected to the idea that teachers would directly contribute to settling social problems, much less help build a new social order, unless they were involved in the settlement of the educational issues in their local communities. As Dewey concluded, "beginning at home is again the lesson to be learned."[23]

In Dewey's address titled "Education for a Changing Social Order" on 23 February 1934 for the American Association of Teachers Colleges in Cleveland, he explained that it was important for educators to recognize where they were at that present time and where education should be throwing its weight. He believed that educators required an understanding of "the facts of the changes that are going on," and knew insightfully "the causes that are producing these changes – the forces that are at work." For him, "an intelligent understanding of actual conditions that will stimulate inquiry" would make it possible to find a substitute for the "fixed indoctrination" that had exercised "an oppression and coercive influence" in the past. Dewey believed that school curriculum should be developed around "a social centre" and oriented towards "social ends" in intellectual organization and unity of purpose.[24]

Dewey published the article "Education and the Social Change" in a pamphlet of the League for Industrial Democracy in 1934. He claimed that schools should embrace "a social purpose," and control methods of teaching, discipline and subject matter through introducing "methods of inquiry and mutual consultation and discussion," instead of imposition and inculcation. He suggested five strategies for processing educational reform. In the first place, it was important to build a school system in which students were given opportunities to learn the present state of society, enabling them to know the conditions of society and forces at work. The second strategy was to demand the organization of the study of economics and social problems in schools. Third, the organization of the school as "a cooperative community" had to be fostered. For Dewey, "re-organization upon a cooperative basis" should not be confined to students; rather, it should be extended to the administration in order to abolish the controlling style of management from above. The fourth strategy was concerned with adult education that would prepare for "intelligent and active citizenship." Fifth, Dewey strove to construct schools that were "genuinely community centres," by reorganizing subject matter and methods that were "linked with social forces."[25]

In the first volume of *The Social Frontier*, Dewey chose to discuss the topic "Can Educators Share in Social Reconstruction?" He was opposed to the fact that schools had been teaching the status quo based on "rugged individualism," assuming that they were living in "a free economic society" at that time in which every individual had an equal chance and liberty. This faction prompted the building of an educational system that prioritized "economic freedom" over "political and cultural freedom." Whereas Dewey did not think that schools can be "the builders of a new social order," he claimed that schools would share in the construction of "the social order of the future" associated with various other social forces. Schools are "partners in the contribution of a changed society" in terms of translating the educational ideal into the conduct of the school in its administration, instruction and subject matter.[26]

Irrespective of the controversial view of whether schools should be a direct agency of social change, the members of *The Social Frontier* shared the idea that there was an explicit link between the school and society. Yet, there was little theoretical consensus as to a concrete way to connect them. In "Education and Social Change," published in *The Social Frontier* in 1937, Dewey stated that there were differences in the members' opinions: some asserted that the schools must simply reflect social changes, while others held that they should take an active part in directing social changes and constructing a new social order. Even among the latter, some thought that schools should assume this role through indoctrination; others opposed this. Around this discussion he intended to refer to "the utopian nature of the idea" that the schools were "neutral." Assuming the neutrality of the schools was not only "an end incapable of accomplishment," but would also perpetuate "disorder" and increase "blind" arguments because it generated unintelligent conflict.

In Dewey's statement, the question was not whether the schools shall or shall not be concerned with the course of future social life, but rather in what direction and how they shall do it; that is, the central issue was whether they process it "blindly and irresponsibly" or with "the maximum possible of courageous intelligence and responsibility." With zeal and dedication, Dewey enunciated that democracy is "a way of living together" which is mediated by "an intelligence that is the outcome of free association and communication with others."[27]

In a broad sense, the members of The Social Frontier of Teachers College raised a comprehensive question as to the relation between schools and social change. In a narrower sense, they discussed education as a means of social reconstruction and strove to build collectivism. Meanwhile, unlike the mainstream of this frontier group, Dewey avoided the dualism of the question as to whether schools should reflect the existing social order or contribute to creating a new social order, rejecting the idea that schools should become the direct agencies of social improvement. The question was not about the advantages and disadvantages of social reconstruction through education, but how education could bring about social changes if schools were not able to maintain neutrality. It was a concrete issue on the measure to link schools to social change, rather than an abstract issue of reconstruction. What Dewey could not share with the frontier group was their admiration of collectivism. In terms of the recognition of collectivism, Dewey's theory and the mainstream of The Social Frontier were displaying a remarkable contrast. Ravitch's interpretation overlooked this point; her analysis was focused too much on Dewey's article "Impressions of Soviet Russia" in 1928, and did not pay sufficient attention to his harsh remarks about the Soviets in the 1930s.

Ironically, there remained a marked difference between Dewey and *The Social Frontier*, even though the group claimed that they had followed Dewey's philosophy. Although Kilpatrick was inaugurated as an editorial board member of the journal and changed its name to *Frontiers of Democracy* in 1940, publication ceased in 1943.[28] Dewey did not trust the Committee of the Progressive

Education Association on Social and Economic Problems, in which Counts served as Chairman. He believed that the formation of a new social order should not be fostered on the assumption of constructing collectivism, much less be prompted by teachers' initiatives to take the leading role.

Individualism and Culture in Education

Dewey was engaged in educational reform in terms of building schools as democratic and public agencies through criticizing the marketization of laissez-faire and the extension of bureaucratic control of the state. His innovative visions consisted of building a network for solidarity and cooperation through participation and communication, and searching for the possibility that the school become a centre that would function as an intelligent and responsible agency amidst a changing society and culture.

In particular, he was involved in recovering a "new individualism" that would contribute to "the free culture of its members," while rejecting "the older economic and political individualism" as expressed in *Individualism, Old and New* (1930). He was opposed to the view that treated "individualism" as if it were something static and fixed, believing instead that the mental and moral factors of individuals, and their desires and purposes, would change along with the changes to social institutions. For him, the tragedy of the "lost individual" lay in the fact that while individuals are caught up in "a vast complex of associations," there is "no harmonious and coherent reflection" that is connected with imaginative and emotional life. He convincingly argued that "all relations are interactions," which include "the give and take of participation, of a sharing that increases, that expands and deepens, the capacity and significance of the interacting factors."[29]

In Dewey's theoretical framework, fostering school reform based on the principle of democracy and the public sphere constituted an educational vision that was more or less concerned with social change and the creation of culture centring on participation and communication by the public. Schools had a significant meaning in this, since they would function as "the agency of important welding and fusing processes." If the school system merely turned out to be "efficient industrial fodder and citizenship fodder" controlled by pecuniary industry, it would not contribute to solving the problem of teaching "a distinctive culture;" then, it would result in acting as "the formal agencies for producing those mental attitudes; those modes of feeling and thinking."

At the same time, schools were not the ultimate and only determinants of such a cultural creation. That would have implied that society and culture are constructed and reconstructed when school education is concerned with social systems, vocations, art, science, technology, lifestyle and so on, and that those elements act on one another. In that sense, it was important that he emphasized the "quality" of culture, as well as its "quantity." Dewey implied that the significance of culture lay not only in increasing the number of those participating in the creation of arts or sciences, but in assessing "quality" as a theme accompanied by political, economic and social considerations. He felt that connecting education to social and cultural reconstruction was promoted when schools cooperated with other political, economic and social agencies, rather than being governed by education of the market principle or the nationalistic system.[30] Dewey stated:

> If, then, I select education for special notice, it is because education – in the broad sense of formation of fundamental attitudes of imagination, desire and thinking – is strictly correlative with culture in its inclusive social sense. It is because the educative influence of economic and political institutions is, in the last analysis, even more important than their immediate economic consequences.[31]

Here, Dewey stressed the correlation between "education" and "culture." In *Freedom and Culture* (1939), the concept of "culture" was discussed more positively. Turning around the idea by Thomas Jefferson that "freedom of culture" is "the final result of political freedom," Dewey developed the idea that "political freedom" cannot be maintained without "freedom of culture." The relations between individuals and all the constituents of culture – industry, communication, science, art and religion – would affect "daily associations" and "the attitudes and habits" expressed in political and legal action, which are an effect, not a cause.[32] Dewey went on further to define culture.

> For this complex of conditions which taxes the terms upon which human beings associate and live together is summed up in the word culture. The problem is to know what kind of culture is so free in itself that it conceives and begets political freedom as its accompaniment and consequence. What about the state of science and knowledge; of the arts, fine and technological; of friendships and family life; of business and finance; of the attitudes and dispositions created in the give and take of ordinary day by day associations? No matter what is the native make-up of human nature, its working activities, those which respond to institutions and rules and which finally shape the pattern of the latter, are created by the whole body of occupations, interests, skills, beliefs that constitute a given culture.[33]

In Dewey's statement, "culture" implied "the system of general ideas" used to justify or blame the conditions underlying law, politics, industry, commerce, science, technology, expressions, transmission of ideas, morality, the sense of values that people think important, their evaluation and the state of interaction. He added that the things that "are concerned with the problem" were more important than how "the problems of freedom" should be solved, and so there was a need to perceive the interactive relation between "human nature" and the "context of the elements that constitute culture" as a problem. He searched for further "cooperative individualities" for creating "a way of living together."[34] Consequently, he protected schools as public agencies that would be connected to promoting social change and the creation of culture.

Reflective Thinking and Project Learning

On 11 March 1931, Dewey gave a lecture titled "The Way out of Educational Confusion" at Harvard University. He was aware of the "educational confusion" that American schools were facing; some insisted that confusion existed in the multiplication of studies and variations in subject matter, while others said that it occurred because of "conflict" between the cultural, or liberal, and the practical. Although there was a difference between conservative educators who perceived a need to return to established standards, and innovative educators who criticized these, both parties were in agreement about the recognition that conditions at that time were unsatisfactory. Dewey's admonition against "educational confusion" applied to his conviction that the problem was not only that "this or that method for securing educational results . . . is attacked" but also "ideals and aims" that would envision a future prospect for education.

As I have indicated in previous chapters, Dewey's educational theory had its foundation in protecting the concept of "learning." He provided a definition of the term "learning" which is distinguished from the terms "a study" and "study." He explained that "study is studying" while "a study" signified "just a definitely aggregated body of subject-matter isolated from others and treated as a unit by itself." For instance, even though a physician might study medicine in medical school, he/she needs to study many other things in practice, including relationships with his/her patients; it is not sufficient for the practitioner of law to study law in order to make their studies effective; likewise, a parent's studies on psychology and social relations, etc. should be applicable to their responsibilities as a parent.

Dewey suggested that the term "learning" also has different meanings. It should not be reduced to "an accumulated and transmitted body of knowledge;" rather, it needs to be acknowledged as "the acts of apprehending, understanding, and retaining in and for subsequent use." He believed that although there was a tendency in "the title" of school programmes (e.g. history, geography, algebra, botany) to assume that "learning" is already at hand, summarized in a proper setting and divided into unified material by isolation from other fields for the act of studying, this premise would break down through learning activities geared towards expanding knowledge and skills. It would be through experiencing these processes that the content change and actuality of variation in subject matter would appear. He added that, in "the actual advance of knowledge and the arts" there needs to be more than a "mere extension of facts and principles;" it should be attended by "constant development of cross references, of interdependencies and interrelations."[35]

> I hope my point has become reasonably clear. In a situation where the skills or arts and the subject-matter of knowledge have become inter-woven and interdependent, adherence to the policy forming the studies of secondary and collegiate instruction on the basis of many isolated and independent subjects is bound to result in precisely the kind of confusion we have at present.[36]

Dewey highlighted that there was a cause for confusion in both conservative and new education; while conservative parties adhered to a traditional classification of subjects, which divided these into isolated contents and did not take into account their correlation and interdependent elements, newer practical subjects resulted in thinness and superficiality by denying traditional divisions and splitting up the subject matter. It was a "failure," he believed, to see the subjects as if they were "complete" themselves, "beginning and terminating within limits fixed in advance."

Against this background, Dewey encouraged an alternative approach to education by the so-called "project," "problem" or "situation" method, which had been adopted by many schools. Subject matter needed to be organized from the perspective of opening "new aims" that would inspire educational efforts and intelligence, and lead to "the wide world" constituted by nature and man, by knowledge, social interests and their uses. He attempted to unify "theoretical subjects" and "practical subjects" vitally, and not formally, through relating theoretical subjects to "the scope of life" and associating practical subjects with "theory and intelligent insight."[37]

In *How We Think* (1933), which was a revised edition of a book published in 1910, Dewey suggested that "reflective thinking" must be "an educational aim," proposing the concept of "reflective thinking" as "the best way of thinking." In other words, "learning is learning to think" and the intellectual side of education is vitally concerned with cultivating "the attitude of reflective thinking."

The inspiring discussion on reflective thinking that Dewey captured entailed concrete processes: reflective thinking arose when an individual faced problematic situations such as perplexity, confusion or doubt. Then, he/she would consider possible solutions to the problem through inquiry. The processes involved in reaching a conclusion involved an active, continuous, participative and careful consideration of knowledge and beliefs through interacting with an environment. It would urge him/her to assess what they knew and what they should know in everyday life. Dewey distinguished between "pre-reflective" and "post-reflective" thinking: while the former indicates "a perplexed, troubled, or confused situation at the beginning," the latter indicates "a cleared-up, unified, resolved situation at the close." Dewey explained "reflective thought" in terms of five phases or aspects: "suggestion," "intellectualization" and "hypothesis" as "guiding ideas" and "reasoning" and "testing the hypothesis by action."[38] What was important for his educational discussion was that he made it explicit that reflective thinking was the aim of education and that learning meant learning to think.

Dewey visited Cape Town and Johannesburg in South Africa to deliver lectures at educational meetings in July 1934. Dewey's visit to South Africa was supported by the New Education Fellowship and Carnegie Foundation. His lectures about "Growth in Activity" and "What Is Learning?" were published in the book *Educational Adaptations in a Changing Society* (1937) that was edited by Ernst Gideon Malherbe, who was one of the founders of the

National Commission of Education.[39] Dewey regarded "learning" as "the product of the exercise of powers needed to meet the demands of the activity in operation;" it represented "an inner pressure in some direction which constitutes the reality of need" and "the existence of materials and objects, or means of realizing impulses." For Dewey, "a genuine school of learning" is "a community" in which individuals find happiness and serve the society by learning to know and use their own powers, as well as disclose their special aptitudes and make the transition to later life.[40]

The Profession of Teaching and Public Responsibility

Dewey devoted a great deal of energy to strengthening the teaching profession as a public responsibility. He said that there were general objectives and specific aims in the educational discourses on the teaching profession; in a general perspective, it aims to secure "a progressive development of capacities" with regard to individual differences on the psychological or individual side, and on the social side, it aims to support the development of individuals through giving "desire and power" to share in "cooperative democratic living" relevant for political citizenship, vocational efficiency and effective social goodwill; the specific aims sought to prepare students to fit efficiently into the existing social life.

Concerned with a definition of the teaching profession, Dewey searched for measures to strengthen "a professional spirit," an "autonomy in education" and "a responsibility for social planning" since, if educational objectives were detached from actual school work, they would become "formal, empty and even verbal" and lose "the closer connection of school with life." What was needed for teachers to enhance the profession of teaching was that they claim autonomy in education and public responsibility in an active and organized way.[41]

In his article "The Teacher and His World" in *The Social Frontier* of 1935, Dewey raised the question of whether teachers should be ahead of or behind their time. One might have asked whether there was a "middle course" for teachers to steer. His response to this question was to promote "intelligent understanding of the social forces and movements," since teachers had to be aware of "a social goal" and understand the "forces at work" and "their direction and the goal to which they point."

Interestingly enough, Dewey emphasized to his contemporaries that "we are also living in times when private and public aims and policies are at strife with each other." Whereas his definition of the "private" could be expressed by Hoover's policy, which referred to "rugged individualism," the "public" was concerned with the organized policy of the Reconstruction Finance Corporation and agencies of public action, in an effort to recover from the tide of depression. By urging school education to meet "public aims and policies" on the basis of "intelligent decision and action," Dewey attempted to organize the social and public responsibility of the teaching profession by encouraging the recognition of various social forces and intelligent actions for the benefit of future society.[42]

On another note, the relation between teachers and the public was questioned by Dewey. In "The Teacher and the Public" (1935), he asked whether teachers are workers and whether there is a common tie to unite workers. Dewey replied to his own question by saying that workers are people who are engaged in "productive activity," especially one that is of "value to others." He mentioned that teachers are workers in that they play an important role in producing a high standard of intelligence in the community, various types of skills for contemporary life, and character. Dewey sought for ways to unite teachers and workers, and build common ties among them. What he believed was important for connecting teachers and the public during that era of vast political, economic and industrial dislocation was to create a cooperative community and take effective measures to restore democracy and education.[43]

Educational Freedom and Equality

In his controversial article "Toward a National System of Education" published in *The Social Frontier* in June 1935, Dewey explained that, unlike "a nationalistic system of education" that is controlled by the welfare of a particular national state and its social–economic system whose concern is to maintain its order, "a national system of education" was a system that put "rights" and "freedom" of education as the cornerstone, secured "the autonomy in education" and built up "a strong unified intelligence and purpose" in accordance with forming "a socialized cooperative democracy."

A national system of education would grow out from "the people." Surely there was government intervention through legislation and administration, yet it followed from "the spontaneous and voluntary efforts of the people." "Autonomy" was not the "indoctrination" of fixed beliefs, but "the right" of teachers to determine the subject matter and methods of school practices. Dewey claimed that concentrating and clarifying "the methods of free mutual discussion and communication among teachers" was indispensable to the educational system, and that those methods should be developed on the basis of the rights to education and free communication, which would ultimately protect the freedom and autonomy of education.[44]

It is worth mentioning that, in practice, Dewey recommended that the Federal Department of Education aid a movement towards a national system of education. This did not mean upholding the building of "a standardized system of education," but rather indicated that all children be provided with fair and equal opportunities, including every phase of child welfare and protection, through introducing federal aid for schools. This was because although the poorest schools spent $78 a year per pupil in New York, only $12 was spent per pupil in Arkansas; on average, boys in the city could go to school for more than five weeks longer each term than boys in the country and, even in the same state, a rich school district was 275 times better able to support its schools than a poor district. On this point, Dewey was not satisfied with the Federal Office of Education since it was mainly an advisory and fact-finding bureau that did not suggest any concrete policies to help children out of educational gaps and inequality. He demanded the establishment of a Federal Department of Education in order to secure an "equal opportunity" for every student.[45]

According to "John Dewey Asks Rotarians to Cooperate with Schools in Character Development," which was also published in *School Management* in 1934, Dewey examined "all the possibilities in education for development of character in children" through building cooperation between schools and the rotarians. He sought possibilities for strengthening the economic background of schools by calling for help from business and professional men, specifically in the areas of promoting growth in the playground movement, determining the treatment of delinquents, improving the educational environment in poor areas, exercising powers to show movies in the community and breaking down the isolation of the classroom from social life.[46] It turns out that Dewey devoted a great deal of energy to inventing a fair and better educational system that would protect children's equal opportunities to learn, by associating education with social life and realizing the cooperation between schools and businesses.

Dewey's short article, titled "Liberty and Social Control" (1935), defined the concept of "liberty" from three angles. First, "liberty" is not just "an idea, an abstract principle," but is "power, effective power to do specific things." Second, the possession of effective power is "a matter of the distribution of power." Last, the relativity of liberty to the distribution of powers of action implies that where there exists liberty at one place, some other place sees its restraint. Dewey grasped "liberty" as "a social question," not "an individual one;" individual liberties are dependent on and conditioned by "the distribution of powers or liberties" that are identical with "actual social arrangements." He called for social control that would contribute to increasing human liberties, instead of that which was executed at the expense of liberty.[47]

Furthermore, in a radio broadcast on WEVD in New York on 14 January 1936, Dewey talked about the issue of building "a genuinely free educational system" that realizes the social ideals of liberty and equality. He said that the social ideals that would change education – democracy, liberty and equality – are not new, but are new in association with the method and means to realize it. Whereas social ideals of liberty and equality had been oriented to realize "democratic ideas of liberty for all and of equality of opportunity to all," they came to be distorted into notions that stood for liberty of economic activities and equality of the law; those people were likely to think that equality already existed, since laws were nominally the same for all. Against this interpretation, Dewey searched for ways to realize the ideals of liberty and equality for "the common and general public good" and to generate a school system that links school education with the ideals of a new social order. A "genuine kind of free school" is the one that is "free in inquiry in teaching and learning" and "intellectually and morally free."[48]

Dewey reflected upon the concept of "freedom," which he felt constitutes the central value of liberalism within the context of school education, since "educational freedom" and "academic freedom" were what he considered should be respected most. He wrote the paper "How Much Freedom in New Schools?," published in *The New Republic* in 1930. In that paper, he discussed the meaning and limits of "freedom" with which progressive education was concerned. Surely, he argued, there is no doubt that progressive education had various diversities in practice, and that there are common directions to escape the restraints of fixed uniform training where traditional education is promoted. He expressed discontent with traditional education and criticized its "formalism and mass regimentation." According to Dewey, the progressive education movement was a "manifestation of a desire for an education at once freer and richer" as a reaction to traditional education. Its importance lay in "the belief in freedom, in esthetic enjoyment and artistic expression, in opportunity for individual development, and in learning through activity rather than by passive absorption."[49] Dewey further explained:

> Upon the whole, progressive schools have been most successful in furthering creativeness in the arts – in music, drawing and picture making, dramatics and literary composition, including poetry. This achievement is well worth while; it ought to assist in producing a generation esthetically more sensitive and alive than the older one. But it is not enough. Taken by itself it will do something to further the private appreciations of, say, the upper section of a middle class. But it will not serve to meet even the esthetic needs and defaultings of contemporary industrial society in its prevailing external expressions. Again, while much has been achieved in teaching science as an addition to private resources in intellectual enjoyment, I do not find that as much has been done in bringing out the relation of science to industrial society, and its potentialities for a planned control of future developments.[50]

Dewey claimed that progressive schools had had remarkable success in respecting freedom of expression in the creative arts. However, since they were ambivalent about industrial and political concerns, or actual social preparation, they lacked freedom of expression through associating with social and political movements. He was involved in securing educational freedom not only from the standpoint of nurturing private appreciation and taste for artistic expression or aesthetic activity, but also within the social and cultural context that these activities would create.[51]

The development of an artistic freedom of expression was prompted by conceptualizing a freedom of social and cultural activities. In "The Social Significance of Academic Freedom" (1936), Dewey claimed that education was a social and political matter not being performed in a void:

> Freedom of education is the thing at issue – I was about to say at stake. And since education is not a function that goes on in the void; but is

carried on by human beings, the freedom of education means, in the concrete, the freedom of students and teachers: the freedom of the school as an agent of education.[52]

Dewey indicated that it was important to include a student's freedom as well as a teacher's freedom in the discussion of educational freedom, and he primarily suggested that a teacher's freedom and a student's freedom cannot be separated. A teacher's freedom was a necessary condition for a student's freedom to learn. Freedom of education was "a social matter," as was "the distribution of effective power." In it, "the struggle for liberty" is important in order to effect "more just, equable, and human relations of men, women, and children to one another." Educational freedom was therefore indispensable for building a democratic society.

For him, it is "a crime against democracy" to deny freedom in education, since "freedom of mind and freedom of expression" are "the root of all freedom." Academic freedom is essentially "a social issue" and is closely related to educating "the future citizenship" that would shape political and economic destinies. It is at the bottom of democratic processes and practices with respect to social, political and economic issues. Dewey indicated that the social significance of academic freedom lies in the fact that there are no freedoms that enable the influence of everything acting on society, or the freedom of teachers and students to be investigated. Social change, which was advancing with the educational process, is founded on "intelligent and orderly methods of directing to a more just, equitable, and humane end." He was committed to introducing "training for good citizenship" through urging the acquisition of educational freedom.[53]

This fact underscores the conclusion of Dewey's arguments, that democracy does not only imply a formal procedure based on political institutions, as his idea of the public sphere symbolically shows, but also is constructed through "a way of living together" constituted by face-to-face interaction and communication. Schools are not to be neutralized in a void space, but need solidarity with other social agencies and networks. He sought the development of the school system as an agency of public action that supports social change and cultural creation. It is conceived of education in democratic processes and practices, in accordance with the public sphere of political and ethical dimensions.

Notes

1   C. A. Bowers, *The Progressive Educator and the Depression: The Radical Years*, New York: Random House, 1969, p.8.

2   Ibid., pp.43–44.

3   George S. Counts, *Dare the School Build a New Social Order?*, New York: Arno Press & *The New York Times*, 1969, pp.7–10.

4   Ibid., pp.34–56.

5   The Committee of the Progressive Education Association on Social and Economic Problems, *A Call to the Teachers of the Nation*, New York: John Day, 1933, pp.12–26.

6 William Heard Kilpatrick (ed.), *The Educational Frontier*, New York: D. Appelton-Century, 1933, pp.v–vi.

7 Ibid., pp.9–10.

8 Ibid., pp.34–56.

9 C. A. Bowers, *The Progressive Educator and the Depression: The Radical Years*, op. cit., pp.96–97.

10 "Editorials," *The Social Frontier: A Journal of Educational Criticism and Reconstruction*, vol.1, no.1, October, 1934, pp.4–5.

11 C. A. Bowers, *The Progressive Educator and the Depression: The Radical Years*, op. cit., pp.101–109.

12 Lucy Sprague Mitchell, *Two Lives: The Story of Wesley Clair Mitchell and Myself*, New York: Simon and Schuster, 1953.

13 The President's Research Committee on Social Trends, *Recent Social Trends in the United States*, McGraw-Hill, 1933, pp.xi–xxxiv.

14 Lawrence A. Cremin, *The Transformation of the School: Progressivism in American Education 1876–1957*, New York: Vintage Books, 1964, p.229.

15 Diane Ravitch, *Left Back: A Century of Battles over School Reform*, New York: Simon & Schuster, 2000, pp.204–206.

16 Robert B. Westbrook, *John Dewey and American Democracy*, op. cit., pp.502–506.

17 John Dewey, Goodwin Watson, "The Forward View: A Free Teacher in a Free Society," *The Teacher and Society*, First Yearbook of the John Dewey Society, New York, London: D. Appleton-Century, 1937, pp.330–345.

18 The John Dewey Society, *Educational Freedom and Democracy*, Second Yearbook of the John Dewey Society, New York, London: D. Appleton-Century, 1938.

19 The John Dewey Society, *Democracy and the Curriculum: The Life and Program of The American School*, Third Yearbook of the John Dewey Society, New York, London: D. Appleton-Century, 1939;

20 The John Dewey Society, *Teachers for Democracy*, Fourth Yearbook of the John Dewey Society, New York, London: D. Appleton-Century, 1940.

21 C. A. Bowers, *The Progressive Educator and the Depression: The Radical Years*, op. cit., p.4.

22 John Dewey, "The Economic Situation: A Challenge to Education," *The Later Works*, vol.6, pp.123–130.

23 John Dewey, "Education and Our Present Social Problems," *The Later Works*, vol.9, pp.127–135.

24 John Dewey, "Education for a Changing Social Order," *The Later Works*, vol.9, pp.158–168.

25 John Dewey, "Education and the Social Order," *The Later Works*, vol.9, pp.175–185.

26 John Dewey, "Can Education Share in Social Reconstruction," *The Later Works*, vol.9, pp.205–209.

27 John Dewey, "Education and Social Change," op. cit., pp.408–417.

28 Progressive Education Association, *Frontiers of Democracy*, vol.10, New York: 1943.

29 John Dewey, *Individualism, Old and New*, op. cit., pp.75–82.

30 Ibid., pp.101–102.

31 Ibid., p.103.

32 John Dewey, Freedom and Culture, *The Later Works*, vol.13, p.67.

33 Ibid., p.67.

34 Ibid., p.79.

35 John Dewey, The Way Out of Educational Confusion, *The Later Works*, vol.6, pp.75–80.

36 Ibid., p.81.

37 Ibid., pp.81–89.

38 John Dewey, "How We Think: A Restatement of the Relation of Reflective Thinking to the Educational Process," *The Later Works*, vol.8, pp.105–352.

39 Ernst Gideon Malherbe (ed.), *Educational Adaptations in a Changing Society*, Cape Town; Johannesburg: Juta and Co., 1937.

40 John Dewey, "What Is Learning?," *The Later Works*, vol.11, pp.238–242.

41 John Dewey, "The Duties and Responsibilities of the Teaching Profession," *The Later Works*, vol.5, pp.326–330.

42 John Dewey, "The Teacher and His World," *The Later Works*, vol.11, pp.339–341.

43 John Dewey, "The Teacher and the Public," *The Later Works*, vol.11, pp.158–161.

44 John Dewey, "Toward a National System of Education," *The Later Works*, vol.11, pp.356–359.

45 "Dewey Favors Federal Department of Education," *School Management*, vol.3, no.4, April, 1934, p.13.

46 "John Dewey Asks Rotarians to Cooperate with Schools in Character Development," *School Management*, vol.4, no.1, October, 1934, pp.6–7.

47 John Dewey, "Liberty and Social Control," *The Later Works*, vol.11, pp.360–363.

48 John Dewey, "Education and New Social Ideals," *The Later Works*, vol.11, pp.167–170.

49 John Dewey, "How Much Freedom in New Schools?," *The Later Works*, vol.5, pp.319–320.

50 Ibid., pp.324–325.

51 Ibid., pp.319–325.

52 John Dewey, "The Social Significance of Academic Freedom," *The Later Works*, vol.11, p.376.

53 Ibid., pp.376–379.

5 Aesthetic Experience and the Public Sphere

As I have discussed in the preceding chapters, Dewey's educational vision of the 1920s and 1930s was oriented towards conceptions of democracy and the public sphere. In an effort to reconstruct the ideas of rights, freedom and equality set by traditional liberalism, he searched for strategies to develop educational reform through democratic processes and practices. In this regard, Dewey often mentioned "art" in connection with the notions of "communication," "public" and "democracy" in *The Public and Its Problems, Experience and Nature, Individualism, Old and New*, and other works. He advanced the ideas of "art" and "aesthetic experiences" in *Art as Experience*, a book that was originally based on a series of 10 lectures held to commemorate William James at Harvard University in 1931. It attracts attention by virtue of the fact that, at the beginning of the book, Dewey wrote "to Albert C. Barnes in gratitude." Barnes, who had collected many works of art at the Barnes Foundation, maintained a friendly relationship with Dewey.

When we look at Dewey's conception of art in relation to his public theory, there appears to be something fundamentally important in the way we reconstruct democratic politics and education. First, art was not an essentially partitioned domain outside of political and social relationships, but a practical arena of human interaction in political, social and cultural life. One of the roles of art was grasped in accordance with a societal transformation in the early twentieth century: urbanization, industrialization and the development of mass society. Second, the conception of art was defined as mediated communication that transcends a barrier of experiences between humans. Dewey pointed out that there was a danger of art becoming detached from human experiences in everyday life, and being separated into fixed and confrontational distinctions such as a producer and a perceiver, a creator and an appreciator, or an artist and an audience. In opposition to that distinction, he understood that art was tied into communication experiences of people in the communities.

Nevertheless, after Dewey's death in 1952, while scientism swept over many fields and academies, Dewey's philosophy of art tended almost to be forgotten. From the standpoint of the analytical philosophy that had a dominant influence on the discipline, pragmatism was criticized as philosophy lacking the scientific method of rigidity. Therefore, while Dewey's successors valued his philosophy, they had to overemphasize his scientism, which was supposed to be inherent in his philosophy. On the other hand, the pragmatism renaissance from the 1980s reawakened interest in Dewey's ideas that contributed to emancipating the potential for philosophy from scientism and relating it to the themes of politics, the economy, art, religion and ethics in social practices and life experiences. Richard Rorty, who took an initiative in leading the pragmatism renaissance movement in the postmodern era, argued that the significance of "contingency," "conversation" and "solidarity" cannot be reduced to the scientism of analytical philosophy, which he did through promoting the aesthetic turn of philosophy inspired by Dewey's pragmatism.[1]

In response to this movement, Thomas M. Alexander claimed that the aesthetic dimension of experience is central and consistent throughout Dewey's philosophy of "the metaphysics of experience."[2] According to Alexander, Dewey considered that "through art man is able to realize the potentiality for meaning and value to be directly embodied in the world."[3] In other words, "art" not only "realizes the community in its fullest sense, as communication," but also "embodies in itself the very quest of the democratic community" through "the creative exploration of the fulfilling meanings and values of experience."[4] Philip W. Jackson also admired Dewey's aesthetics, saying that the arts are necessary within curriculum neither because "they offer a means of self-expression," nor because they provide students with "different ways of knowing," but because they are "educative." That is, "they open the door to an expansion of meaning and to an enlarged capacity to experience the world" by teaching "how to live richer and fuller lives."[5] In this chapter, I focus on Dewey's theory of bridging aesthetic experience and the public sphere, which lay deep within the roots of his ideas of democratic politics and education.

Art and Politics in the 1930s: The Transformation of Art in the Age of Mass Culture

There were many responses to *Art as Experience* after its publication. Herbert Read, a British art critic, remarked that "I regard it as one of the curiosities of philosophy that when John Dewey, late in life, came to the subject of aesthetics (*Art as Experience*, London, 1934), he nowhere, in the course of an imposing treatise, established a connection between aesthetics and education."[6] Stephen Pepper indicated there was a conflict between the factors of "idealism" and "pragmatism" in Dewey's aesthetics, while expressing his support for the concept of the book.[7]

In particular, one of the stimulating dialogues that developed about *Art as Experience* was between Dewey and Benedetto Croce, who was a prominent Italian thinker and aesthetician in the first half of the twentieth century. As a Hegelian idealist, Croce began his criticism with reference to Pepper's point of argument. For Croce, despite pragmatism being a theory of "conflict" and regarding every solution as the beginning of a new problem, *Art as Experience* appeared to be a theory of "idealism" aiming to form an ultimate harmony. Croce considered Dewey's aesthetic theory as a mixture of incompatible, inconsistent and self-contradictory ideas between naturalist and idealist. Croce was also dissatisfied with Dewey's reply, since he answered only that he was a pragmatist and not an idealist, without an explicit explanation of the relationship between the two.[8] Dewey was opposed to Croce's aesthetics, which took only the "mind" as real, believing that intuition and expression stemmed from "idealism;"[9] however, Dewey showed his respect for Croce for courageously expressing his anti-fascist position and attacking the conclusion of the Lateran Treaty under the Mussolini Administration.[10] Thus, the argument between Dewey and Croce ended without reaching a conclusion.

Alexander refuted the charges against Dewey's aesthetics made by Pepper and Croce by labelling them the "Pepper–Croce thesis." Alexander protected Dewey's aesthetics as a theory founded on "naturalistic metaphysics."[11] However, contrary to Alexander's interpretation that discussed Pepper and Croce within the same framework, it is also important to note that unlike Croce, who was inclined to attack Dewey from an idealist perspective, Pepper was a strong proponent of Dewey's theory of aesthetics, seeing it as "contextualism" rather than "metaphysics."[12] In this regard, Rorty's work is important since he urged an increased interest in pragmatism in light of abandoning the metaphysical aspect of its theory. Reinterpreting Dewey's *Experience and Nature*, which had been grasped from a metaphysical point of view as an acclaimed work of "historic-sociological" study, Rorty prompted a turn "from a 'metaphysics of experience' to a study of cultural development."[13] Rorty's theory was suggestive: it also offered a new way to interpret Dewey's aesthetics that inquired into political, social and cultural experiences.

When we turn our attention to the international situation in the 1930s and 1940s, it is clear that the theory of art became a new and controversial theme in accordance with the rise at that time of mass media and popular culture. For example, Walter Benjamin discussed the connection of "aesthetics" and "politics" in the advent of film and photography in 1936, in an inspiring essay titled "The Work of Art in the Age of Mechanical Reproduction."[14] Theodor W. Adorno wrote about the relationship between "art" and a "culture industry" while he was exiled in the US in the mid-1940s.[15] In addition, Paul F. Lazarsfeld and several Jewish political refugees, including Adorno, were engaged in research about mass media and popular culture in the late 1930s and 1940s. Thus, a growing concern is observed in the research of that time which interpreted art from political, social and cultural contexts by paying attention to its critical function. Daniel J. Czitrom, who researched the history of media studies and the transformation of culture in the US, evaluated Dewey in depth because the latter's theory included the roles of the media and communication as associated with the development of democracy.[16]

Despite the fact that there were not necessarily theoretical exchanges and arguments between Dewey and these thinkers, aside from those between Dewey and Croce, all others seemed to share a common perspective in discussing aesthetics – namely, the theme of relating a theory of art with politics. However, this does not mean that every thinker asserted the same opinions. What Adorno saw in the American "culture industry," such as film, radio and magazines, were uncritical and unreflective factors of commoditized art, which produced standardized commercial goods. He offered a pessimistic diagnosis based on the tendency of a germ to turn into totalitarianism. It was symbolic that he used the term "culture industry" rather than "mass culture" – he avoided expressing the term in a way that suggested the "mass" was bearing the subject of culture. On the contrary, he believed that people had turned into objects that are passively operated and manipulated.[17] For Benjamin, regardless of the fact that the spread of the mechanical reproduction of mass culture had brought about the decay of the "aura" and "the here and now" of art by destroying its uniqueness and authenticity, it led to emancipating art from its parasitical dependence on rituals to "another practice – politics." Benjamin used the term "mass" in a positive way, by urging people to become involved in the emancipation of art through the "politicization of art," which constituted an alternative to the "aestheticization of politics" seen in fascism.[18]

How can we interpret Dewey's aesthetics in this context? Dewey considered that aesthetic experience is concerned with the creation of the public sphere through generating community and association. He did not use the term "mass" – rather, he advanced use of the word "public." Dewey claimed that the "articulate public" would be created by the "art of communication."[19] For him, public education is related to education of the public in the communities, and art is at the basis of the public sphere.

It would be interesting to know the background of Dewey's attempt at theorizing art in the US, because it might have presented an opportunity to pursue a more positive definition of American culture and its potentiality to emerge from the predominance of European "fine art" which appeared at that time to be firm and unchangeable. Richard Shusterman, who employs "the pragmatist project in aesthetics," affirms "popular art" positively. Using the historical context of the US, where people had to "fight for political and economic independence from Europe" as "a New World," and taking into consideration its inclination to resist "high art" (perceiving it as "an aristocratic European import"), Shusterman criticizes the "aesthetic ideology" of "the museum conception of art" or "the beauty parlor of civilization" in Dewey's sayings, because it provides "a devastating strategy" by which "the socio-cultural elite" can "disguise and assert its proud claim to intrinsic superiority thorough privileged association with high art's illustrious tradition." For him, despite the incapacity to appreciate that "high art" is "relative and socially determined," it is "projected as a sign of a more intrinsic inferiority," which suggests "natural and not socio-economic disability." However, his pragmatist project is not to abolish or destroy "the institution of art" but to "open and enlarge" it through defining "art" as "experience," as Dewey did, rather than understanding it as a "cultural practice."[20]

Emergence of Aesthetic Experience

Dewey associated "art" with "ordinary experience," rather than confining it in the framework of "fine art." His theory aimed to bridge art and the public sphere through constructing aesthetic experiences in social and cultural practices.

According to Dewey's explanation, "impulsions" are distinct from "an impulse" and are "the beginnings of complete experience." An "impulse" is "specialized and particular" and "simply a part of the mechanism" used to adapt to the environment; "impulsion" is at once "the movement of the organism in its entirety" and "the initial stage of any complete experience." However, "the act of expression" is taken a step further by Dewey: it differs from "emotional discharge." Although with "emotional discharge" there is an urge "from within outwards," it must "be clarified and ordered by taking into itself the values of prior experiences" in order to become "the act of expression." At the same time, these values are called into play through "objects of the environment" that resist the direct discharge. For Dewey, "discharge" is "to get rid of, to dismiss," but "expression" is "to stay by, to carry forward in development, to work out to completion." He explained this further by pointing out the erroneous thinking that "emotion is complete in itself within;" it is, in actuality, "to or from or about something objective, whether in fact or in idea." Dewey stated that "the connection between a medium and the act of expression is intrinsic."[21]

To recognize "the act of expression" as a "medium" involves a re-examination of the traditional notion of art in Western culture. According to Alexander, art has been interpreted as "*mimesis*, an imitation or representation of some object or action" since the ancient Greek philosophies of Plato and Aristotle, which were followed by the theoreticians of romanticism like Schelling, Schopenhauer and Coleridge. Alexander asserts that Dewey's idea of "expression" was in contrast to that of romanticism; while the latter regards "Spirit" as "the true source of being," the former considers "art" as arising from "the natural interaction of an organism with the world" and from "the cultural interaction of members in a society."[22] As we have also seen in the controversy between Dewey and Croce, this constitutes a fundamental difference in the understanding of art.

Dewey believed that the problem of existing theories is in the fact that they start from "a ready-made compartmentalization" or from "a conception of art that 'spiritualizes' it out of connection with the objects of concrete experience." For him, the alternative to "spiritualization" is not "a degrading and Philistinish materialization" of works of art, but "a conception that discloses the way in which these works idealize qualities found in common experience." According to his theory, "experience" is "the fulfilment of an organism" that continuously and accumulatively interacts with "environment." In this sense, "the junction of the new and old" is not "a mere composition of forces" but is "a re-creation" in which the impulsion obtains form and solidity while the old material is "revived, given new life and soul" in meeting a new situation. Dewey insisted that through "the rhythm of loss of integration with environment and recovery of union," that is, through "all interactions that effect stability and order in the whirling flux of change," the interactions bear "the germ of a consummation akin to the esthetic" which is essential to living.[23]

Dewey illustrated this idea through the activities of an infant. As the infant grows, he learns that particular acts, such as smiling or crying, induce definite responses around him. The infant begins to be aware that his different acts effect different consequences and thus grasps the meaning of the act. If he knows that his crying will attract his parents' attention, he might learn to cry intentionally. He comes to control his acts in consideration of the consequences they might cause. These consequences offer to him the meaning of the acts, and unite them to the subsequent acts. Through this experience mediated by interaction, expression is practised and performed.[24] Dewey understood the expression of art in the context of communication.

Expression of experience is public and communicating because the experiences expressed are what they are because of experiences of the living and the dead that have shaped them. It is not necessary that communication should be part of the deliberate intent of an artist, although he/she can never escape the thought of a potential audience. But its function and consequence are to effect communication, and this not by external accident but from the nature he/she shares with others. Expression strikes below the barriers that separate human beings from one another. Since art is the most universal form of language and because it is constituted, even apart from literature, by the common qualities of the public world, it is the most universal and freest form of communication.[25]

The theory of "expression of experience" as "public" and "communicating" is noteworthy. Dewey thought that "art" is "communication" of "the common qualities of the public world" that destroy "barriers" between human beings by urging interactions and exchanges of experiences. In *Experience and Nature*, Dewey asserted that "of all affairs, communication is the most wonderful" and that "the fruit of communication should be participation, sharing," in which "all natural events are subject to reconsideration and revision."[26] Interestingly, he added that "impartial and disinterested thinking, discourse in terms of scru-tinized, tested, and related meanings, is a fine art."[27] For Dewey, one of the potentialities of aesthetic experience was to urge a sharing and participating communication in political, social and cultural communities.

However, what was important for Dewey in the discussion of art is that "communication to others" is not "the intent of an artist" but is "the conse-quence," and that this communication exists by working through the experience of others. For him, the work of art would become "universal" only when it could "continuously inspire new personal realizations in experience." Whether the Parthenon, a work by Tolstoy or a symphony by Beethoven, a work of art needs to live in "some individualized experience" and be "recreated every time it is esthetically experienced."[28] According to Dewey's statement, we are likely to suppose that the perceiver and the appreciator merely take in artworks in their "finished form," but that reception actually involves activities that are comparable to those of the creator. He asserted that "receptivity is not passivity;"

it is "a process consisting of a series of responsive acts that accumulate toward objective fulfillment," and also "an act of reconstructive doing" in which "consciousness becomes fresh and alive."[29] It is through these processes and practices that "expression of experience" becomes "public and communicating."

Comprehending art from the viewpoint of experience and communication is to open up a conception of art that is connected with political and social practices through which various people interact with each other, rather than putting it in a narrow and exclusive domain separate from everyday life. Dewey placed emphasis on the role of media in expanding the dialogue between members of the public and blowing life into a community. Because art has its own media, it is suitable as a mode of communication. He observed that "sensitivity to a medium as a medium" is at "the very heart of all artistic creation and esthetic perception." For example, although a phonographic disc might be "a vehicle of an effect and nothing more," the music of the disc is also "a vehicle but is something more:" it becomes one with what it carries and coalesces with what it conveys. Dewey elaborated upon the idea of art as media by saying that "the medium is a mediator," that is, "a go-between of artist and perceiver." Art becomes the "consummation of an experience" when it mediates aesthetic experiences through interactive communication.[30]

Dewey remarked that it is "unfortunate" that there is no single word in English to express both "artistic" and "esthetic" together, and explained the existing distinction between the two words: while "artistic" refers primarily to "the act of production," "esthetic" refers to "perception and enjoyment." The effect of having two different terms is to "separate" the experiences of the "production" and the "perception" and to think that there is "nothing in common" between the two.[31] According to Shusterman, "the practice of art" has been preoccupied by the "model of making" since Aristotle – we might call it "the productive model" or "the fabricational model" – but it has led to "the fetishization of art's objects" as well as "an essential division between artist and audience, between the active maker or author and the contemplative receiver or reader." In opposition to this trend, Dewey's redefinition of "art" as "experience" involved a "fullness of art" that is "both receptive undergoing and productive doing" and "both absorbing and responsively reconstructing what is experienced, where the experiencing subject both shapes and is shaped."[32] Rather than supporting a tradition that distinctly separated receptive and productive elements in art, Dewey attempted to construct an idea of community that reconciled them along with people's ordinary experiences.

> Every art communicates because it expresses. It enables us to share vividly and deeply in meanings to which we had been dumb, or for which we had but the ear that permits what is said to pass through in transit to overt action. For communication is not announcing things, even if they are said with the emphasis of great sonority. Communication is the process of creating participation, of making common what had been isolated and singular; and part of the miracle it achieves is that, in being communicated,

the conveyance of meaning gives body and definiteness to the experience of the one who utters as well as to that of those who listen.[33]

In *The Public and Its Problems*, Dewey stated:

The freeing of the artist in literary presentation, in other words, is as much a precondition of the desirable creation of adequate opinion on public matters as is the freeing of social inquiry. Men's conscious life of opinion and judgment often proceeds on a superficial and trivial plane. But their lives reach a deeper level. The function of art has always been to break through the crust of conventionalized and routine consciousness.[34]

Central to Dewey's concept of art was the need to bridge aesthetic experience and the public sphere in a democratic community. He wrote that "a subtle, delicate, vivid and responsive art of communication" would breathe life into the physical machinery of transmission and circulation. It was his belief that art enriches people's ordinary, everyday experiences, broadens their consciousness and brings familiar things to a deeper level of meaning. In addition, it induces participation in generating a meaning for the articulation of experience through interactive processes of communication. In his view, "democracy is a name for a life of free and enriching communion" and "it will have its consummation when free social inquiry is indissolubly wedded to the art of full and moving communication."[35] It can be inferred from this that Dewey comprehended "art" as "a precondition" for "public matters." By removing "art" from the conventional way of understanding it, Dewey attempted to have it seen from the perspective of interactive participation that mediates people, and builds democracy and the public sphere on the basis of aesthetic experience.

Art and the Public Sphere

It was when the US was facing rapid social changes that Dewey developed his theory of art. The mode of art and people's lives were transformed by the emergence of a society of mass consumption that was accompanied by technological developments in film, photography, radio, print media and others. Irrespective of the fact that art was "what the product does with and in experience," it came to be understood as existing apart from human experiences in social and cultural contexts. Historically, "dancing and pantomime, the sources of the art of the theater" were "part of religious rites and celebrations;" "musical art" derived from "the fingering of the stretched string, the beating of the taut skin, the blowing with reeds;" and even in "the caves," human habitations were "adorned with colored pictures." Thus, the drama, music, painting and architecture of the past were closely bound to "the lives of humans" and were "part of the significant life of an organized community;" it was not that they had a "peculiar connection" with theatres, galleries and museums, as in Dewey's era. On the other hand, the tradition of separating works of art from social connections and setting them on "a far-off pedestal" did not arise within "the realm of art."[36] Dewey grasped processes or phases that separated art from ordinary life, as expressed by the following five factors.

Initially, one of the historical reasons for a separation occurring between art and ordinary life – Dewey called it "the compartmental conception of fine art" – could be found in the "nationalism" and "imperialism" of modern society. The "modern institutions of museum and exhibition gallery" to which works of art were moved and stored caused a segregation of art from temple, forum and community life. As Dewey remarked, most European museums are "memorials of the rise of nationalism and imperialism," and "museums of paintings, sculptures, etc." decorating every capital exhibit "the loot gathered by its monarchs in conquest of other nations" and "the greatness of its artistic past." To illustrate his point, Dewey used the Louvre, which displayed the accumulations of the spoils of Napoleon, as an example. At the same time, he wrote that in Japan, art treasures had avoided being exploited by other countries because of that country's "nationalizing the temples that contained them" during the process of Westernization. In this regard, we might say that Dewey was seeing the ambivalence of "nationalism." However, the point that concerned him most was the isolation of art from everyday experiences in life, and its functioning as a sign to show off its "greatness" with the development of modern society. The establishment of modern institutions such as museums and galleries fostered and strengthened such ideas of "nationalism" and "imperialism."[37] Dewey's theory of art correlated to the decline of the public sphere through these processes.

The second process that caused the separation of art from ordinary experiences of everyday life was the expansion of the "market" that accompanied the rise of "capitalism." Dewey's ideas on this point can be seen in his statement that "works of art" lost much of their "intimate social connection" and "the conditions of their origin" because they were mainly produced "for sale in the market" and incorporated into "the impersonality of a world market." The way he saw it, the nouveau riche collected works of art – like stocks and bonds – that for them acquired the new statuses of "specimens of fine art," "insignia of taste" and "certificates of special culture" for the sake of showing them off as "evidence of good standing in the realm of higher culture." He argued that artistic products took on "the air of something independent and esoteric" and were valued in the realm of the impersonality of the market economy, while deviating from the "common experience." As a result, artists were set apart from the "common life" and became absorbed in "self-expression," feeling obliged to "exaggerate their separateness to the point of eccentricity." Collections of works of art acquired a new meaning as "certificates," by which the member of a newly risen class could show "his standing in the economic world."[38]

The third is a dimension related to the appearance of industrialization and mechanization. Dewey praised Daniel Bell's essay "Adjusting Men to Machines: Social Scientists Explore the World of the Factory" (1947)[39] as "epoch-making," as Bell criticized the industrialized society that urges men to adjust to machines rather than adjusting machines to men.[40] In *Individualism, Old and New*, Dewey denounced the situation of industrialized society, where few workers know "what they are making" or "the meaning of what they do" and in which the "'impersonalization' of the human soul" would cause the "quantification of life" with its disregard of "quality." In the process of the dissemination of mass production and mass consumption, "agreement," "similarity" and "homogeneity of thought and emotion" became "ideal" while "differences," "distinctions" and "critical thinking" were ignored. He asserted that the "quantification, mechanization and standardization" that conquered American society "have invaded mind and character, and subdued the soul to their own dye."[41] Nevertheless, he was not fundamentally making charges against industrial society, referring to the fact that "science and technology is relevant because they are the forces of present life which are finally significant." He aimed to create "a new type of individuality" through "art," since "art" is "sensitive to the technology and science that are the moving force" in "the expansive, the social, culture."[42] Thus, Dewey's theory of art had a significant meaning in relation to the labour and technology of industrial society.

The fourth is in regard to the rise of "the totalitarian state." In *Freedom and Culture*, Dewey stated that in "totalitarian countries," works of art become "the most compelling of the means of communication by which emotions are stirred and opinions formed." For instance, the theatre, the movie and music hall, the picture gallery, eloquence, popular parades, common sports and recreational agencies in those countries are brought under "regulation as part of the propaganda agencies," by which "dictatorship is kept in power without being regarded by the masses as oppressive." It is not "information and reason" but "emotions and imagination" that more potently shape "public sentiment and opinion." In this sense, churches were no exception; in a totalitarian dictatorship, the church took over "esthetic appeal" and incorporated the public sentiments into its "structure" by gaining and maintaining "the allegiance of the mass." The object of strengthening a totalitarian regime by using the "ability to reach emotions and imagination" would be extended to include "rites and ceremonies" and "legend and folklore." In Dewey's view, people should not hold the "delusion" that "totalitarianism rests upon external coercion alone;" a "totalitarian state" has to be "total" in that it is involved in controlling "the whole life of all its subjects," including "feelings, desires, emotions, as well as opinions."[43]

Regardless of Dewey's critical comments on the social changes and inconsistencies brought about by the rise of the market economy, industrial society and totalitarianism, by which the concept of art was segregated from ordinary experiences of common life and divided into a fixed distinction between a producer and a perceiver, a creator and an appreciator, or an artist and an audience, he was not necessarily looking only at the negative aspect of these changes. This is related to the fifth aspect, of connecting art with democracy and the public sphere based on the media and community. During the 1920s and 1930s, mass culture and a society of consumption expanded as accompaniment to the development and spread of movies, radio and print media.

In the face of society's transformation, Dewey interpreted "the arts" and "the fine arts" in terms of "the cultural bases of democracy." He pointed out that there was a tendency to reject the view that art is "an important part of the social conditions that bear upon democratic institutions and personal freedom." Despite the people who were inclined to see literature, music, painting, drama and architecture as "adornments of culture," Dewey aimed to reconstruct the arts in the light of an "intimate connection with the cultural bases of democracy."[44] His statement that the "expression of experience is public and communicating" was formed by reflecting social changes such as the rise of mass media and popular culture.

The viewpoint of pragmatism that related art to mass culture and life experience was also introduced in Japan after World War II. *Studies of Marginal Art* (1956) by Shunsuke Tsurumi, who had contributed to introducing pragmatism to Japan, was a typical instance of this. While touching upon Dewey's notion of "aesthetic experience," Tsurumi advocated "marginal art" that was broader in distinction than "fine arts" and "popular art" and lay at the "boundary line between life and art." "Marginal art" was pushed into the corners and included examples such as children's play and scribbling, card games and folk songs; it sat on a "boundary" between "art" and "non-art" that was difficult to distinguish. According to Tsurumi, these examples of "marginal art" were considered to be the "origin of art" and had the power to produce "fine art" and "popular art." "Art" should not be directed by the principle of "non-socialization" and "non-politicization" that separates it from "other activities," nor should it be grasped from the "excessive socialization and politicization" that serve and subordinate art to other activities. Instead, Tsurumi felt that it enters into "other activities" through its relationships with politics, labour, family life, social life, education and religion, and is considered to redirect human actions as a whole.[45]

Shusterman aims to establish aesthetics on the basis of a conception of "the art of living," while criticizing an "essential and unbridgeable divide" between "high art" and "popular art." Indicating the "paradox" that "the aesthetically refined Nazi officers who would weep at Beethoven to express their human emotions while inhumanly orchestrating the wholesale slaughter of innocent children," Shusterman raises a question of the inclination of "fine art" to divide society through "its privileging distinction from craft, entertainment, and popular art" rather than "unequivocally uniting society."[46] Thus, Dewey's regarding "arts" as "experiences" criticized not only the concept of art as being separate from everyday life in the community, but also denounced the idea of a fixed and confrontational distinction between a producer and a perceiver, a creator and an appreciator, or an artist and an audience.

In this chapter, I have explored Dewey's attempts to bridge aesthetic experience and the public sphere in connection with media and communication in democratic politics. He interpreted art from the viewpoint of ordinary experiences of common life, which enlarge the aesthetic quality of "a democracy as a way of living together." He was not necessarily arguing how to bridge art and the public sphere in an explicit way. Rather, Dewey's theoretical outline becomes visible when taking the theories of mass society and the media into account. Dewey aimed to open the avenue of the potentiality of art to cross the borders of separated social relationships through mediating between individuals, and creating and recreating communities inspired by aesthetic experiences offering fuller and richer meanings of life. He presented the idea that the public sphere is constructed through the process of face-to-face communications of aesthetic experiences, in which various people interact as the public in democratic politics.

Notes

1 Richard Rorty, *Contingency, Irony, and Solidarity*, op. cit; *Objectivity, Relativism, and Truth*, op. cit.
2 Thomas M. Alexander, *John Dewey's Theory of Art, Experience & Nature: The Horizon of Feeling*, Albany: State University of New York, 1987; "The Art of Life: Dewey's Aesthetics," *Reading Dewey*, Larry A. Hickman (ed.), Bloomington: Indiana University Press, 1998.
3 Alexander, Thomas M., *John Dewey's Theory of Art, Experience & Nature: The Horizon of Feeling*, op. cit., p.185.
4 Ibid., p.273.
5 Philip W. Jackson, "If We Took Dewey's Aesthetics Seriously, How Would the Arts Be Taught?," *The New Scholarship on Dewey*, Jim Garrison (ed.), Dordrecht; Boston: Kluwer Academic Publishers, 1995, p.195.
6 Herbert Read, *Education Through Art*, London: Faber and Faber, 1943, p.245.
7 Stephen Pepper, "Some Questions on Dewey's Esthetics," *The Philosophy of John Dewey*, Paul Arthur Schilpp (ed.), *The Philosophy of John Dewey*, Chicago: Northwestern University Press, 1939, p.389.
8 Benedetto Croce, "On the Aesthetics of Dewey," *The Journal of Aesthetics & Art Criticism*, vol.6, March, 1948, p.205.
9 John Dewey, *Art as Experience*, op. cit., p.299.
10 John Dewey, "A Comment on the Foregoing Criticism," *The Journal of Aesthetics & Art Criticism*, vol.6, March, 1948, p.207.
11 Thomas M. Alexander, *John Dewey's Theory of Art, Experience & Nature: The Horizon of Feeling*, op. cit.
12 Stephen Pepper, "The Development of Contextualistic Aesthetics," *Antioch Review*, vol.28, 1968, pp.169–185.
13 Richard Rorty, "Dewey's Metaphysics," *New Studies in the Philosophy of John Dewey*, Steven M., Cahn (ed.), Hanover, NH: University Press of New England, 1977, pp.45–75.
14 Walter Benjamin, *Das Kunstwerk im Zeitalter seiner technischen Reproduzierbarkeit*, Berlin: Suhrkamp, 2013.
15 Theodor W. Adorno, *Minima Moralia: Reflexionen aus dem beschädigten Leben*, Frankfurt am Main: Suhrkamp, 1962.
16 Daniel J. Czitrom, *Media and the American Mind: From Morse to McLuhan*, Chapel Hill: University of North Carolina Press, 1982, pp.91–121.
17 Kiyoshi Abe, *Public Sphere and Communication: A New Horizon of Critical Research*, Kyoto: Minerva Shobo, 1998, pp.49–50.
18 Walter Benjamin, *Das Kunstwerk im Zeitalter seiner technischen Reproduzierbarkeit*, op. cit.
19 John Dewey, *The Public and Its Problems*, op. cit., pp.304–350.

20 Richard Shusterman, *Pragmatist Aesthetics: Living Beauty, Rethinking Art*, Oxford; Cambridge, MA: B. Blackwell, 1992.
21 John Dewey, *Art as Experience*, op. cit., pp.64–73.
22 Thomas M., Alexander, *John Dewey's Theory of Art, Experience & Nature: Horizon of Feeling*, op. cit., pp.214–215.
23 John Dewey, *Art as Experience*, op. cit., pp.17–28.
24 Ibid., p.68.
25 Ibid., p.275.
26 Dewey, John, *Experience and Nature*, op. cit., p.132.
27 Ibid., pp.158–159.
28 John Dewey, *Art as Experience*, op. cit., pp.109–117.
29 Ibid., pp.58–61.
30 Ibid., pp.203–204.
31 Ibid., p.53.
32 Richard Shusterman, *Pragmatist Aesthetics: Living Beauty, Rethinking Art*, op. cit.
33 John Dewey, *Art as Experience*, op. cit., pp.248–249.
34 John Dewey, *The Public and Its Problems*, op. cit., p.349.
35 Ibid., p.350.
36 John Dewey, *Art as Experience*, op. cit., pp.9–13.
37 Ibid., p.14.
38 Ibid., pp.14–16.
39 Daniel Bell, "Adjusting Men to Machines: Social Scientists Explore the World of the Factory," *Commentary*, vol.3, no.1, January, 1947, pp.79–88.
40 John Dewey, "Comment on Bell and Polanyi," *The Later Works*, vol.15, p.361.
41 John Dewey, *Individualism, Old and New*, op. cit., pp.45–52.
42 Ibid., pp.88–89.
43 John Dewey, *Freedom and Culture*, op. cit., pp.69–71.
44 Ibid., p.69.
45 Shunsuke Tsurumi, *Studies of Marginal Art*, Chikuma Shobo, [1956] 1999.
46 Richard Shusterman, *Pragmatist Aesthetics: Living Beauty, Rethinking Art*, op. cit.

6 Education through Art and Democracy

Dewey's Art Education Project at the Barnes Foundation

This chapter considers how Dewey attempted to create democratic education and the public sphere through aesthetic experience by focusing on his involvement in the art education project at the Barnes Foundation. The central questions for consideration are: is it possible to reconstruct democratic education through art? How can we connect the concept of aesthetic experience to the idea of the public sphere? How can we lead the art education practice on the basis of democracy and the public sphere? In the 1920s and 1930s, Dewey and Albert C. Barnes, a physician, chemist and art collector, devoted their efforts to advancing art education and democracy in Philadelphia. The Barnes Foundation was established as an educational institution in 1922 and Dewey was in charge of its art education section. However, their practices of building democratic education through art faced various difficulties. I will look at the challenges faced by Dewey in his attempts to bridge democracy and art in the art education project of the Barnes Foundation.

Barnes and Dewey

After earning a medical degree from the University of Pennsylvania in 1892, Barnes engaged in the study of chemistry and pharmacology at the universities of Berlin and Heidelberg. Through his research activities in Germany, Barnes developed the antiseptic Argyrol, which had powerful effects against decay. He then established the A. C. Barnes Company in Philadelphia where he developed the manufacture and sale of Argyrol. Having become extremely wealthy, Barnes established the Barnes Foundation in Merion, a suburb of Philadelphia, in December 1922. What was emphasized in the inauguration was that the Barnes Foundation was an educational institution.[1]

Barnes visited Europe frequently and purchased impressionist and post-impressionist paintings and African sculptures. In his collection there were works by Pierre-Auguste Renoir, Paul Cézanne, Édouard Manet, Edgar Degas, Claude Monet, Vincent van Gogh, Henri Matisse, Pablo Picasso, Amedeo Modigliani and others. Through purchasing these paintings, Barnes came to be recognized as one of the world's greatest collectors of French contemporary art. He was also eager to write on art criticism. Barnes not only published *The*

Art in Painting in 1925,[2] but also wrote *The French Primitives and Their Forms* (1931),[3] *The Art of Henri Matisse* (1933),[4] *The Art of Renoir* (1935)[5] and *The Art of Cézanne* (1939),[6] with Violette de Mazia. Barnes was also engaged in the "New Negro Movement" and protection of Native American artworks in sympathy with the ideal of racial equality in the 1920s.

Dewey and Barnes were close personal and intellectual friends. Dewey deepened his perspective and understanding of art through his friendship with Barnes. Paintings of Renoir's *The Bathers*, Cézanne's *Still Life with Peaches*, Matisse's *The Joy of Life* and African artworks and sculptures that Dewey had discussed in his book *Art as Experience* were in the possession of the Barnes Foundation. In the "Preface" of *Art as Experience*, Dewey showed his gratitude to Barnes:

> My greatest indebtedness is to Dr. A. C. Barnes. The chapters have been gone over one by one with him, and yet what I owe to his comments and suggestions on this account is but a small measure of my debt. I have had the benefit of conversations with him through a period of years, many of which occurred in the presence of the unrivaled collection of pictures he has assembled. The influence of these conversations, together with that of his books, has been a chief factor in shaping my own thinking about the philosophy of esthetics. Whatever is sound in this volume is due more than I can say to the great educational work carried on in the Barnes Foundation.[7]

The friendship between Dewey and Barnes went back to the 1910s, when Barnes had been impressed by reading Dewey's *Democracy and Education* and attended his seminar on Social Philosophy at Columbia University in 1917, one year after its publication. Barnes was inspired by Dewey's philosophy of democracy, experience and education. One of the motives behind Barnes becoming interested in Dewey's theory was that Barnes felt repulsion towards cubism in general, though he had purchased Picasso's *Composition: Farmers* in 1913. Barnes published "Cubism: Requiescat in Pace" in *Arts & Decoration* in January 1916, criticizing cubism as academic, repetitive, mediocre and dead. Barnes believed that art should be linked to experiences that are continuously reconstructed.[8] This assertion prompted him to approach Dewey's theory of experience, while making it hard for him to accept cubism.

In order to attend Dewey's weekly seminars at Columbia University, Barnes took a train from Philadelphia to New York every week. Through Dewey's lecture on Social Philosophy, Barnes studied various issues such as international politics, education and philosophy. On 7 November 1917 Barnes sent a letter to Dewey, announcing that he was moved by Dewey's lecture of the previous day with regard to the "plan to organize enlightened liberal thought for the intelligent prosecution of the war." Barnes suggested he would offer "some of the means which college professors do not always have at their disposal – money, business organization and the assistance of practical men of affairs." Barnes wrote that he would like to have Dewey come to his house, exchange general ideas and attend a symphony concert by the Philadelphia Orchestra the following Saturday and Sunday.[9]

Although they were not able to coordinate their schedules to meet at that time, it was an opportunity to deepen their mutual friendship. Dewey visited Barnes' house in response to his invitation in January 1918, when Dewey gave a lecture at Swarthmore College in the suburb of Philadelphia. Barnes wrote to Dewey: "I feel sure that there are enough interesting things here for you to see and for us to talk about that the time will not seem long" and "it is very quiet where I live, so that you will be free from all excitement, even that of meeting any strange people."[10] After the visit, Dewey expressed his sincere appreciation to Barnes, saying that "I want to thank you for the extraordinary experience which you gave me. I have been conscious of living in a medium of color ever since Friday – almost swimming in it. I can but feel that it is a mark of the quality of your paintings that there has been no nervous exasperation or fatigue accompanying this sensation."[11]

When Dewey visited Japan and China between 1919 and 1921, he often sent letters to Barnes concerning his impressions and experiences of his stay in those countries. In a letter to Barnes on 5 December 1920, Dewey described his meeting with Bertrand Russell in Beijing. According to Dewey's letter to Barnes, Russell was also visiting Beijing to give lectures on analysis of the mind and the problems of philosophy. Russell declined to give lectures on social reconstruction in China, since he thought he should have studied more about China first.[12] In response to Dewey's letter, Barnes wrote: "I never thought that Russell understood pragmatism."[13] Barnes told Dewey with full irony that "we read in the newspapers that Bertrand Russell died in your arms and a month later read that the death was only of his marriage."[14]

While Dewey taught Barnes philosophy and educational theory, Barnes encouraged Dewey to pursue his interest in art. Dewey introduced Walter Lippmann and Herbert Croly, who had been engaged in the editing of *The New Republic*, to Barnes. In a letter to Alice Chipman Dewey, Dewey's wife, Barnes reported that "Croly is the dullest person I ever met in a prominent position and Lippmann is an artist only in dressing up platitudes."[15] Dewey and Barnes trusted and respected each other. After reading Dewey's *Reconstruction in Philosophy* (1920), Barnes informed Dewey that "it is not a bit like philosophy, but like a talk among ourselves – just the way we do talk among ourselves – of what happens in the office, the laboratories, our homes, newspapers, concerts, picture exhibitions, and everywhere" and "when you find, pragmatically, a method to reach the unconscious self of each individual, Democracy and Education won"t be a book or a philosophy, but will be spontaneous, joyful living."[16]

Barnes was dedicated to collecting French paintings at the time the Barnes Foundation was established in 1922. After Degas passed away in 1917 and Renoir in 1919, their works were sold on the market. Whenever Barnes purchased works of art, he sent letters to Dewey expressing his joy. On 30 June 1920,

Barnes told Dewey, who was in China at that time, that he had bought 13 paintings by Cézanne from the museum in Amsterdam. He expressed his joy by saying that they are "masterpieces of rare power" and he is "terribly excited about a windfall brought about by the war."[17] In a letter to Alice Dewey on 1 July, Barnes said that he could not decide whether Renoir or Cézanne was "the biggest man of the last century in art," since Cézanne was "intense, passionate, almost cruel in his insight into reality" while Renoir's work was "charming, human, lyric – sheer beauty and feeling."[18] On 29 January 1921, Barnes told Dewey in a letter that he had purchased four oil and four pastel paintings by Degas. According to Barnes, these pictures would normally have cost him about $100,000, but he could purchase them for just a trifle under $30,000.[19] In his letter of 14 May, Barnes mentioned that he possessed over a hundred of Renoir's works (one was purchased at a cost of $80,000) and over 30 of Cézanne's works.[20] Taking these letters as a clue to his character, Barnes seems to be filled with confidence yet the way he expressed himself might give the impression of a man with a self-centred character. Nevertheless, Dewey was kind and generous to such attitudes. Dewey wrote to Barnes: "Tell us more about Cezannes when you feel like it, what period etc. We enjoyed your article very much."[21]

Barnes appointed Paul Guillaume, a French art dealer, as the main Parisian art supplier of the Foundation and purchased works of art at Guillaume's gallery. Barnes' collection contained more than 400 paintings: approximately 150 works by Renoir, 50 by Cézanne and works by Picasso, Matisse, Degas, Modigliani, Manet and Van Gogh, in addition to 53 works by Chaim Soutine, a young Russian painter, works by William Glackens, who had been a high school classmate of Barnes and had graduated from the Pennsylvania Academy of the Fine Arts, works by Thomas Eakins, a painter whose works focused on the landscape of Philadelphia, and African sculptures. According to the 5 February 1923 edition of the *Public Ledger*, a local newspaper in Philadelphia, Barnes had bought every canvas by Soutine that he had heard of, being attracted by Soutine's work that, according to him, "resembles Van Gogh's, but is more powerful and its color is more brilliant." Furthermore, Barnes' collection of African sculptures, which he had collected from the Guillaume museum, exceeded the collection of the Congo Museum in Brussels and the British Museum, and was the "most comprehensive in the world."[22]

However, the problem was that there was not sufficient space to display those paintings and sculptures in Barnes' house in Merion. According to the *Public Ledger* of 13 January 1923, "works of art were housed in his home, which is so crowded with paintings that many had been placed in the bathroom and on closet doors." Barnes eventually undertook a plan to establish a new museum with an investment of $6 million. Barnes purchased a 12-acre tract of land on North Latch's Lane in Merion from Joseph Lapsley Wilson. The contract stipulated that Barnes had to preserve and utilize Wilson's arboretum, which was one of the finest private arboretums in the country. Paul Philippe Cret, who was born in France and was Professor at the University of

Pennsylvania, was contracted to build the new museum. According to the newspaper, Barnes intended to build a museum that would "eventually become public property."[23]

The Barnes Foundation as an Educational Institution

From the foregoing, we are likely to conclude that Barnes was a member of a newly risen class, a parvenu of capitalist society. Apparently, he had an inclination to act in some ways to give this impression. When we look at the way Barnes amassed his collection of artwork, it cannot be denied that he was a child of capitalism. However, to regard him as a snobbish parvenu would be drawing an overhasty conclusion, for the establishment of the Barnes Foundation was intended not as simply the opening of a museum for personal appreciation, but rather the development of art education. Even from the outset, Barnes did not have the intention to build a traditional type of art museum. Dewey's criticism of "the museum conception of art," discussed in the previous chapter, was derived from the ideas of art education in the Barnes Foundation.

On 4 December 1922, the Barnes Foundation was chartered as "an educational institution" by the state of Pennsylvania. The purpose, as stated in the charter, was the "advancement of education and the appreciation of the fine arts."[24] Initially, Barnes initiated the organization of the art education section while Dewey was inaugurated as the first Director of Education of the Foundation in 1923. It was announced that "the educational work of the Barnes Foundation will be conducted in connection with the departments of fine arts and aesthetics of several universities and colleges."[25] Students who were enrolled in the education programme at the Barnes Foundation studied the theory, history and method of art.

In the Foundation, Dewey was expected to promote art education based on the theory of democracy and experience. Lawrence Buermeyer, Thomas Munro and Mary Mullen served as Associate Directors of Education of the Foundation. Munro was a student of Dewey's at Columbia University and it was Dewey who had introduced Munro to Barnes. Barnes expressed his initial impression of Munro as a young man who was an "intellectual star" and had a "practical knowledge of plastic art and psychological aesthetics."[26] Barnes and Buermeyer had been involved in both "the study of the psychology of aesthetics" and "the practical application of those principles to the paintings" since 1915.[27] Barnes was attracted to Buermeyer's "rare talents." A few years prior to that, Barnes had told Dewey that "Buermeyer is the only young man I know wedded to philosophical teaching of your work," and asked Dewey to find a teaching position for Buermeyer at Columbia University; Buermeyer had been seeking employment because his contract with Princeton University had expired.[28] In particular, Barnes was worried about "the restrictions and religious oppressions" that Buermeyer had endured at Princeton University.[29] Thus, Barnes was pleased to have a chance to hire Buermeyer as the Associate

Director of Education at the Barnes Foundation after the expiration of his term at Princeton University.

Between 1923 and 1925, three books were published by the Barnes Foundation Press: Mullen's *An Approach to Art* (1923),[30] Buermeyer's *The Aesthetic Experience* (1924)[31] and Barnes' *The Art in Painting*. Mullen insisted that "art and life are one and the same thing, they cannot be separated." According to Mullen, "art" is not "a phase of life that transcends life itself" but is "as much a part of reality as the imagination is a part of actual existence." More concretely, "art is simply the revelation of those activities embodied in perceptible forms capable of communicating the emotional content of the experience to us." Mullen stated that her view was founded on the psychology of James, Dewey, Russell and George Santayana.[32]

Buermeyer also opined that "the aesthetic experience" is related to "the various realms of human activity." He denounced the view that looked upon art as something detached from business life: a relaxation, distraction or dissipation akin to books, concert halls and museums. For him, "art is woven into the whole texture of life," and "aesthetic experience" is "active throughout" and "enters into activities which are not solely or predominantly those ordinarily associated with the word 'art.'" Buermeyer illustrated this with "the analogy between scientific and aesthetic experience:" both are "pervasive of life in all its departments;" both "must be singled out from the mass of our experience and deliberately cultivated" in order to attain their fullest development. He then analysed aesthetic experience in the light of expression, medium, creativity, satisfaction, morality and religion. It was Dewey's philosophy of experience that gave inspiration to Buermeyer's theory of aesthetic experience.[33]

At the beginning of *The Art in Painting*, Barnes offered the following dedication: "To John Dewey whose conceptions of experience, of method, of education, inspired the work of which this book is a part."[34] *The Art in Painting* is a voluminous book that amounts to 500 pages, with 122 illustrations of paintings. The purpose of the book was to discuss "esthetic experience in general" and "the intelligent appreciation of the paintings." In Barnes' view, "beauty" as "the roots of art" is not "something which exists independently in nature, like magnetism or gravitation," but should be sought in "psychological principles" that are related to "human wants and interest" in ordinary experiences. After analysing "the elements of painting" such as "plastic form," "subject-matter," "colour," "drawing" and "composition" from this perspective, he introduced the history of painting of the Italian Renaissance, the artistic traditions of Germany, Flanders, France, Spain and the Netherlands, impressionism, post-impressionism, American painting and the contemporary painting of Matisse and Picasso.[35] On 27 January 1925, Dewey sent a letter to Barnes giving his comments on *The Art in Painting*. Dewey wrote that "it does something which no other book on art criticism with which I am familiar has done and that it will be useful, indeed indispensable to those who want to get beyond erudition on one side and sentimentalism on the other."[36]

An Approach to Art, The Aesthetic Experience and *The Art in Painting* were used as textbooks in the art classes of the Barnes Foundation. At the centre of these art education classes lay art appreciation of works of art. According to Buermeyer's article "An Experiment in Education," published in *The Nation* in 1925, the Barnes Foundation as an educational institution grew out of "a community plan" that was in connection with "the administration of a business," and its main goal was to study "the view of art and [. . .] the relation of art to life." Buermeyer remarked that "this view is the same as that which is associated with the name of John Dewey." The students who came to the Barnes Foundation were not necessarily people with special knowledge of, or capabilities in, the fine arts. Rather, a "method of investigating plastic art and of finding a way to its intelligent appreciation" that Barnes yielded was first applied to "people whose academic education was of the slightest."

Furthermore, it was not improvement in painting skills or capabilities that the classes of the Foundation tried to teach; the art education programme mainly focused on the "appreciation of art" that lay at the heart of the "life" and "business" of common citizens and workers. Buermeyer placed an emphasis on "democracy in industry" and "cooperation" in "art." Through this, "the free expression of personality takes the place of rigid subordination of inferior to superior" and "foregoes the mechanical efficiency of an autocratic administration;" it would require "a different kind of knowledge, a more liberal, a more imaginative frame of mind" by harmonizing "the purposes of responsible individuals," rather than fitting together "the parts of a machine." In his theory, "the realm of industry" and "the realm of art" are not different. If the "industry [is to] be animated by intelligence and so humanized," then "the transition to art is not only easy and natural but inevitable."[37] The book review for Buermeyer's *The Aesthetic Experience* published in *The Nation* introduced his view as one pursuing "art as intelligence."[38]

The background to the Barnes Foundation relating "art" to "business" and "industry," and stressing the importance of intelligence and humanization, overlapped with the development process of the Foundation, which originated in the A. C. Barnes Company factory. According to John Anderson, the working day at the A. C. Barnes Company factory was "remarkably humane:" eight hours, of which only six were devoted to manufacturing and two to the discussion seminars that Barnes held every day for workers. There had never been more than 20 employees, comprising both men and women, and both whites and African-Americans. In the seminars, attendants not only studied psychology, pragmatism and James' theory of religious experience, but also read works by Dewey, Santayana and Russell.[39]

Barnes stated that "a community plan" of the A. C. Barnes Company was "the most valuable asset of the Foundation" in which "education" was seen as "a means of growth, of direction, of personal development cooperated in by a group of people." He introduced nine employees to the group: five white women, three African-Americans and one white man. The educational background was varied; the white man had a university degree, three of the women were high school graduates, the other two women and two of the African-Americans had primary school educations, and the other middle-aged man could neither read not write, aside from signing his name.[40] At that point, the educational activities of the Foundation derived from Barnes' seminar at the A. C. Barnes Company factory, which was mixed gender and with a racially integrated workforce. The practice of workers' education was already underway during the time of the A. C. Barnes Company's operations, prior to the establishment of the Barnes Foundation. Such programmes formed the basic policy of the Foundation as an educational institution for the common people who had not necessarily been educated in the school system.

Barnes asked Dewey to attend the formal opening ceremony of the new building of the Barnes Foundation, which would take place on 19 March 1925, and to give an address as the Foundation's Director of Education. Barnes explained that "our interest in plastic art grew out of our discovery that doing the everyday things of life, for the sake of the things themselves, was an aesthetic experience" and that "art is intelligence, all pervasive of experience, not compartmental." Barnes requested Dewey to emphasize in the address that "the Foundation is an educational institution and not an entertainment bureau for 'aesthetes'" and that "anybody serious can link up with us – but nobody is rich enough or prominent enough to get in with us on those qualities."[41] Several hundred people attended the ceremony, and both Dewey and Leopold Stokowski, who was conductor of the Philadelphia Orchestra, gave addresses.[42]

Dewey talked about the importance of the Barnes Foundation as an educational institution, saying that "an artistic or aesthetic educational enterprise" should not be interpreted in the "narrow and exclusive sense of the word." He told the audience that "art is not something apart, not something for the few, but something which should give the final touch of meaning, of consummation, to all the activities of life." He further expressed the thought that art is not the preference of the individual made accessible to only privileged people, but should be related to "all human activity." According to Dewey's speech, the intention of opening a new building was neither for the display of "the collection of pictures," nor for "the dissemination of knowledge about pictures," but for "the expression of a profound belief that all the daily activities of life" might be "made intrinsically significant" and be "made sources of joy," so that they can put "their whole beings," including their hands and brains as well as feelings and emotions, into "what they are doing."

Dewey's address dealt with the theme of the reform of public schools. He considered that the theory of the Barnes Foundation, which conceived of art as ordinary experiences of everyday life, would play a significant role in school education since "one of the weakest points in our public school educational system" was that while it gave "some training in mechanical, technical things," it did not yet "touch what is most common, most fundamental, most demanding public recognition." For Dewey, it would be important to restore "an appreciation of the place occupied in all human activity" by "intelligent method which is the essence of art" and by "the liberated and enjoyable methods which are the result of the presence of art." He expressed his deep appreciation of the honour of participating in "the initiation of this genuinely monumental and epoch-making enterprise," mentioning that the work of the Foundation would be "one of the most important educational acts, one of the most profound educational deeds, of the age in which we are living."[43]

The Advancement of the Art Education Project at the Barnes Foundation

Barnes undertook the plan to build a new art education centre that would advance the innovative research and education of art in Philadelphia through fostering a collaboration between the Barnes Foundation and the School of Fine Arts at the University of Pennsylvania. Barnes sought concrete means for realizing the purpose of the Foundation: the "advancement of education and the appreciation of the fine arts." He thought that he could effectively utilize the Foundations' properties, such as its paintings, sculptures and the arboretum, for its educational activities. In particular, if paintings, trees or objects that represented human values were appropriately used by teaching organizations, they could be made "more interesting, more vital, more valuable." In order to put the plan into effect, Barnes suggested that it was necessary for the Barnes Foundation to develop new curriculum in cooperation with universities and colleges.[44] Barnes' attempt to do so deserves attention in that it had the potential to develop an innovative educational practice by forming a collaborative network between the Foundation, universities and colleges.

Barnes had a desire to build a cooperative alliance between the Barnes Foundation and the University of Pennsylvania, from which he himself had graduated. He made contact with Josiah H. Penniman, President of the University of Pennsylvania, and Warren P. Laird, Dean of the School of Fine Arts at the University of Pennsylvania in preparation for this cooperation. In January 1924, Barnes sent a letter to President Penniman enclosing his article about the Foundation that had been published in *The New Republic*, and Mullen's *An Approach to Art*. Barnes' letter was about the proposal to establish "a Chair of Modern Art" at the University of Pennsylvania with Buermeyer serving as full professor of the subject. According to Barnes' plan, Buermeyer would give two lectures a week at the university and two practical talks at the Foundation's gallery. Barnes pointed out that Princeton, Harvard and Columbia all had courses in "Modern Art" but that "those who teach it bewail the absence of available modern paintings which are indispensable to make the subject a living reality." He stated, on the other hand, that "our [Foundation's] collection of modern paintings is the most important in existence," and "our buildings will be ready for the practical instruction in art in about a year." Barnes also wrote that the Foundation had "ample funds" without aid from the university, the state or other sources.[45] In any event, Barnes was pleased to utilize the Foundation's immense property and collection by building cooperation, and expected that the university would develop a leading and advanced art education practice through adopting the educational programme provided by the Barnes Foundation. Barnes speculated that he would construct a comprehensive and innovative research centre of art education by introducing an educational programme about modern art at the university.

The University of Pennsylvania responded to the proposal of the Barnes Foundation when, on 4 April 1924, Penniman conveyed his deepest appreciation of Barnes' offer, suggesting an alternative plan that would "render possible a co-operative arrangement between the Foundation and the University" and "realize in effect the purposes of your [Barnes'] plan." He went on to state that the university staff members "recognize and value fully the importance of the collection of Modern Art which you [Barnes] have assembled and the sincerity and earnestness of purpose with which you have organized and endowed the Barnes Foundation to promote the teaching of art as represented by this collection." Penniman's suggestion included the university's acceptance of members belonging to other educational institutions, such as exchange professors or visiting lecturers: the university would receive the Professor of Modern Art of the Foundation and give him facilities in accordance with faculty members, open his courses to students and accept credit from the course towards a degree in Fine Arts from the university. Penniman explained that "this plan of cooperation" might signify an "operation between foremost educational institutions here and abroad," but "we here propose its application in a more intimate and extended form than is usually found possible."[46]

Through these processes, the Barnes Foundation and the University of Pennsylvania reached an agreement in May 1924. In a letter from the university to the Foundation, the following five points were confirmed for incorporation into the agreement. First, the university would receive an appointee of the Barnes Foundation as a visiting lecturer to the School of Fine Arts during the academic seasons 1924–1925 and 1925–1926 and give "a course of lectures on Modern Art as exemplified in the Barnes collections" by delivering the lectures at the university and demonstrating them at the galleries in Merion. Second, the lecturer's title would be "the Barnes Foundation Professor of Modern Art." Third, "the course in Modern Art" would consist of two lectures each week plus demonstrations, and the evaluation would be determined by the Barnes Foundation's Director of Education and the Dean of the School of Fine Arts. Fourth, the university would include these courses among the subjects open to election and give credit to the candidates for the degree of Fine Arts. Fifth, tuition fees for this course would be the property of the university, while the Foundation assumed all costs of instruction and equipment. The university also stated that they were glad to accept either Buermeyer or Munro as lecturer.[47] On 3 May Barnes notified Penniman that the Board of Directors of the Foundation had ratified the suggestions unanimously. He declared that "one thing sure is that no human power can stop Philadelphia from becoming the only place in the world where plastic art can be adequately studied objectively and scientifically."[48]

In January 1925, the staff of the Barnes Foundation, including Barnes, Dewey, Buermeyer and Munro, started talking about the extension of the art education projects of the Foundation. Barnes informed President Penniman that they had been considering "ways and means of increasing the value of the Foundation from an educational standpoint." According to Barnes, the outcome of these conferences by the education section was that the Foundation would promote the incorporation of its course of Psychological Aesthetics in the Department of Philosophy at Columbia University through professors of Columbia University such as Dewey and John Jacob Coss. Barnes told Penniman that he was preparing to shift lecturers of the courses in the Department of Fine Arts at the University from Munro to Buermeyer.[49]

In the meantime, Dewey backed the cooperation between the Barnes Foundation and Columbia University. On 27 January, Dewey wrote to Barnes: "I hope that the arrangements Munro made with Coss about work at Columbia are satisfactory to you."[50] According to a letter dated 23 February from Barnes to Penniman, there were about 30 attendants at Munro's class and they would come to the Barnes Foundation gallery for the first time the following Thursday. Barnes made the following proposal to Penniman: "since it is the first meeting of the class, and the real launching of our mutual project, we feel that it would be most fitting if you would talk to the class for about five minutes."[51]

Seen from this perspective, the Barnes Foundation enjoyed great prosperity during this period. In April 1925, the Foundation began to publish the *Journal of the Barnes Foundation*. According to the first volume of the journal, the educational programme of the Foundation comprised the following components. The Foundation conducted "general courses in the appreciation of art" at the University of Pennsylvania, Columbia University and the Barnes Foundation. Munro took charge of the courses of "Modern Art" at the University of Pennsylvania and "Applied Aesthetics" at Columbia University. Munro's courses included "a study of the principles of aesthetics" that analysed concrete data by comparing recent paintings and sculptures with those of the past. Munro also took over the course "Research in Plastic Art" at the University of Pennsylvania, which was primarily for graduate students, though other persons were admitted if they were prepared to study painting and sculpture.

Buermeyer conducted the course "The Aesthetic Experience" at the University of Pennsylvania, which combined modern psychology, art criticism and literary criticism with educational methods on the appreciation of art and the aesthetic aspects of all experiences. Other advanced courses in the appreciation of art were conducted at the building of the Barnes Foundation by Barnes, Mullen, Buermeyer, Munro and Sala Carles. Various people such as painters, teachers, critics, writers and museum directors attended the advanced seminar of the course, which was conducted through both "theoretical discussion of aesthetic principles" and "practical talks in front of pictures."[52]

The Barnes Foundation was also eager to foster a collaborative relationship with the Philadelphia Museum of Art, which was originally founded as a legacy of the Centennial Exposition of 1876 held in Fairmont Park. The Memorial

Hall opened as a museum on 10 May 1877, and the Pennsylvania Museum School of Industrial Art opened on 17 December 1877. Barnes sent a letter to Fiske Kimball, who was the Director of the Museum, asking whether Munro could be one of the lecturers of the public course offered by the institution.[53] Kimball informed Barnes that he was pleased to comply with this offer.[54]

The Barnes Foundation continued to extend its influence in the field of art education. Mullen's *An Approach to Art*, Buermeyer's *The Aesthetic Experience* and Barnes' *The Art in Painting* were used in 35 universities and colleges from Maine to California, in the public school systems of six important cities and in classes conducted in art galleries including the Louvre and the Metropolitan Museum in New York. In the arboretum of the Foundation, research in arboriculture and horticulture was conducted under the guidance of Laura Leggett Barnes, who was the wife of Albert Barnes, and John W. Prince. They established a department of floriculture, in which students could engage in research about new species of flowers and plants. Thus, the art education project of the Barnes Foundation became comprehensive.[55]

On the other hand, Barnes showed an unwillingness to exhibit the collection of the Foundation to the general public, as an art museum would have done. On 22 October 1924, Barnes told Laird that though the Foundation had carefully discussed opening the gallery to the public, they had decided not to exhibit the collection at least for the next couple of years, since their "educational program" might be "seriously handicapped by admitting the public." According to Barnes, "the general educational plan which has materialized in the Foundation" was a result of discussion with Dewey over seven years, which Barnes detailed to Laird by saying that "he [Dewey] believes that if we can carry out the educational plan which Mr. Buermeyer, Mr. Munro and myself have worked out under his direction, we will have something of monumental importance to American culture."[56] In response to Barnes, Laird wrote that "I am glad to have your careful statement" and that "the reasons for a negative decision are logically determined and must, I think, satisfy reasonable people."[57] Barnes claimed that the Foundation was not an art museum but an educational institution.

Public Education Reform in Philadelphia

Barnes' interest in education encompassed public education reform in Philadelphia. He wanted the collection of the Foundation to be utilized effectively in the schools of Philadelphia. Barnes told Dewey that he wanted to talk about this by meeting him in Merion on 1 February 1925. Barnes provided the following details to Dewey at that time: "you take the train that leaves New York at 9 A.M.," "get off at West Philadelphia where my car will meet you" and "the Foundation will pay the fare of the guests [you] like."[58] Whenever Dewey came to Merion, Barnes gave him a warm and hearty welcome. The letter to Dewey was about the necessity for the educational reform in Philadelphia that Barnes had in mind.

On 2 March, Barnes wrote to Dewey that "we are at a crisis in the public education system in Pennsylvania." In Philadelphia, Gifford Pinchot, who was Governor of Pennsylvania, was then struggling to devise state employment retirement, old-age pension systems and other reforms. Barnes asked Dewey whether it would be possible to arrange a meeting with Cornelia Bryce Pinchot, the wife of Gifford Pinchot.[59] Dewey accepted Barnes' offer to introduce him to Mrs Pinchot, saying that "I am not sure whether an approach to her through me will do more harm or good."[60] In response to this, Mrs Pinchot sent a letter to Barnes on 15 March. She stated: "I have the greatest belief in John Dewey" and "I am, apriori [sic], interested in any and all attempts to translate his philosophy into action."[61]

Notwithstanding Barnes' efforts, his plan to build a cooperative network between the Foundation and the universities raised opposition from artists and teachers in Philadelphia. One of the educators who severely criticized the Foundation was Theodore Milton Dillaway, who had studied at the Pennsylvania Academy of the Fine Arts and was Director of Art Education for the Philadelphia public schools. In "Art Critics Flay Barnes Foundation" published in *North American* on 20 May 1924, Dillaway criticized the method of teaching Modern Art by the Foundation as being extremely harmful and likely to bring about "anarchy."[62]

Barnes reacted swiftly to Dillaway's criticism, choosing the topic "The Shame in the Public School of Philadelphia" as an essay for the first volume of the *Journal of the Barnes Foundation* in 1925. Barnes' opposition was declared against the "obsolete system" of instruction in the public schools of Philadelphia. In particular, he accused art education in Philadelphia of lacking "any intelligent purpose" and losing "order" or "method." In his view, though "industrial art" such as the designing of costumes, interior decoration and so on was instructed in the high schools for girls, "the aesthetic phase" was neglected by "the mechanical methods that rob art of its indispensable personal and expressive element;" even when drawing and the use of watercolours were instructed, the students were "merely taught to copy literally, or to relate a narrative." Hence, art education made "no appeal to individual interest or self-expression" and "it cannot function as art at all, and the teaching of it is aesthetically futile." According to Barnes, "these defects" were caused by the "obsolete system" of teaching and were seen in Dillaway's personality and opinions. Introducing Dillaway's criticism of the Foundation that was published in *North American*, Barnes declared that "the opinion that modern art is demoralizing to students and repulsive to all cultured persons, shows a complete inability to grasp the purposes, the essential art values," and that "modern art is only anarchic to one aesthetically blind, or to one who confuses all self-expression with anarchy." For him, students were able to understand "the essentials in art" through appreciating modern art; for instance, one can see in Renoir a modernized version of Greek traditions, in Matisse the Persian and Hindu traditions, in Picasso the Florentine tradition, and in Soutine the Egyptian and Venetian traditions. Barnes asserted that "Mr. Dillaway's public statement that the work of the modern artists leads to 'anarchy' shows his closed mind to the new, his hostility to it." He stated that Dillaway's viewpoint was "not education" but "demagoguery."[63]

In order to find a way out of the difficulties that the Foundation faced in terms of public education reform in Philadelphia, Barnes often relied on Dewey for appropriate advice. On 1 April 1925, he wrote to Dewey that Mr Dillaway "was guilty of all these offences" since he was aiding "mob hysteria" and displaying "a complete indifference to the interests of teachers and students of art." Barnes added that "we have no personal animus against Mr. Dillaway" and "we are willing to work with him if we are guaranteed a genuine spirit of cooperation and freedom from his supervision." He was eager to advance "fruitful cooperation" with the Philadelphia public schools.[64] Responding to Barnes' request, Dewey met with Dillaway for half an hour on 21 April. Dewey informed Barnes: "I think the ground is set for some cooperation," because when Dewey proposed to Dillaway that he meet with Buermeyer and Munro to talk about the matter, Dillaway "was more than agreeable." For Dewey, Dillaway was "not a strong man, rather neutral in his makeup" and "had been trying to change methods and conditions in the schools there."[65]

Nonetheless, the situation did not improve readily, mainly because Barnes directed his criticism at Samuel S. Fleisher, an art teacher who founded the Graphic Sketch Club. Fleisher, one of the pioneers of art education, had opened art classes for children in poverty in the Jewish Union Building at 422 Bainbridge Street in Philadelphia, in 1898. The Graphic Sketch Club was an institution that offered free and collaborative art classes for both adults and children. Barnes pointed out that Dillaway's prejudices against modern art were caused by Fleisher's educational thought, since many of the art teachers of Philadelphia had attended the classes conducted in the Graphic Sketch Club in the 1920s. He insisted: "Mr. Dillaway's grotesque vaudeville performances in the public class-rooms and his acceptance of Graphic Sketch Club standards for the public schools of Philadelphia make him impossible to fit into any educational plan that can be considered intelligent."[66]

Barnes told Dewey that a man like Dillaway "so bitterly prejudiced against all novelty" was "obviously a bar to any effective cooperation between the Barnes Foundation and the public schools," and that Dillaway was mainly affected by Fleisher, who had maintained "a soup kitchen for nourishing commercial painters."[67] Buermeyer also attacked Fleisher, criticizing the latter's art education as "the fortress of conventionalism" and saying that "what it has contributed to real education is substantially nothing," though the stated goal of the Graphic Sketch Club was primarily to "diffuse an appreciation of art."[68]

In any event, Barnes was a contentious person. He spread his provocative utterances to museums and educational institutions. For instance, Barnes rejected the art theory of Denman Ross, Professor of Art at Harvard University and Trustee of the Museum of Fine Arts in Boston, for reflecting "ignorance of human nature" and "of science and art."[69] Barnes accused American painter Jay Hambidge of not having "real aesthetic sensitiveness." For Barnes,

Hambidge's method corresponded to a "system of mechanics" that trained memory and strengthened the will "with no imagination and no aesthetic feeling." Barnes also cast a critical eye towards Walter Pach, saying that he had elaborated "pseude[sic]-scientific dressing to platitudes" and substituted "for aesthetic perceptiveness and comprehension a mystical adoration of the great names of painting" by overlooking "the distinctive and important features in contemporary painting."[70] Furthermore, Barnes denounced Huger Elliot, Director of Educational Work at the Metropolitan Museum in New York, due to the fact that Elliot's teachings in both the classroom and the field of industrial art were conducted not as "suggestions" but as "dogmas" that were "fatal to either appreciation or creation of works of art."[71] It is thus clear that Barnes initiated contentious disputes with authorities in the field of fine arts and art education, one after another.

Munro suggested nine fundamental principles of education of the Barnes Foundation in "A Constructive Program for Teaching Art" (1925) in *Journal of the Barnes Foundation*: (1) the purpose of education is to urge the harmonious development of native abilities; (2) aesthetic growth involves freedom for individual thought and feeling; (3) genuinely rational control and analysis furthers aesthetic growth; (4) artistic and other activities should be mutually correlated; (5) specific values and interests should be distinguished; (6) teaching should follow natural growth; (7) the order should not be rigidly systematic; (8) it is important to consider the stages in art education; and (9) it would require practical steps in reform of the public school system. According to Munro, "intelligent art instruction" should not be completed by "change in the school system" but by "change in spirit, aims and methods of individual teachers."[72]

Munro also advocated the reform of art education in universities and colleges in "College Art Instruction: Its Failure and a Remedy" in 1925. According to him, the "failure" of art education lay in the fact that though painting and sculpture were briefly taught in courses on Aesthetics, they were "usually entirely abstract, without observation of concrete examples;" and courses in the History of Art were based on both "the names and dates of artists" and "anecdotes." It was the "academic system of mass instruction, of marks, examinations and credits" that was "antithetic and destructive to the spirit of art." Besides, the vast majority of students on the art courses were "ignorant of the fundamentals necessary for appreciation" because of "false teaching" in the schools and in the outside environment. According to Munro, what was needed was to replace "passive absorption" by "spontaneous activity," and "remote abstraction" by "concrete problems." Art education, he said, should be neither "coercive" nor "anarchic," but should be involved in "native preference and character" that encourage "breadth and catholicity, as well as intensity of experience." Munro proposed that there should be courses of "intellectual history," "aesthetic psychology," "history of art," "practical art construction," "applied and industrial arts," etc. in college art instruction.[73]

With regard to art classes at the Barnes Foundation, these were conducted according to the principle of democracy. Mullen depicted a concrete scene of this at the first meeting of the class, in which one of the students asked the question: "What do you mean by beauty?" Although the other students' immediate answers were "vague, confused, or irrelevant," each person had expressed "his own opinion" and contributed to sharing in "the general discussion." Finally, attendants reached the conclusion that "as far as beauty could be defined at all, it is 'pleasure objectified'" and "it is a value which can be made concrete only by relating it to something in one's own experience." Mullen stressed that "a common understanding of the meaning of beauty" was not imposed as "a definition to be accepted without question," but was developed by "free discussion" irrespective of whether the definition was right or wrong. For Mullen, "the exchange of ideas is one of the most important means of a real education" because it would guard against "the closed, academic mind which is fatal to intellectual progress." She concluded that "the appreciation of art" thus becomes "real, genuine, personal" and "intelligent."[74]

In the *Journal of the Barnes Foundation*, Dewey's address at the opening ceremony of the new building of the Barnes Foundation,[75] as well as his articles "Experience, Nature and Art" (1925),[76] "Individuality and Experience" (1925)[77] and "Affective Thought in Logic and Painting" (1926),[78] were published. Dewey mentioned in "Individuality and Experience" that the history of schools had shown "a swing of the pendulum between extremes," such as "external imposition and dictation and 'free-expression.'" For Dewey, the metaphor of the pendulum was itself "faulty" and what was really needed was "a change in the direction of movement." He regarded "freedom" or "individuality" not as "an original possession or gift" but as "something to be achieved, to be wrought out" that must come from "a sympathetic and discriminating knowledge of what has been done in the past and how it has been done."[79]

Dewey expressed his eagerness to support the educational projects of the Barnes Foundation, saying "that art and its intelligent appreciation as manifested especially in painting is itself an integrating experience [and] is the constant implication of the work of the Barnes Foundation." It was obvious for Dewey that "the genuine intelligent realization of pictures" is not only "an integration of the specialized factors," but also "a deep and abiding experience of the nature of fully harmonized experience" that forms "a standard" and "a habit for all other experiences."[80] Thus, Dewey supported the educational works of the Foundation through his opinions in the *Journal of the Barnes Foundation*.

Difficulties in Forming Cooperative Networks

Dark clouds descended over the art education project of the Barnes Foundation right at the beginning, even as the project was in the ascendancy. Barnes devoted himself to carrying out educational reform in Philadelphia by building collaborative networks between the Barnes Foundation and universities, colleges and museums. However, his plan to form an innovative research base for art education, which was supposed to be in cooperation with the University of Pennsylvania and should have been established before other institutions could do so, did not progress. In fact, Barnes' plan stagnated and the collaboration between the Foundation and the university itself became unreliable, partly because they had not shared sufficient time, effort and cooperation for the establishment of the programme.

In addition, harsh criticism against Dillaway and Fleisher by the Barnes Foundation was not acceptable to the University of Pennsylvania because if they admitted that these individuals, who had an influence on the public schools of Philadelphia, were to blame, their relationship with other institutions might be strained, thereby causing damage to the prestige of the university as an educational institution. Many of the attacks conducted by the Barnes Foundation hindered the cooperative relationship; those criticisms were beyond the level that the university could consent to and accept. The University of Pennsylvania made its stand on the issue known to the Barnes Foundation through Edgar A. Singer Jr, who had graduated from the same high school as Barnes and was teaching at the university.[81]

The Barnes Foundation often triggered bitter controversies between other educational institutions. Whether Barnes' provocative and belligerent attitudes were appropriate or not, it is not hard to imagine that such offensive remarks might have caused the isolation of his project and hindered the establishment of cooperation by expanding mutual doubt between the Foundation and other institutions and deepening the confusion. On the other hand, irrespective of his criticism, it was by no means easy at that time to build collaboration with influential academicism or any institution that exercised authority in the traditional way.

Mullen and Munro described the difficulties that the Barnes Foundation had faced in forming cooperative networks with other educational institutions. According to Mullen, several professors of the Pennsylvania Academy of the Fine Arts brought their students to the Foundation's gallery. The Pennsylvania Academy of the Fine Arts, located in the central part of Philadelphia, was founded in 1805 and is the oldest art school in the US. While visiting the Barnes Foundation's gallery, the professors of the academy asked the educational staff of the Foundation to attend the regular talks given in front of the paintings. Then, in order for the students to be guided towards "an intelligent approach to paintings," the Foundation's staff suggested to the most intelligent member of the faculty of the Pennsylvania Academy of the Fine Arts that it would be more effective to work out a plan to build cooperation between the Foundation and the academy. However, the professor confessed that "no such plan had even been attempted at the Academy" and "its mere suggestion by him would be likely to cause his dismissal from its faculty."[82]

Munro also described difficulties and problems that the Foundation had encountered in cooperating with academic institutions. According to Munro, because several members of the faculty of the Pennsylvania Academy of the Fine Arts and the members of the Art Students League of New York had enjoyed the privilege of bringing their students to the Barnes Foundation's gallery, the Foundation proposed to build "cooperation" to the extent of having one or more classes study regularly at the gallery, explaining that "the Barnes Foundation is not a public gallery, but an educational institution which has its own courses and its own requirements for admission to those courses." However, there was no response to the Foundation's offer, nor were similar suggestions forthcoming from these institutions. Munro mentioned disappointedly that "we are reluctant to close the door to any cooperation that promises valuable results," but "the conditions under which such cooperation is possible . . . are not easy of attainment."[83]

Dewey was aware of the difficulties that the Barnes Foundation faced in building cooperation with universities, public schools and museums. On 16 April 1925 Dewey wrote a letter to Barnes, advising the Foundation to seek a more intelligent strategy to advance connections and cooperation, while showing an understanding of the Foundation's intention to increase "an educational influence." Dewey was deeply distressed by the assaults and conflicts that the Barnes Foundation had initiated. Dewey warned that "the policy of negative criticism" would result in "rendering the Foundation isolated as an educational influence." He cautioned that "bringing the Univ. of Penn into your controversy with Dillaway" is "wholly contrary to University conventions," and he continued to say that "they may be poor conventions but they exist, and every University is very sensitive at being involved in outside controversies." Dewey told Barnes that "it seems to me essential to consider just what the University connection – I mean generically not just this one university – stands for and is worth, both intrinsically and representatively."[84] He attempted to persuade him by saying:

> Supposing that aside from the university connection you have broken off by controversial methods . . . relations with the state educational people, with the local people, and with Philadelphia, besides the incidental effect on their friends, connections, and the influences which they can set in motion, and this procedure goes on. What is the outcome to be? With whom and what is the Foundation to cooperate? I do not know how many letters of individual approval you get, nor what are the motives and standing of those who write them, but I have great difficulty in believing that they offset the isolation produced by these alienations.[85]

Dewey believed that there was no benefit for the Barnes Foundation in becoming involved in controversial disputes against the universities and schools. Dewey proposed in another letter of the same day that the Foundation should seek a moderate way to solve the situation. He advised Barnes to "realize the positive strength of the Foundation and of your position" rather than wasting "time and energy in unnecessary controversies." For him, this did not imply conciliating the dissension, still less catering to opposing institutions, but meant encouraging and fostering cooperative connections. Dewey concluded: "That way you will get sure and cumulative results – that is growth and education."[86]

In response to Dewey, Barnes wrote that "what I like best about you are two things;" one is "you speak frankly and bring home a man's own weaknesses in a way that he sees them intellectually" and the other is "I"ve never seen you lack courage in a big situation," adding that "you have I"ve told you, personal timidity."[87] However, in another letter to Dewey, Barnes did not forget to insist that the Foundation aims at "a liberalizing, a loosening up of the academic tightness termed propriety" because "intelligent bar-room methods have subjugated parlor manners."[88]

Dewey made an effort to improve the cooperative relationship between the Barnes Foundation and the University of Pennsylvania by sending a letter to Singer. Dewey explained to Singer that "he [Barnes] was primarily concerned with the relations between Penn and the Foundation," and promised that "if you have Barnes Foundation Journal in mind, I should certainly, if it were needed, urge upon Barnes the propriety of publishing and answer."[89] Dewey also sent a letter to Leo Stein, who was an art critic and close friend of Barnes, telling him that "Barnes's method has a value in creating a challenging attitude on the part of students – not just a passively acquiescent one" and it would raise a "challenge of an intelligent and directed kind in the mind of any intelligent auditor."[90] Thus, Dewey strove to resolve the conflicts by resurrecting the trust and honour of the Barnes Foundation.

Barnes sought for a way to maintain and develop a cooperative relationship with the School of Fine Arts of the University of Pennsylvania in 1926. However, the plan remained stagnant and showed no effective progress. Barnes consulted the university regarding the expiration of the contract between the Foundation and the university that was signed in May 1924. On 20 May 1926, the university sent a letter to the Foundation to say: "should you desire a renewal of this agreement for the ensuing two years the University will be glad to approve it."[91] However, the response of the university to the Foundation was by no means favourable. Barnes' intention was to build an innovative research base for art education by reorganizing the collaboration between the Foundation and the university.

On 21 May, Barnes told Penniman: "We shall be glad to renew our arrangements with Penn for another two years," but also stressed "that Penn and ourselves together can do something for art education that has never been approached before, I am absolutely certain." Barnes wanted to exchange opinions about forming a permanent alliance without reserve. He was worried about what would happen to his properties and collections after his death since, according to him, the Foundation owned a 12-acre park, buildings that were worth $1 million at that time, paintings that could be sold for more than $6 million and a yearly income of about $600,000. He hoped that the University could make use of them effectively by strengthening the cooperative relationship with the Foundation. Barnes told Penniman that "the proposed scheme of cooperation between your courses in Philosophy and our courses in art appreciation, if put into effect, would produce something worthwhile; but it would not alter the situation in Fine Arts because it leaves untouched certain fundamental defects of organization to use our common resources intelligently and adequately for the general good."[92] Barnes was disappointed that the existing institutions had no intention to bring about changes in education. He was not satisfied with the situation where credits and degrees were the only things upheld, or with the reduced cooperation between the Foundation and the university. Barnes was determined to dedicate his energy to creating an innovative centre that would reconstruct art education research and practices, by renewing the collaborative relationship.

Nevertheless, the University of Pennsylvania did not respond to his proposal. Barnes' plan was disregarded by the university. The Barnes Foundation announced that they would suspend the cooperative arrangement with the university in the middle of the term since they did not receive any response from the university, even though six months had passed since Barnes had suggested the plan. The Barnes Foundation told the University of Pennsylvania that "since a de facto enforcement of the suspension in mid-season would work injury to innocent and needy students, our gallery will continue to be open to the regular University class every Thursday afternoon until the end of the present semester."[93]

Singer wrote to Barnes: "You are right; it is a public pity as well as a personal disappointment that plans which promised so much and so permanent good should have come to shipwreck." He added: "had we succeeded in working together along the lines we planned together, I believe the future would have had occasion to bless us a little."[94] Laird's response was more euphemistic, explaining that though he had agreed with Barnes' letter dated 21 May to Penniman, "its suggestion of co-operation between the Foundation and the University in the development of art appreciation" necessitated "most careful consideration by members of University faculties," and therefore took so much time to send a response that, he pointed out to Barnes, "seemed to you to be an undue delay."[95] Out of consideration for the honour of the schools and educational institutions that had become targets of criticism by the Foundation, the University of Pennsylvania induced a suspension of the contract from the Foundation's side, by both ignoring and fending off its assaults.

Impatient with the conflict, Barnes could not hide his irritation and described his sincere dissatisfaction to the university. He informed Dewey that the university had shown its "antagonism and jealously" to the Foundation, and told him that "there is not an educated, cultured person in the whole faculty." According to Barnes, even when "Tom [Munro] outlined the plan, invited criticism, and pleaded for cooperation," "absolutely nothing resulted." Besides, he indicated, Penniman never responded to Barnes' request to explain to the Board of Trustees "the plan for the distant future," even though he had asked Penniman several times to visit the Foundation. Barnes believed that the students of the university lacked "knowledge of the absolute necessities of psychology" and "of the principles of aesthetic." Yet, the university seemed to be organized for "self-protection against the penetration of new ideas." Barnes mentioned that "this balking of a great future for art at Penn is nothing short of a public disgrace and crime."[96] The crack between the Barnes Foundation and the

University of Pennsylvania became decisive and the Foundation was put in a predicament in losing the backing and support of the university. Thus, Barnes' plan to utilize the Foundation's collection effectively in the university and public schools was frustrated and ended in failure.

Barnes assumed a strong attitude towards both the Philadelphia Museum of Art and the University of Pennsylvania. At that time, the Philadelphia Museum of Art was highly trusted by the people who were concerned with art education in the city. For instance, Fleisher of the Graphic Sketch Club decided to transfer the real estate and management of the art education programme to the Philadelphia Museum of Art. However, Barnes did not concede to the museum when negotiating the opening of the Foundation's gallery to the public. He told Kimball, Director of the Museum, that the Barnes Foundation would not accept "casual visitors, whatever their alleged qualifications" because it was "an educational institution" that provided means for all classes of people with sufficient interest in attending "the classes organized for systematic study."[97] In response to this, Kimball wrote that "it is clear I have failed to realize your policy and practice about visitors" but "I am sorry you did not tell me earlier that this annoyed you," and warned that it might "injure our first friendly relations."[98] The tension between the Barnes Foundation and the Philadelphia Museum of Art had reached breaking point.

At this point, Dewey did not comprehend the controversial events going on in the Foundation in detail, since he had resigned from his position as Director of Education at the Barnes Foundation. On 11 December 1926, Dewey confessed to Singer that "I am not however 'Director of Education' in the Barnes Foundation," and "I do not know the critic or distinguished writer of whom Barnes spoke" in the *Journal of the Barnes Foundation*.[99] Buermeyer also resigned from his post as the Foundation's Associate Director of Education after he became an Assistant Professor at New York University in 1926, the same year that the *Journal of the Barnes Foundation* ended publication in April. Although Dewey left his post, he continued to support Barnes and offered his support for the development of the Foundation's art education project.

Art Education in Public Practice

Barnes was eager to give students a chance to appreciate paintings in art museums by taking his Barnes Foundation students to museums in other countries. The Foundation conducted the classes of Munro, Mullen and Buermeyer around the art galleries of France, Italy, Spain and the UK from June to September, 1925. Munro taught the tradition of paintings, which included the study of Byzantine art, Giotto, Michelangelo, Titian, Tintoretto, El Greco, Rubens, Fragonard, Renoir, Cézanne, Picasso, Matisse, Modigliani and Soutine; Mullen taught an advanced class in which students analysed "the plastic form" of the principal painters through visiting the galleries of Spain, France, Italy, and the UK; Buermeyer conducted classes in Paris, Madrid and Toledo that studied the aesthetic principles underlying the paintings of the Italian Renaissance and their influence on the Spanish tradition, and modern paintings.

The Barnes Foundation provided scholarships for this study in Europe, including the course in Aesthetics at the Sorbonne, to two of the students of Mullen's advanced class. Blanche Crawford, a teacher at Swarthmore College, and Sala Carles, a painter and painting teacher, were chosen as recipients.[100] Dewey also joined the Foundation's European study tour at selected venues in Europe, writing to Barnes that he hoped to attend one of the lectures at the Louvre.[101] Dewey visited art museums in Paris, Madrid, Vienna, Copenhagen and other cities. After coming back to the US, Dewey told Barnes: I "came back by London and enjoyed the galleries, especially the [John] Constables."[102]

Dewey published an essay titled "Art in Education and Education in Art" in *The New Republic* in February 1926.[103] By introducing the work of Alfred North Whitehead that pleaded for "the inclusion of aesthetic appreciation in the scheme of life and of education,"[104] Dewey insisted that "aesthetic appreciation" and "art" are not "additions to the real world," much less "luxuries," but "the only ways in which the individualized elements in the world of nature and man are grasped." For him, it was "disastrous" that, because the era was governed by "science" and "industry," in which education was conducted on the basis of "professionalism" and "technical training," "aesthetic appreciation inspired by art" tended to be driven to the periphery. Dewey emphasized that the establishment of the Barnes Foundation as "an educational institution" had a prominent meaning, since its art education project raised the following question: "Is art in painting so foreign to education and education so foreign to art that they must be kept apart, or is art intrinsically educative, intrinsically, by its very existence, and not by virtue of any didactic purpose to which it is subordinated?"

Dewey stated that "the answer to the question is clear," criticizing art that was apart from "values inherent in all experiences of things in their full integrity" and "the constant needs of the everyday man," by means of "the customs of institutionalized museums" and "the habits of professional critics." Dewey was convinced that "art as displayed in painting is inherently educative." In this regard, he said, the Barnes Foundation's assertion, that "aesthetic appreciation inspired and directed by art" is a "rightful and imperatively urgent demand of the common man," as well as the Foundation's "method" and "intelligence," should be employed not only by "a few critics" but by "everyone" who is educated to obtain it.[105] Dewey explored a way to connect art and education by supporting the art education project of the Barnes Foundation.

In 1929, Dewey, Barnes, Buermeyer, Mullen and Violette de Mazia published *Art and Education* through the Barnes Foundation Press.[106] Dewey's articles "Experience, Nature and Art" and "Individuality and Experience," which had been earlier published in the *Journal of the Barnes Foundation*, were included in the book. In it, Barnes explained the Foundation's intention in conducting an art education project as follows.

The Foundation from the start was intended not only to offer instruction to individual students enrolled in its own classes or in those of allied institutions, but also to put before the public a tried and tested method for education in art, and an outline of what such education should be.[107]

The Barnes Foundation had the intention to make art accessible to the public, though their way of doing so was not by exhibiting works of art in the museum. What they pursued instead was a way to interpret art from the perspective of human experiences that lay at the heart of everyday life, which is why the Foundation explored the possibility of becoming an educational institution. Therefore, the art courses of the Foundation aimed not only to teach art appreciation and theory to the students, but also to reveal its method of art education to the public. While Barnes searched for a strategy to put Dewey's theory of democratic education into practice, Dewey's conceptions of art and the public sphere developed through his engagement in the art education project of the Barnes Foundation.

The Barnes Foundation on Thin Ice

The Barnes Foundation encountered a turning point at the end of the 1920s. *The New Yorker* of 22 September 1928 published A. H. Shaw's article entitled "De Medici in Merion," in which Barnes was introduced as an "eccentric, forceful Philadelphia physician" who assembled "the finest collection of modern paintings in the world with the one possible exception of a rich museum in Moscow." According to the article, Barnes was deeply inspired by Dewey's philosophy and attended his lecture, and at that time there seemed to be no one aside from Dewey from whom Barnes took advice. Shaw added that after Dewey, Buermeyer and Munro had resigned their posts at the Foundation and cooperative arrangements between the Foundation and universities were discontinued, Barnes did not go out so often (except for concerts of the Philadelphia Orchestra with his wife), much less meet with visitors, but was indulged in reading books and studying the paintings that the Foundation owned.[108]

In November 1928, Barnes and Dillaway, who had experienced a serious dispute over the reform of art education in Philadelphia's public schools, began to talk to each other again. They discussed the treatment of Allan Randall Freelon, who was attending a class of the Barnes Foundation while serving as the Assistant Director of Art Education in Philadelphia. Freelon was the first African-American appointed to the Department of the Superintendent in Philadelphia schools. A problem had arisen over whether it was appropriate for Freelon to participate in the Foundation's class during the office hours of the public school. On 28 November, Barnes reported to Dewey that he had talked about the treatment of Freelon with Dillaway. Barnes said that "the public school incident turned out better than I expected." According to Barnes' letter, Dillaway had told him that, though one faction of superintendents and assistant superintendents supported the law prohibiting a teacher from attending outside activities during the hours he/she is supposed to be in the school, the other faction insisted that the rule be suspended. Barnes reported to Dewey that Dillaway had led the latter faction and that Freelon would continue to attend the Foundation's class. He explained that "the solution" might be "only temporary," but "we are going to do our best to make the course productive to Dillaway and Freelon."[109]

Barnes started to withdraw from the enterprise of the A. C. Barnes Company, in order to dedicate most of his time to the Foundation. In July 1929 Barnes sold off the A. C. Barnes Company factory, after which manufacture of the antiseptic Argyrol was taken over by the Zonite Products Corporation. The selling price was as high as $6 million, which was fortunate for the Foundation since this transaction was concluded three months before the crash of the New York Stock Market in October 1929. Barnes would have concentrated solely on the study of art after selling the factory, but the situation did not go satisfactorily.

In 1930, while Barnes was travelling to California and New Mexico with Dewey, the city of Philadelphia ordered the Barnes Foundation to pay property taxes for the new building at 4525 Spruce Street, which amounted to $50,000. Before selling off the factory, the Foundation had used the office of the Argyrol factory as their administrative headquarters before moving to the new building on Spruce Street. The tax imposed on the office of the three-storey brick house was $756. However, Barnes was not convinced of the validity of the taxation and decided to contend the law over payment: Barnes insisted that the building should be tax-exempt because the purpose of the Foundation was to advance art education, and the office was the administrative headquarters that managed courses and published books and a journal. The city's claim was that the building did not qualify for exemption from the property tax since the building of Spruce Street, which was furnished with a kitchen, bathroom and electric cabinet, looked more like a residence than a place of business, and was also distant from the Foundation in Merion.[110]

Barnes asked Dewey to testify in court that the Foundation was an educational institution. He said: "As you know all of our books were written in that old business building" and "naturally when we left we had to have a place to continue that work and that's what we have been doing at Fortieth Street ever since."[111] The office was indeed a location indispensable to writing and editing the publications of the Foundation. On 30 September, Dewey served as a witness for the Barnes Foundation in court, with Buermeyer and Mazia also appearing. Barnes explained that the reason why the office was not adjoined to the Foundation in Merion was because it was more convenient for them to be located in the city area. He also told of the necessity to have a place to write by introducing the Foundation's new plan to publish *The French Primitives and Their Forms* with Mazia. This lawsuit over the property tax was known to the people in Philadelphia through an article entitled "Foundation Fights Tax: A. C. Barnes Protests City Levy on Property in Suit," published in the *Philadelphia Inquirer* of 1 October 1930.[112] Barnes sent a letter of gratitude to Dewey, enclosing a clipping from the newspaper. He mentioned that "I want to say again how deeply grateful I am for your wonderful help" and "if we win I think other public questions now barred by the prestige and power of the opposing factions from intelligent exposition in Court will get an airing and probably a victory."[113] As a result, the Barnes Foundation won the case through trials at the Superior Court of Pennsylvania and the Supreme Court that admitted the Foundation's role as an educational experiment. Dewey wrote to Barnes: "I was glad to get the clipping that you won your suit; you certainly did a good job in preparing the case. I wish a stenographic report of your testimony could be put on permanent record or published. It was a valuable piece of history."[114]

Matisse, Dewey and Barnes

In 1930 there was another major event for the Barnes Foundation, which was that Henri Matisse visited the Foundation in Merion. Matisse was staying in the US in order to serve as the judge for the Carnegie International Exposition held in Pittsburgh. Having been fascinated by Matisse's work, Barnes introduced the collection of the Foundation to him. Dewey also met Matisse. Matisse invited Dewey to his room at the Plaza Hotel in New York, and drew his portrait in charcoal. Dewey's portrait by Matisse, which was 24 inches high and 19 inches wide, later came under the possession of the Museum of Modern Art in New York. In a letter to Barnes on 26 December, Dewey said: "I'm enjoying . . . Matisse immensely," adding that "it was interesting to see Matisse's hands move in the rhythm of his forms" (Figure 6.1).[115]

During Matisse's visit to Merion, Barnes had a plan to request a great work of Matisse, which was the creation of a mural painting to be placed in the main hall of the gallery. The mural had to be designed across three canvases that would nestle into the arched spaces reaching to a vaulted ceiling, which was more than 12 feet in height and stretched about 47 feet in width. In addition to this vast space, there were exhibited great works of art in the main hall of the gallery; this collection included Cézanne's *The Card Players* and *Woman in a Green Hat*, Renoir's *The Artist's Family*, Georges Seurat's *The Models*, Picasso's *Composition*, Matisse's *Seated Riffian* and others. Barnes agreed to pay $30,000 for the mural and promised to protect Matisse's free will in creating the mural. Such a proposal presented favourable conditions for Matisse and he finally accepted the offer of the Foundation. Matisse chose to create *The Dance* as the motif for the mural. In May 1933, *The Dance* was installed in the enormous space of three lunettes in the main gallery.[116]

That the huge mural by Matisse was exhibited at the main gallery led to enhancement of the prestige of the Barnes Foundation. On the other hand, Barnes was involved in another dispute over Matisse's work, which was with the Philadelphia Museum of Art. That incident was initiated by Barnes' refusal of the museum's request to lend it a work of El Greco then in possession of

Figure 6.1 Henri Matisse (1869–1954), John Dewey, 1930, New York, Museum of
Modern Art (MoMA). Charcoal on paper, 24 3/8 × 19" (61.9 × 48.4 cm).
Gift of Pierre Matisse. Acc. n.: 149.1962. © 2015. Digital image,
The Museum of Modern Art, New York/Scala, Florence

the Foundation. Then, the main contention occurred when R. Sturgis Ingersoll,
who was a friend of Barnes and Chair of the museum's Committee on Modern
Art, consulted Barnes about purchasing Matisse's *Three Sisters* of 1917 because
he thought Barnes was an expert on Matisse. Ingersoll and Kimball had seen
Three Sisters at Valentine Dudensing's gallery in New York. On 17 February
1931, Ingersoll asked Barnes to have lunch with him at the Midday Club in
the Fidelity-Philadelphia Trust Company Building.[117] At this lunch meeting,
Barnes responded to Ingersoll's request by saying that he would promise to
cooperate with the Philadelphia Museum of Art and loan the cost of $15,000
that Ingersoll conveyed he could not immediately raise; on the other hand,
Barnes told him that the term of this option would be short. On 25 February,

which was the day before the term ended, Ingersoll telephoned Barnes to ask for one week's delay of the payment because he could not cover the expense. However, Barnes replied that he could not adjourn the term, since Dudensing had demanded immediate payment for the purchase and, if payment was delayed, the dealer would sell it to another client. On 26 February, the day of the term's expiration, Ingersoll and Kimball finally raised $15,000 through aid from the Provident Trust Company.[118] Although Ingersoll telephoned Barnes immediately, Barnes informed Ingersoll that he had already purchased *Three Sisters* and would not transfer the picture to the Museum. Kimball, who heard the telephone call between Barnes and Ingersoll, transcribed their communication on an envelope.

Ingersoll:	We take the picture.
Barnes:	You"re just too late. Dudensing said that he had to have cash at once and I have paid for it.
Ingersoll:	But Dr. Barnes . . .
Barnes:	I have the picture.
Ingersoll:	You"re going to let us have it?
Barnes:	The hell I will.
Ingersoll:	I am very much disappointed.
Barnes:	It is a peach of a picture. I told you I could not obligate myself. Yesterday you told me you couldn"t get the money.
Ingersoll:	You say the door is closed?
Barnes:	Yes.
Ingersoll:	I have the check for $15,000 to your order on my desk.
Barnes:	There is nothing I can do about it.[119]

Barnes made an enemy of the Philadelphia Museum of Art through this incident involving Matisse's work. He decided to purchase Matisse's picture from Dudensing. Barnes' conduct inspired in Ingersoll distrust and confusion. Ingersoll suspected that Barnes had bought *Three Sisters* while he was trying to make contact with the dealer, though Barnes denied this and maintained that he had kept his word. However, according to Howard Greenfeld, it is supposed that the truth lay somewhere else, even for the museum: namely, the reason why Ingersoll consulted Barnes and revealed the museum's information to the Foundation was "a deception" by which the trustee tried to get Barnes to buy the painting and donate it to the museum.[120] Therefore, the expectation of the museum ended in failure. While the Foundation and the museum were engaged in mudslinging, a series of smear campaigns had begun. In Philadelphia, the reputation of the Barnes Foundation became tarnished, and citizens flew into a rage at the damage to the honour of the museum. Regarding the dispute, Barnes stated that "the rumor" that he had "double-crossed" Ingersoll was "a lie."[121] Matisse had by that point already returned to Nice, in France, and was not involved in the contention.

Barnes appeared to be glowing with pride in obtaining *Three Sisters* and informed Dewey that "I bought a good Matisse in New York the other day . . . I beseech your aid in adjusting these goods to worthy physiological and psychological purposes."[122] Barnes had told Ingersoll that he had appropriately waited until the term of the option was finished before buying Matisse's work, but the letter to Dewey proved that he had purchased it without honouring the due date that he had set. This is because his letter to Dewey was sent on 23 February 1931, two days before the term of the option was to end. Furthermore, that date was the day before Ingersoll had asked Barnes for one week's adjournment of the payment, indicating that Barnes had purchased the painting prior to Ingersoll's request. From this fact, although it remains a matter of speculation as to whether Barnes had seen through the expectation of the museum or not, it is clear that he had presumed to purchase the picture before the date of the promise. To be sure, the museum's tactics that apparently sought the donation from the Barnes Foundation by intentionally revealing information were underhanded, but Barnes' manoeuvre was as shrewd as Ingersoll's.

After the series of disputes over Matisse's work, Dewey and Barnes maintained a firm friendship, calling each other "Jack" and "Al." When Dewey published *Art as Experience* in 1934, Barnes gave advice to him such as suggestions for the correction of spelling and content prior to the work's going to print.[123] Barnes wrote to Dewey that he had talked about the book to a group at the Foundation two days after its publication, and 50 copies had been sold. Three weeks later, he asked purchasers for their comments on the book and many of them replied that, although "it was helpful," "much of the contents required reading and reading which fatigued them before they could get the purport." Barnes told Dewey: "Of course, the difficulty is not with the book but with the chaotic mental state created by the world" and "I had no trouble in reading the book and, as I told you before, found it smoother sailing than anything else you have published."[124]

The Friends of Art and Education and the Federal Art Project

During this period, the Friends of Art and Education was established at an office in a building on Walnut Street in Philadelphia. The Friends of Art and Education was an organization that aimed to foster the development of culture, art and education by Philadelphia citizens, wherein Dewey served as Honorary President, Barnes as President, Robert Gwathmey as Vice-President and Henry Hart as Secretary. On 13 December 1937, Barnes told Dewey that he had contributed an essay titled "A Disgrace to Philadelphia" to *The Nation*, in which he introduced the political intentions of the Friends of Art and Education. Although Barnes believed that "if they publish it, the plans of the Friends of Art and Education will come in on the public rebound with overwhelming evidence,"[125] *The Nation* refused to publish it. In a letter to Dewey, Barnes complained that the reasons why *The Nation* turned down his article were "fishy," saying "I imagine it will be the most explosive and most comprehensive bomb ever dropped in the community."[126]

In regard to the Friends of Art and Education, Dewey responded to Barnes to say that "I think of nothing finer than linking together Art and Education," and "I believe you have a great future before you and it is an honor to me to be connected with the organization even in an honorary capacity."[127] In a letter to Dewey on 31 January 1938, Barnes explained the reform plan for Philadelphia through the work of the Friends of Art and Education. He stated that he would be involved in "the analysis of the Museum's outrages in the name of art and education" and a "study of the vicious practices of the local WPA Art Project," as well as issues such as "the drastic cut in the teachers" pay" and "the exclusion of Negroes from public matters." Although Barnes requested Dewey to attend the meeting to be held on 18 February,[128] Dewey could not participate because he was supposed to visit his daughter's house in Key West, Florida.[129]

In particular, the Friends of Art and Education attacked the artist relief project of the Works Progress Administration (WPA) initiated by President Roosevelt. The WPA was one of the central policies of the New Deal, and it promoted the relief of millions of unemployed people that had resulted from the Great Depression. Through that policy, the Federal Project Number One started in 1935 for the purpose of employing unemployed artists and consisted of four projects: the Federal Music Project (FMP), the Federal Theatre Project (FTP), the Federal Writers' Project (FWP) and the Federal Art Project (FAP). The FAP was a large-scale government policy that offered financial support for artists by urging employment in the fields of literature, music, art, theatre, performing arts and others, while introducing a tax deduction for the companies and organizations that contributed to art organizations and activities. The FMP employed around 16,000 musicians at its peak, and presented 5,000 performances, such as orchestral music, chamber concerts, dance bands and theatre concerts, before three million people each week; the FTP employed 12,700 theatre people and gave more than one thousand public performances for one million spectators every month; the FWP employed 6,686 writers in 1936 and had published 3,500,000 copies of 800 books by 1941; the FAP employed 5,300 artists and experts in 1936, most of which were registrants of the artists' relief list. The artists employed received a salary ranging from $23 to $25 per week.[130] Works of art created by the FAP, such as mural paintings, posters, pictures and sculptures, decorated public facilities including the surfaces and walls of buildings, public schools, public offices, stations, libraries, post offices and hospitals, with the purpose of enhancing opportunities for citizens to come into contact with the arts.

Initially, Barnes supported the Roosevelt Administration and the New Deal, a stand that differed from that of Dewey. Barnes was apprehensive about the artists' plight following the Great Depression and showed a positive attitude to the FAP. However, Barnes made critical utterances against the project conducted in Philadelphia, and the Friends of Art and Education came to be used as the institution for his criticism. In 1938, the Friends of Art and Education released the following publications: "A Disgrace to Philadelphia" by Barnes,[131] "Philadelphia's Shame: An Analysis of Un-American Administration of the Federal Art Project in Philadelphia" by Henry Hart[132] and "The Progressive Decay of the Pennsylvania Museum of Art" by Harry Fuiman.[133] The essays of Hart and Fuiman appeared to stand proxy for Barnes' opinions, since Hart was a journalist and secretary for the group and Fuiman a lawyer who had studied at the Barnes Foundation.

The Friends of Art and Education protested against the art education projects initiated by the FAP. They especially criticized the Pennsylvania FAP, where Mary Curran was appointed Regional Director. The Friends of Art and Education regarded Curran's policy as "un-American administration"[134] that would be "a hindrance to a genuine art movement in this community."[135] Hart opposed Curran's "inhumanly, inefficiently and illegally administered" method and insisted that "she should be dismissed immediately."[136] Hart's opposition was due to the fact that, in the Pennsylvania FAP, artists were obliged to work in a fixed studio during the daytime on weekdays, which restricted their free and creative working and prohibited their attending the Barnes Foundation courses. Curran had formerly been a high school teacher of English literature, yet she had also been dismissed from the art course at the Barnes Foundation because other students stated that her inappropriate attitudes presented an obstacle to the ordered management of the class. Following that, Curran organized the New Student League that aimed to support young working women and men. In 1928, this league hosted the First Philadelphia Independent Artists' Exhibition and established the Little Gallery of Contemporary Art at Spruce Street, which was close to the Barnes Foundation's headquarters.

Taking advantage of the opportunity to host the Exhibition, Curran set about the undertaking of art education projects in Philadelphia. She was on good terms with Kimball of the Philadelphia Museum of Art. When the Public Works of Art Program (PWAP), which was funded by the Civil Works Administration (CWA) of the United States Treasury Department, started in December 1933, Kimball served as chairman and Curran as clerk. The PWAP was the government's first relief project encouraging unemployed artists to decorate public buildings with paintings, murals and sculptures. Curran organized another Philadelphia Independent Artists' Exhibition in January 1934 and hosted an exhibition of 600 works of the PWAP at the Lincoln-Liberty Building in April. The PWAP had ended by June 1936 and was taken over by the FAP, Philadelphia. Although 1,200 works of art decorated public offices, schools, libraries, post offices and department stores through this project, the Friends of Art and Education criticized it as not actually making a contribution to the development of "true art" in Philadelphia.

In fact, Curran's projects appeared to have clashed with the Barnes Foundation and the Philadelphia Artists' Union. When the Artists' Union consulted Curran about the hosting of the exhibition in 1937, she refused the idea completely. However, surprisingly enough, Curran decided to hold the exhibition without including prominent artists in Philadelphia. Since the artworks exhibited were limited to the creations of the four artists who were close friends of Curran, the exhibition was referred to as "Curran's pet shop." She also severely criticized the Barnes Foundation. For instance, Charles Gardner, who attended the Pennsylvania Academy of the Fine Arts, was employed with a salary of $240 per month; nonetheless, A. L. Chanin, who participated in the Barnes Foundation's class once a week, had his work at CWA cancelled. From that time, Curran had excluded artists who attended the Foundation's classes from the FAP. Hart stressed that she should be immediately dismissed because of her "favoritism" and "discrimination." Barnes did not regard the situation calmly, either. He stated that "Miss Curran is not only profoundly ignorant of what constitutes a work of art but is so handicapped mentally that she is incapable of obtaining the experience that would enable her either to form an intelligent option of art values, or to direct any project participated in by normal human beings."[137] Though it was not clearly mentioned, by talking of Curran's incapability of obtaining "the experience," Barnes was possibly making reference to Curran's dismissal from the art course of the Barnes Foundation.

The Friends of Art and Education criticized Philadelphia's relief exhibition of the WPA that Curran and Kimball had arranged in February 1938 as a "waste" of public funds and a "fraud" against its citizens. Furthermore, they felt that it was because of their "incompetence and malfeasance" that they could not meet the "responsibility" of the museum to the public, despite the fact that the museum should have been for the public an educational institution that would enrich citizens' perspectives and experiences. The Friends of Art and Education declared that the project of the Philadelphia Museum of Art was an "educational crime" and had a "fundamental defect."[138] However, according to the art critic Dorothy Grafly, "the general level is higher than that displayed in many a non-relief exhibition."[139]

On 13 February, Barnes, together with 60 picketers from both the Artists' Union and the Barnes Foundation, staged a protest against the project near the entrance of the Philadelphia Museum of Art where the exhibition was held.[140] The protest heated up when it was found out that a petition was circulating, which was to be signed by artists who would engage in the exhibition, disclaiming membership from the Artists' Union. Although the WPA of Philadelphia ordered a stop to this petition, Curran's anti-union position became evident. Curran criticized artworks by members of the Artists' Union and blamed the opinions of the association.[141] The protesters' signs proclaimed: "New York has 36 WPA art exhibits in one week – Philadelphia only ten in a year." Barnes told reporters that they would picket the museum and the Art Project "in protest against the Fascistic way it is being operated."[142]

Regarding the accusations made by the Friends of Art and Education, Kimball of the Philadelphia Museum of Art also broke his silence and argued that "'Argyrol' Barnes' complaints were rubbish." Barnes was irritated by

Kimball's utterances and advocated at a meeting of Philadelphia's Leftist People's Forum that "if you are really interested in painting go out and raise hell at the museum." Meanwhile, the Pennsylvania Academy of the Fine Arts was steadily preparing the 133rd Annual Exhibition of US Art while disregarding the noise from the other side of the Parkway leading to the Museum.[143] The Barnes Foundation's relationship with the Philadelphia Museum of Art and the Pennsylvania Academy of the Fine Arts became irreparable. As a result of the request to dismiss Curran, she was transferred from her position as Director in Philadelphia to Harrisburg, the state capital, by July 1938. She was then demoted to Assistant State Director for Western Pennsylvania by September, and her position was eventually terminated in December of the same year. On 31 January 1938, Barnes wrote to Dewey that "we have two good jobs already done: an analysis of the Museum's outrages in the name of art and education, and a thoroughly documented study of the vicious practices of the local WPA Art Project."[144] Dewey responded to Barnes: "Glad to hear F.A & E [Friends of Art and Education] is going so flourishingly. If I were anywhere in the neighborhood I"d be there."[145] But, the Friends of Art and Education was dissolved after these activities.

On the other hand, the FAP of the WPA that had hired so many unemployed artists remained in existence until 1943 as one of the primary policies of the New Deal. By displaying numerous works of arts in public facilities, the FAP contributed to the expansion of citizens' opportunities to broaden their appreciation of the arts and deepen their aesthetic experiences. According to Holger Cahill, who served as the National Director of the FAP, its aim was not nurturing the "solitary genius" but promoting art as a "cultural project" wherein every citizen could participate in experiencing art. Cahill further elaborated that the FAP was meant to connect art and life, and break the unbridgeable difference between artists and citizens. In this sense, the philosophy of the FAP came close to Dewey's theory of art. Indeed, Cahill had taken Dewey's courses at Columbia University and was greatly influenced by his philosophy.[146]

The FAP was composed of three kinds of project. The first was the creation of the fine arts. The Graphic Arts Division made 240,000 prints and two million posters of 35,000 different kinds; the Mural Division produced more than 2,500 murals that were displayed in schools, hospitals and other public facilities; the Easel Painting Division created 108,099 paintings; and the Sculpture Division produced 17,744 pieces. The second was the promotion of art education, through which hundreds of teachers were employed by the Art Teaching Division in community centres and settlement houses, 100 community art centres were established in 22 states and art education programmes were carried out through galleries, classrooms and community workshops. The third was the sponsoring of the Index of American Design that created 20,000 photographic records of American art, painting, sculpture, handicraft and folk art. Although the FAP was federally funded and its administrative expenses were shared between the state and the federal government, the project was conducted in 48 states. Bringing works of art, including murals, paintings, posters and sculptures, out from the art museums and galleries and into public spaces in cities and communities promoted the expansion of citizens' opportunities to connect art with public life.

The FAP brought about changes to the conception of art in society through its influence on artists, art producers and educators. When the artists produced their works, they had to be conscious not only of devotees and collectors, but also the common people, since their artwork was placed and displayed in the communities of the public sphere. Nevertheless, this conversion created ambivalence around the function of art. That is, although the project contributed to reducing the social unrest of people during the Great Depression by regarding art as public goods and inducing support for art and culture by the government, the way was paved for controlling communities through art by means of governmental intervention into people's everyday experiences in their public lives. This was because the government managed the contents of artists' expressions in murals, paintings and sculptures in schools, post offices, hospitals and other public spaces, and partly censored them. The arts came to be used as a means of transferring political ideologies, in that the artists were asked to be accountable while huge amounts of public funds were invested in the production of their art.[147] In Philadelphia, the members of the Artists' Union were likely to be removed from the list of candidates for the relief programme by the Pennsylvania FAP. Curran thoroughly rejected the works of art by union members and persuaded one of them to state that the declaration of the union was against his will.[148]

Consequently, the policy of the Pennsylvania FAP differed from Dewey's theory of art education and the public sphere. In *Art as Experience*, Dewey argued that art had become a means of "propaganda" to maintain "power" and gain "the allegiance of the mass." Although he interpreted art as everyday experiences of human life and encouraged art's potential in a democratic community, the project promoted by the government was inclined to utilize art as some kind of political justification. During this period, Dewey and Barnes strove to reconstruct art education through the Friends of Art and Education. Nonetheless, they could not persuade the Roosevelt Administration to reconsider its art policies.

Bridging Art and the Public Sphere

A trusting relationship between Barnes and Dewey was maintained continuously. When Dewey turned 80 in 1939, Barnes offered to him his sincere blessings. In *The Philosophy of the Common Man: Essays in Honor of John Dewey to Celebrate His Eightieth Birthday*, which was published in 1940 by Dewey's friends and colleagues out of respect for him, Barnes wrote an essay titled "Method in Aesthetics." He stated that Dewey's theory of art was connected with "intelligence" and "science" on the basis of "ordinary experience." According to Barnes, in experience, "a living being is in the closest possible interaction with an objective situation," to which "every thought, feeling, and act" was related, and experience is "intelligent" insofar as "their coordinated interaction" continues to achieve "his needed adjustment to an environment." He regarded that at the heart of Dewey's definition of "intelligence" lies "the purposeful reorganization through action of the matter of experience," and that it constituted "the germ of the thesis of every contribution of Dewey, including his *Art as Experience*."[149]

In Barnes' essay "Art as Experience" (1939), which shared its title with Dewey's book, he stressed that the Barnes Foundation owed "its origin to the ideas which he [Dewey] has contributed to human thought" and that its pro-gramme had benefited at times "too numerously[sic] to mention by suggestion and advice from him [Dewey]." Barnes wrote that the Foundation's 17 years of educational practices had made "the value of Dewey's conceptions and principles ever more apparent." In his interpretation of Dewey's theory, "the value of art" ultimately transcends "far beyond the satisfaction derived from the experience of actual works of art," and "works of art" suggest "what experi-ence is at its best," by revealing "possibilities of sensitive insight, of harmonious exercise of powers, of union of the self with the world." Barnes concluded that "genuine aesthetic experience" requires "long-continued effort," "the use of methods systematically elaborated" and "a reorientation of the whole personality," and it is "the business of education in art" that guides this "reorientation."[150] In 1940 Laura Barnes founded the Foundation's Arboretum School, in which she, John M. Fogg of the University of Pennsylvania and Frederick W. G. Peck of the American Society of Landscape Architects con-ducted classes focusing on horticulture, plants and design.[151]

The Barnes Foundation made strenuous efforts to promote art education on the basis of democratic ideals. However, they had restricted the opening of the gallery to casual visitors because they regarded the Foundation as an educational institution. One of the misfortunes of the Barnes Foundation was that, as much as they wanted to, they were not able to utilize their collection in educational reform in Philadelphia in spite of its prominent value and properties. This was because no one in the Foundation suspected Barnes' talent or could give suitable advice to him except for Dewey. Instead of stopping Barnes' attacks, Buermeyer, Munro and Mullen stirred them up. On this point, Sydney Hook was severely contemptuous of Barnes.[152]

Arthur Danto, an art critic, pointed out that Barnes had contributed to closing "the gap between fine and practical art" and "between primitive and Western art" by reducing to "a matter of degree the differences between high art and decoration," which derived from Dewey's theory of art. However, Danto indicated that Barnes' personality was defined by "a degree of irascibility so outside the common measure that his crusade for esthetic education was accompanied by an obbligato of fits and tantrums comically disproportionate to their many occasions," and that "he was a man to find quarrel in a straw when the honor of his theories was at stake."[153] Thus, Barnes was opposed to the governing class and fought with the mainstream art circles. It was because of the controversies and conflicts provoked by Barnes that his projects resulted in deepening confusion and made unavoidable the increasingly unfavourable criticism by other institutions.

Dewey supported the Barnes Foundation's art education projects irrespective of the contentious disputes in which they were involved. The friendship between Dewey and Barnes continued until Barnes died in July 1951. Dewey

Figure 6.2 John Dewey and Albert C. Barnes, 1942, Special Collections Research Center, Morris Library, Southern Illinois University Carbondale

sought the reconstruction of the theory of art by associating it with democratic education and the public sphere. One of the focuses of his theory was to form communities by mediating aesthetic experiences and urging the art of communication. Art for him lay at the depths of the public sphere and should be considered as "the cultural bases of democracy." From this perspective, Dewey defended the educational and cultural projects of the Barnes Foundation. Considering their attempts to create innovative art education practices, their difficulties and problems in connecting art with the public sphere can be confirmed. Despite Dewey' and Barnes' endeavours to relate art to democratic education, their projects encountered difficulties and ended in failure. However, Dewey saw the potential of art that lay at the heart of constructing the public sphere. Thus, Dewey's practice involving art education bore an important meaning for understanding his theory of democracy and the public sphere (Figure 6.2).

Notes

1   Albert C. Barnes, "The Barnes Foundation," op. cit., p.65.
2   Albert C. Barnes, *The Art in Painting*, Merion, PA.: The Barnes Foundation Press, 2000.
3   Albert C. Barnes and Violette de Mazia, *The French Primitives and Their Forms: From Their Origin to the End of the Fifteenth Century*, Merion, PA.: The Barnes Foundation Press, 1931.
4   Albert C. Barnes and Violette de Mazia, *The Art of Henri Matisse*, New York: Charles Scribner's Sons, 1933.
5   Albert C. Barnes and Violette de Mazia, *The Art of Renoir*, New York: Minton, Balch & Co, 1935.
6   Albert C. Barnes and Violette de Mazia, *The Art of Cézanne*, Marion, PA: The Barnes Foundation Press, 1939.
7   John Dewey, *Art as Experience*, op. cit., pp.7–8.
8   Albert C. Barnes, "Cubism: Requiescat in Pace," *Arts & Decoration*, vol.6, January, 1916, p.121.
9   Albert C. Barnes to John Dewey, 7 November 1917, John Dewey Papers; *The Correspondence of John Dewey*, vol.1.
10   Albert C. Barnes to John Dewey, 10 January 1918, John Dewey Papers; *The Correspondence of John Dewey*, vol.1.
11   John Dewey to Albert C. Barnes, 22 January 1918, John Dewey Papers; *The Correspondence of John Dewey*, vol.1.
12   John Dewey to Albert C. Barnes, 5 December 1920, John Dewey Papers; *The Correspondence of John Dewey*, vol.2.
13   Albert C. Barnes to John Dewey, 29 January 1921, John Dewey Papers; *The Correspondence of John Dewey*, vol.2.
14   Albert C. Barnes to John Dewey, 14 May 1921, John Dewey Papers; *The Correspondence of John Dewey*, vol.2.
15   Albert C. Barnes to Alice Chipman Dewey, 1 July 1920, John Dewey Papers; *The Correspondence of John Dewey*, vol.2.
16   Albert C. Barnes to John Dewey, 7 January 1921, John Dewey Papers; *The Correspondence of John Dewey*, vol.2.
17   Albert C. Barnes to John Dewey, 30 June 1920, John Dewey Papers; *The Correspondence of John Dewey*, vol.2.

18   Albert C. Barnes to Alice Chipman Dewey, 1 July 1920, op. cit.

19   Albert C. Barnes to John Dewey, 29 January 1921, op. cit.

20   Albert C. Barnes to John Dewey, 14 May 1921, op. cit.

21   John Dewey to Albert C. Barnes, 5 December 1920, op. cit.

22   "African Art Work for Merion Museum Is Most Comprehensive in the World," *Public Ledger*, February 5, 1923, p.3.

23   "Dr. Barnes Gives $6,000,000 for Art Museum in Merion," *Public Ledger*, 13 January 1923, p.1.

24   Albert C. Barnes, "The Barnes Foundation," op. cit., pp.65–67.

25   "African Art Work for Merion Museum Is Most Comprehensive in the World," op. cit., p.3.

26   Albert C. Barnes to Josiah H. Penniman, 18 April 1924, Office of the Provost, Josiah H. Penniman Records (UPA 6.2 P), Box 2, Folder 35, University of Pennsylvania Archives, Philadelphia, PA.

27   Albert C. Barnes to Josiah H. Penniman, 27 January 1924, Penniman Records, Box 2, Folder 35.

28   Albert C. Barnes to John Dewey, 17 January 1921, John Dewey Papers; *The Correspondence of John Dewey*, vol.2.

29   Albert C. Barnes to John Dewey, 30 June 1920, John Dewey Papers; *The Correspondence of John Dewey*, vol.2.

30   Mary Mullen, *An Approach to Art*, Merion, PA.: The Barnes Foundation Press, 1923.

31   Laurence Buermeyer, *The Aesthetic Experience*, Merion, PA.: The Barnes Foundation Press, 1924.

32   Mary Mullen, *An Approach to Art*, op. cit., pp.5–25.

33   Laurence Buermeyer, *The Aesthetic Experience*, op. cit., pp.1–184. Buermeyer and Munro published *An Introduction to Reflective Thinking* with Columbia Associates in Philosophy in 1923. Columbia Associates in Philosophy, *An Introduction to Reflective Thinking*, Boston: Houghton Muffin, 1923.

34   Albert C. Barnes, *The Art in Painting*, op. cit., p.v.

35   Ibid., pp.1–522.

36   John Dewey to Albert C. Barnes, 27 January 1925, John Dewey Papers; *The Correspondence of John Dewey*, vol.2.

37   Laurence Buermeyer, "An Experiment in Education," *The Nation*, vol.120, no.3119, 15 April 1925, p.442.

38   Irwin Edman, "Art as Intelligence," *The Nation*, vol.120, no.3112, 25 February 1925.

39   John Anderson, *Art Held Hostage: The Battle over the Barnes Collection*, New York: W. W. Norton, 2003, pp.23–24.

40   Albert C. Barnes, "The Barnes Foundation," op. cit., p.65.

41   Albert C. Barnes to John Dewey, 14 March 1925, John Dewey Papers; *The Correspondence of John Dewey*, vol.2.

42   The Barnes Foundation, "Notes and Comments," *Journal of the Barnes Foundation*, vol.1, no.1, April, 1925, p.47.

43   John Dewey, "Dedication Address of the Barnes Foundation," *The Later Works*, vol.2, pp.382–385.

44   Albert C., Barnes, "The Barnes Foundation," op. cit., pp.65–67.

45   Albert C. Barnes to Josiah H. Penniman, 27 January 1924, op. cit.

46   Josiah H. Penniman to Albert C. Barnes, 4 April 1924, Penniman Records, Box 2, Folder 35.

47   Josiah H. Penniman to Albert C. Barnes, 2 May 1924, Penniman Records, Box 2, Folder 35.

48   Albert C. Barnes to Josiah H. Penniman, 3 May 1924, Penniman Records, Box 2, Folder 35.

49   Albert C. Barnes to Josiah H. Penniman, 20 January 1925, Penniman Records, Box 2, Folder 35.

50   John Dewey to Albert C. Barnes, 27 January 1925, John Dewey Papers; *The Correspondence of John Dewey*, vol.2.

51   Albert C. Barnes to Josiah H. Penniman, 23 February 1925, Penniman Records, Box 2, Folder 35.

52   The Barnes Foundation, "The Educational Program of the Barnes Foundation," *Journal of the Barnes Foundation*, vol.1, no.1, April, 1925, p.1; Mary Mullen, "The Barnes Foundation: An Experiment in Education," *Journal of the Barnes Foundation*, vol.1, no.1, April, 1925, p.6.

53   Albert C. Barnes to Fiske Kimball, 5 October 1925, Fiske Kimball Records, 1908–1955, Box 1, Folder 8, Philadelphia Museum of Art Archives, Philadelphia, PA.

54   Fiske Kimball to Albert C. Barnes, 7 October 1925, Fiske Kimball Records, Box 1, Folder 8.

55   The Barnes Foundation, "The Educational Program of the Barnes Foundation," op. cit., p.1; Mary Mullen, "The Barnes Foundation: An Experiment in Education," op. cit., p.7.

56   Albert C. Barnes to Warren P. Laird, 22 October 1924, Penniman Records, Box 2, Folder 35.

57   Warren P. Laird to Albert C. Barnes, 27 October 1924, Penniman Records, Box 2, Folder 35.

58   Albert C. Barnes to John Dewey, 28 January 1925, John Dewey Papers; *The Correspondence of John Dewey*, vol.2; Albert C. Barnes to John Dewey, 30 January 1925, John Dewey Papers; *The Correspondence of John Dewey*, vol.2.

59   Albert C. Barnes to John Dewey, 2 March 1925, John Dewey Papers; *The Correspondence of John Dewey*, vol.2.

60   John Dewey to Albert C. Barnes, 4 March 1925, John Dewey Papers; *The Correspondence of John Dewey*, vol.2.

61   Cornelia Bryce Pinchot to Albert C. Barnes, 15 March 1925, C. B. Pinchot Papers, Container 39, Albert C. Barnes File, Library of Congress, Washington, DC; *The Correspondence of John Dewey*, vol.2.

62   "Art Critics Flay Barnes Foundation," *North American*, 20 May 1924.

63   Albert C. Barnes, "The Shame in the Public School of Philadelphia," *Journal of the Barnes Foundation*, vol.1, no.1, April 1925, pp.13–17.

64   Albert C. Barnes to John Dewey, 1 April 1925, John Dewey Papers; *The Correspondence of John Dewey*, vol.2.

65   John Dewey to Albert C. Barnes, 21 April 1925, John Dewey Papers; *The Correspondence of John Dewey*, vol.2.

66   Albert C. Barnes, "The Shame in the Public School of Philadelphia," op. cit., pp.16–17.

67   Albert C. Barnes to John Dewey, 1 April 1925, John Dewey Papers; *The Correspondence of John Dewey*, vol.2.

68   Laurence Buermeyer, "The Graphic Sketch Club and Art Education." *Journal of the Barnes Foundation*, vol.1, no.1, April, 1925, pp.18–25.

69   Albert C. Barnes, "Art Teaching that Obstacles Education," *Journal of the Barnes Foundation*, vol.1, no.2, May, 1925, pp.44–47.

70   Albert C. Barnes, "Art Teaching that Obstacles Education," *Journal of the Barnes Foundation*, vol.1, no.3, October, 1925, pp.41–48.

71   Albert C. Barnes, "Educational Disorder at the Metropolitan Museum," *Journal of the Barnes Foundation*, vol.2, no.1, January, 1926, pp.45–48.

72   Thomas Munro, "A Constructive Program for Teaching Art," *Journal of the Barnes Foundation*, vol.1, no.1, April, 1925, pp.26–38.

73 Thomas Munro, "College Art Instruction: Its Failure and a Remedy," *Journal of the Barnes Foundation*, vol.1, no.2, May, 1925, pp.34–43.

74 Mary Mullen, "A First Requisite in Art Education," *Journal of the Barnes Foundation*, vol.1, no.2, May, 1925, pp.31–33.

75 John Dewey, "Dedication Address," *Journal of the Barnes Foundation*, vol.1, no.2, May, 1925, pp.3–6.

76 John Dewey, "Experience, Nature and Art," *Journal of the Barnes Foundation*, vol.1, no.3, October, 1925, pp.4–10.

77 John Dewey, "Individuality and Experience," *Journal of the Barnes Foundation*, vol.2, no.1, January, 1926, pp.1–6.

78 John Dewey, "Affective Thought in Logic and Painting," *Journal of the Barnes Foundation*, vol.2, no.2, April, 1926, pp.3–9.

79 John Dewey, "Individuality and Experience," op. cit., pp.1–6.

80 John Dewey, "Affective Thought in Logic and Painting," op. cit., p.9.

81 Edgar A. Singer to Albert C. Barnes, 10 April 1925, Penniman Records, Box 2, Folder 35.

82 Mary Mullen, "Learn to See," *Journal of the Barnes Foundation*, vol.2, no.1, January, 1926, pp.8–13.

83 Thomas Munro, "The Art Academies and Modern Education," *Journal of the Barnes Foundation*, vol.2, no.2, April, 1926, pp.36–37.

84 John Dewey to Albert C. Barnes, 16 April 1925, Presidents' Files, Albert C. Barnes Correspondence. The Barnes Foundation Archives, Merion, PA.; *The Correspondence of John Dewey*, vol.2.

85 Ibid.

86 John Dewey to Albert C. Barnes, April 16, 1925, Presidents' Files, Albert C. Barnes Correspondence; *The Correspondence of John Dewey*, vol.2.

87 Albert C. Barnes to John Dewey, 16 April 1925, Presidents' Files, Albert C. Barnes Correspondence; *The Correspondence of John Dewey*, vol.2.

88 Albert C. Barnes to John Dewey, 20 April 1925, John Dewey Papers; *The Correspondence of John Dewey*, vol.2.

89 John Dewey to Edgar A. Singer, 1 December 1926, Penniman Records, Box 2, Folder 35.

90 John Dewey to Leo Stein, 22 February 1926, Leo Stein Papers, The Yale Collection of American Literature, Beinecke Rare Book and Manuscript Library, Yale University, New Haven, CT; *The Correspondence of John Dewey*, vol.2.

91 Josiah H. Penniman to Albert C. Barnes, 20 May 1926, Penniman Records, Box 2, Folder 35.

92 Albert C. Barnes to Josiah H. Penniman, 21 May 1926, Penniman Records, Box 2, Folder 35.

93 N. E. Mullen to Edward W. Mumford, 10 December 1926, Penniman Records, Box 2, Folder 35.

94 Edgar A. Singer to Albert C. Barnes, 21 December 1926, Penniman Records, Box 2, Folder 35.

95 Warren P. Laird to Albert C. Barnes, 4 December 1926, Penniman Records, Box 2, Folder 35.

96 Albert C. Barnes to John Dewey, 24 December 1926, Presidents' Files, Albert C. Barnes Correspondence; *The Correspondence of John Dewey*, vol.2.

97 Albert C. Barnes to Fiske Kimball, 27 October 1926, Fiske Kimball Records, Box 1, Folder 8.

98 Fiske Kimball to Albert C. Barnes, 28 October 1926, Fiske Kimball Records, Box 1, Folder 8.

99 John Dewey to Edgar A. Singer,11 December 1926, Penniman Records, Box 2, Folder 35.

100   The Barnes Foundation, "Notes and Comments," op. cit., p.46.
101   John Dewey to Albert C. Barnes, 29 May 1925, John Dewey Papers; *The Correspondence of John Dewey*, vol.2.
102   John Dewey to Albert C. Barnes, 21 September 1925, John Dewey Papers; *The Correspondence of John Dewey*, vol.2.
103   John Dewey, "Art in Education and Education in Art," *The Later Works*, vol.2, pp.111–115.
104   Alfred North Whitehead, *Science and the Modern World*, Cambridge: Cambridge University Press, 1925.
105   John Dewey, "Art in Education and Education in Art," op. cit., pp.111–115.
106   John Dewey, Albert C. Barnes, Laurence Buermeyer, Mary Mullen and Violette de Mazia, *Art and Education*, Merion, PA: The Barnes Foundation Press, 1954.
107   Albert C. Barnes, "Preface to First Edition," John Dewey, Albert C. Barnes, Laurence Buermeyer, Mary Mullen and Violette de Mazia, *Art and Education*, op. cit., p.ix.
108   A. H. Shaw, "De Medici in Merion," *The New Yorker*, 22 September 1928, pp.29–34.
109   Albert C. Barnes to John Dewey, 28 November 1928, John Dewey Papers; *The Correspondence of John Dewey*, vol.2.
110   Mary Ann Meyers, *Art, Education, and African-American Culture: Albert Barnes and the Science of Philanthropy*, New Brunswick, N.J.: Transaction Publishers, 2004, pp.165–166
111   Albert C. Barnes to John Dewey, 19 September 1930, John Dewey Papers; *The Correspondence of John Dewey*, vol.2.
112   "Foundation Fights Tax: A. C. Barnes Protests City Levy on Property in Suit," *Philadelphia Inquirer*, 1 October 1930, p.3.
113   Albert C. Barnes to John Dewey, 1 October 1930, John Dewey Papers; *The Correspondence of John Dewey*, vol.2.
114   John Dewey to Albert C. Barnes, 20 February 1931, John Dewey Papers; *The Correspondence of John Dewey*, vol.2.
115   John Dewey to Albert C. Barnes, 26 December 1930, John Dewey Papers; *The Correspondence of John Dewey*, vol.2.
116   Mary Ann Meyers, *Art, Education, and African-American Culture: Albert Barnes and the Science of Philanthropy*, op. cit., pp.173–193.
117   R. Sturgis Ingersoll to Albert C. Barnes, 17 February 1931, Fiske Kimball Records, Box 26, Folder 7.
118   Valentine Dudensing to Albert C. Barnes, 22 November 1934, Fiske Kimball Records, Box 26, Folder 7.
119   Fiske Kimball, "Conversation Between R. Sturgis Ingersoll and Dr. A. C. Barnes, February 26, 1931 Regarding Matisse & Three Sisters," Fiske Kimball Papers, 1874–1957, Box 160, Folder 17, Philadelphia, PA.
120   Howard Greenfeld, *The Devil and Dr. Barnes: Portrait of an American Art Collector*, New York: Penguin Books, 1989, pp.165–166.
121   Albert C. Barnes, "To Whom It May Concern," 26 November 1934, Fiske Kimball Records, Box 26, Folder 7.
122   Albert C. Barnes to John Dewey, 24 February 1931, John Dewey Papers; *The Correspondence of John Dewey*, vol.2.
123   Albert C. Barnes to John Dewey, 29 March 1934, John Dewey Papers; *The Correspondence of John Dewey*, vol.2; Albert C. Barnes to John Dewey, 2 April 1934, John Dewey Papers; *The Correspondence of John Dewey*, vol.2.
124   Albert C. Barnes to John Dewey, 16 April 1934, John Dewey Papers; *The Correspondence of John Dewey*, vol.2.
125   Albert C. Barnes to John Dewey, 13 December 1937, John Dewey Papers; *The Correspondence of John Dewey*, vol.2.

126 Albert C. Barnes to John Dewey, 24 December 1937, John Dewey Papers; *The Correspondence of John Dewey*, vol.2.

127 John Dewey to Albert C. Barnes, 27 December 1937, John Dewey Papers; *The Correspondence of John Dewey*, vol.2.

128 Albert C. Barnes to John Dewey, 31 January 1938, John Dewey Papers; *The Correspondence of John Dewey*, vol.2.

129 John Dewey to Albert C. Barnes, 22 February 1938, John Dewey Papers; *The Correspondence of John Dewey*, vol.2.

130 Yasuyo Kudo, *The Public Art Policy: The Transformation of the Publicness of Art and Cultural Policy in America*, Tokyo: Keiso Shobo, 2008, pp.39–42.

131 Albert C. Barnes, "A Disgrace to Philadelphia," Friends of Art and Education, 1938, Fiske Kimball Papers, Box 160, Folder 19.

132 Henry Hart, "Philadelphia's Shame: An Analysis of Un-American Administration of the Federal Art Project in Philadelphia," Friends of Art and Education, 1938, Fiske Kimball Papers, Box 160, Folder 19.

133 Harry Fuiman, "The Progressive Decay of the Pennsylvania Museum of Art," Friends of Art and Education, 1938. Fiske Kimball Papers, Box 160, Folder 19.

134 Henry Hart, "Philadelphia's Shame: An Analysis of Un-American Administration of the Federal Art Project in Philadelphia," op. cit.

135 Friends of Art and Education, "Program of Friends of Art and Education," *1212*, vol.2, no.2, The Artists' Union 1212 Walnut St., Philadelphia, PA, March, 1938, Fiske Kimball Papers, Box 160, Folder 19, pp.22–23.

136 Henry Hart, "Philadelphia's Shame: An Analysis of Un-American Administration of the Federal Art Project in Philadelphia," op. cit.

137 Ibid.

138 Harry Fuiman, "The Progressive Decay of the Pennsylvania Museum of Art," op. cit., pp.7–18.

139 "Art," *Time*, 14 February 1938, p.43.

140 Ibid., p.43.

141 Henry Hart, "Philadelphia's Shame: An Analysis of Un-American Administration of the Federal Art Project in Philadelphia," op. cit., p.7.

142 "Art," *Time*, op. cit., pp.43–44.

143 Ibid., pp.43–44.

144 Albert C. Barnes to John Dewey, 31 January 1938, op. cit.

145 John Dewey to Albert C. Barnes, 3 February 1938, John Dewey Papers; *The Correspondence of John Dewey*, vol.2.

146 Holger Cahill, *New Horizons in American Art*, New York: The Museum of Modern Art, 1936, pp.46–49.

147 Yasuyo Kudo, *The Public Art Policy: The Transformation of the Publicness of Art and Cultural Policy in America*, op. cit., pp.46–49.

148 Henry Hart, "Philadelphia's Shame: An Analysis of Un-American Administration of the Federal Art Project in Philadelphia," op. cit., p.7.

149 Albert C. Barnes, "Method in Aesthetics," *The Philosophy of the Common Man: Essays in Honor of John Dewey to Celebrate His Eightieth Birthday*, New York: G. P. Putnam's Sons, 1940, pp.87–105.

150 Albert C. Barnes, "Art as Experience," *The Educational Frontier*, no.13, 1939, pp.13–25.

151 Mary Ann Meyers, *Art, Education, and African-American Culture: Albert Barnes and the Science of Philanthropy*, op. cit., pp.238–239.

152 Sidney Hook, *Pragmatism and the Tragic Sense of Life*, New York: Basic Books, 1974, p.108.

153 Arthur Danto, "Every Straw Was the Last," *New York Times Book Review*, 22 November 1987.

7 Education for Democracy and Civil Liberties

Dewey aimed to develop an innovative school system that connected the conception of democracy to education, while criticizing the traditional liberalism of "rugged individualism." In the mid- to late 1930s, he energetically took up the issue of reconstructing liberalism and education that is related to the idea of the public sphere. In this chapter, I will clarify his vision of democratic education and discuss its practices in the late 1930s and early 1940s.

Democratic Education and Civil Liberties

In "A Liberal Speaks Out for Liberalism," Dewey described how "a conscious and aggressive movement" of liberalism had arisen in Great Britain as "two different streams flowed into one." That is, the one stream was "the humanitarian and philanthropic zeal" of the late eighteenth century and the other was "the principle of laissez-faire" that had derived from "freedom of production" and "freedom of exchange." Dewey claimed that though the two streams came together as a social and political movement, "they never coalesced" and there had been "an inner split in liberalism." According to Dewey, this "split" was embodied in the principle of "the greatest happiness of the greatest number" (originally derived from the "philanthropic and humanitarian movement") advocated in the nineteenth century by Jeremy Bentham, who positioned himself as a supporter of "laissez-faire liberalism" when it came to realizing this goal. On the other hand, on the European continent, "liberal parties" meant "the political representatives of big industry, banking and commerce."

Dewey went further to argue that liberalism in the US was divided into two schools. One school was identified with Square Deals and New Deals that supported government intervention to "help equalize conditions between the wealthy and the poor, between the over-privileged and the underprivileged," and the other school stood in opposition to the former, attacking it as "pink socialism" and "disguised radicalism" and promoting laissez-faire liberalism. However, Dewey believed that regardless of "the extreme clash," both schools declared "the same ultimate ideal and goal" which could be expressed as "the utmost possible liberty of the individual." For him, the difference between the two was related to "the province in which liberty and individuality are most important" and "the means by which they are to be realized:"[1]

Humane liberalism in order to save itself must cease to deal with symptoms and go to the causes of which inequalities and oppressions are but the symptoms. In order to endure under present conditions, liberalism must become radical in the sense that, instead of using social power to ameliorate the evil consequences of the existing system, it shall use social power to change the system.[2]

Becoming "radical" for Dewey did not imply "the change of the present system by violent overthrow." On the contrary, it was committed to "democratic methods of effecting social change" wherein "freedom" was not "something that can be handed to men as a gift from outside," but "something which can be had only as individuals participate in winning it." In other words, "liberty" was the "the means" as well as the "goal," and "the development of individuality" could be made secure by "the development of individuals in their voluntary cooperation with one another."[3]

Dewey took up the relationship between "a liberal education" and the "common schools" in "The Meaning of Liberalism." He mentioned that the term "liberal," as in "a liberal education" or "the liberal arts," had historically denoted "the education of a free man" as opposed to "the training of mechanics." However, he argued that "the liberal arts and a liberal education were confined to persons who occupied a superior social status" and belonged to "gentlemen as distinct from the 'lower classes.'" Instead, Dewey placed emphasis on the role of "the free and common schools," whose ideas came from the principle that "a nation of truly free men and women required schools open to all and hence supported by public taxation." His theory of liberalism was associated with the ideal that makes "schooling accessible to all," and he believed that the means of attaining the goals of liberalism demanded "a radical change in economic institutions and the political arrangements," which might accrue to "the liberation of all individuals associated together" in building a life that promotes "human liberty." Dewey pursued reconstruction to achieve a "new liberalism" that bore "the theme of liberal education and free schools" of the "common schools."[4]

The idea of the school that is "open to all" raises the question of how to make compatible "freedom" and "equality" in education. In "Liberalism and Equality," Dewey critically examined one school of social philosophy that insisted: "liberty and equality are so incompatible that liberalism is not a possible social philosophy." According to Dewey, this school argued that if "liberty" were the dominant goal then "the natural diversity and inequality of natural endowments will inevitably work out to produce social inequalities," and if "equality" were the goal, there must be "important restrictions put upon the exercise of liberty." Dewey claimed that the belief in "the incompatibility of liberty and equality" had resulted in "the school of liberalism that identifies liberty with laissez faire."

Synthetically considered, we might be able to imagine Dewey's conclusion overlapping his criticism against laissez-faire liberalism. He criticized "the common assertion of the mutual incompatibility of equality and liberty" as an idea that rests upon "a highly formal and limited concept of liberty" and conceives of "liberty" in a "completely abstract way." Specifically, rather than identifying "liberty" with "the maximum of unrestrained individualistic action in the economic sphere," he recognized that "actual and concrete liberty of opportunity and action is dependent upon equalization of the political and economic conditions under which individuals are alone free in fact."[5] Dewey encouraged the realization of "liberty" and "equality" through the reconstruction of liberalism that secures a democratic way of living.

In "Liberalism and Civil Liberties," Dewey remarked that the idea of "civil liberties" had been formulated in "the Bill of Rights" enacted by the English Parliament in 1689, and had been contained in the first 10 amendments to the US Constitution in 1791. He classified the notion of "civil liberties" into two principles. While the first emphasized "theoretical justification of freedom of conscience, of choice of worship, of freedom of speech . . . and of publication" based upon "the theory of natural rights," which was inherent in "individuals prior to political organization and independent of political authority," the second, opposing principle stressed "the idea of citizenship" that contributed to the "welfare of the community." In regard to the latter, the idea of "civil liberties" was interpreted as being different from both "those which individuals are supposed to possess in a state of nature" and "political rights such as the franchise and the right to hold office." Dewey stated that "the only hope for liberalism" is to surrender "the doctrine that liberty is a full-fledged ready-made possession of individuals independent of social institutions and arrangements" and to create "social control" that secures "the liberties of the individual, including civil liberties."[6]

The reconstruction of liberalism for Dewey was associated with the restoration of democracy and education. In "The Challenge of Democracy to Education" (1937), he insisted that "the greatest mistake" was to conceive of democracy as "something fixed, fixed in idea and fixed in its outward manifestation." Dewey defended Horace Mann's statement that "the Common School is the greatest discovery ever made by man" and declared that Mann was "the prophet of the idea of the absolute necessity of free public education" supported by public taxation and open for all children in order to preserve "a democratic way of life." However, for Dewey, Mann's ideal had never been realized completely.

It must be borne in mind that democracy for Dewey was always going through a process of construction and reconstruction. Dewey articulated that the "idea of democracy" must "be continually explored afresh," and has to "be constantly discovered, and rediscovered, remade and reorganized." He added that "democracy as a form of life cannot stand still," and pointed out that "in the fact that democracy in order to live must change and move" we have "the challenge that democracy offers to education." According to Dewey, "schools in a democracy" must undertake the "reorganization of studies, of methods of teaching, of administration" in regard to "the relation of pupils and teachers to each other, and to the life of the community." He believed that schools meet "the challenge of democracy" only when they provide "an understanding of the movement and direction of social forces" and "an understanding of social needs and of the resources."

Here, it is of interest that Dewey used the term "understanding" rather than "knowledge." While "knowledge" for him was associated with "information," an "understanding" related to "action" was related to "how things work and how to do things." He asserted that "the isolation of the school" was "the isolation of knowledge from action," and that it was necessary to connect "knowledge, information, and skills with the way things are done socially and how they may be done." He considered that communicative interactions and cooperative activities had the potential to restore democratic education in schools.[7] In "Democracy and Education in the World of Today," published in the *Journal of the Society for Ethical Culture* in 1938, Dewey wrote:

> It is obvious that the relation between democracy and education is a reciprocal one, a mutual one, and vitally so. Democracy is itself an educational principle, an educational measure and policy.[8]

Regarding Dewey's theory of democracy, Nel Noddings interpreted this as a "dynamic conception" in contrast to "the static notion;" that is, "a democracy" is not "given," nor is "the outcome of a common set of words and customs," but is "an achievement – one that depends on the desire to communicate and the goodwill to persist in collaborative inquiry." Achieving a democracy for Noddings meant that "we must try things out, evaluate them without personal prejudice, revise them if they are found wanting, and decide what to do next through a process of reasoned consensus or compromise." She said that "the same advice" applied to "education" on the grounds that, "for Dewey education, too, is a constructive achievement" that is "a matter of trying things out with the valued help of experts (teachers), of evaluating, revising, comparing, sharing, communicating, constructing, choosing."[9]

What Noddings indicated was a reciprocal relationship between "democracy" and "education," which overlapped Dewey's belief that "democracy" is "an educational principle, an educational measure and policy." For Dewey, the school was "the essential distributing agency" for values wherein "free individuals for intelligent participation in a free society" were prepared. He thought that it was important to express "the significance of democracy as the educational process" in the classroom. In other words, when only the textbook and the teacher had the power, "learning which develops intelligence and character" does not occur, but when every child has "an opportunity to contribute something from his own experience," which comes "from the give and take, from the exchange of experiences and ideas," he will become educated. Schools needed to make clear the meaning of "public spirit" and "good citizenship" in all facets of life.

By criticizing "racial intolerance" of being "exaggerated, one-sided nationalism," Dewey defended the idea that democracy would teach "the method of intelligence of understanding, the method of goodwill and of mutual sympathy." "The cause of democracy" for Dewey was concerned with "the moral cause of the dignity and the worth of the individual," through which "mutual respect, mutual toleration, give and take, [and] the pooling of experiences" were formed.[10] The ideal of democratic education for him was considered as something to be continuously created and recreated, and was associated with learning "a way of living together" through social action and cooperative intelligence.

The Bertrand Russell Incident

In 1940, Dewey's involvement in the reconstruction of education and the public sphere faced major problems as at that time the very system of democracy was at stake. There was growing pressure on international society due to the expansion of fascism and Naziism. The disquieting signs turned into reality when Nazi Germany invaded Poland on 1 September 1939, and Britain and France declared war on Germany on 3 September. The German army invaded and occupied most European countries. This conquest culminated when France surrendered to German invasion and Hitler held a victory parade in Paris in June 1940. The heightening of pressure on international society instilled fear in the American people. Although the Roosevelt administration stressed that the US should not become involved in infringement of human rights and the oppression of civil liberties as during World War I, the government's message was still reflective of the conservative and exclusive tone of arguments among the general public. The situation was explosively unstable, with educational institutions strained almost to breaking point because of the growing pressure on universities and schools.

This pressure surfaced through what became known as the Bertrand Russell case, which was brought about by the announcement by New York's Board of Higher Education to employ Russell as Professor of Philosophy at the College of the City of New York in February 1940. Russell, who was in the US to teach at the universities of Chicago and California, had gained fame in the fields of logic, mathematics and philosophy. He had frequently discussed moral issues surrounding the freedom of love, extramarital sex and divorce in his books *Principles of Social Reconstruction* (1916),[11] *Marriage and Morals* (1929)[12] and *The Conquest of Happiness* (1930).[13] However, at a time when the influence of religious authorities was strong and the conventional view of marriage predominated in society, Russell's way of thinking about love and marriage seemed to involve extremely radical content, especially for those who cherished conservative values.

The Christian community began to criticize New York's Board of Higher Education because of its determination to employ Russell. William T. Manning, Bishop of New York, blamed Russell for promoting adultery, thereby

destroying religious attitudes and offending moralities. The opposition movement that attacked Russell and asked for the withdrawal of his appointment
to the academic post then spread throughout society.[14] The anti-Russell
bandwagon reached its peak when Jean Kay, who was a devout Catholic and
mother of a female student, filed a suit against New York's Board of Higher
Education in the New York Supreme Court. Though her daughter was not
a student of the college, Kay was afraid that her daughter might be adversely
affected by Russell's ideas. John E. McGeehan, Justice of the New York
Supreme Court, accepted the justification of the plaintiff's opinion and judged
in favour of the withdrawal of Russell's appointment. The grounds for this
decision were that Russell's views regarding pre- and extramarital sex and nudity
were so extraordinarily indecent that it would be morally unsuitable for him
to teach at the college, and that his appointment might be an insult to both
New York citizens and the academies.[15]

However, regarding the judgement, there was suspicion of mutual interest
having been shared between the judge and the anti-Russell groups, since Justice
McGeehan was an Irish Catholic and the movement demanding the withdrawal
of Russell's appointment was largely swayed by Catholic and Protestant
opinions. Russell was amazed and disappointed at the exclusive situation that
was spreading throughout the US, his demand for an appeal was rejected by
the court and his appointment as Professor of the College of the City of New
York was thus blocked.

On the other hand, there arose a movement comprising associations of the
universities, societies of philosophy, and the staff and students of the College
of the City of New York to support Russell and appeal for the justification of
his appointment at the College. Dewey, who had been a friend of Russell,
reacted to this issue by playing the central role in protecting the latter. Besides
Dewey, Albert Einstein, Robert Maynard Hutchins, Horace Meyer Kallen,
Albert C. Barnes, Alfred North Whitehead, Thomas Mann, Aldous Huxley
and others expressed their support for Russell. The key point of their insistence
was to defend educational freedom and autonomy, which was at risk from
interference by external pressures. It was impermissible that educational freedom
should be submitted to such political and religious oppression by silencing
academies in the universities and colleges.

Dewey wrote an essay in *The Nation* of 15 June 1940 raising two points
regarding the Russell incident. The first related to "the legal authority of a
court to overrule and nullify the action of an administrative board created
according to the statutes of New York State." The second was whether "writings upon matters of great social importance" could be used to "deprive the
author of the power to teach his own special and very different subject" in
higher education. According to Dewey, if courts have "the power" over
them, educational institutions are deprived of "power" and "responsibility"
and would be thrown into "a state of uncertainty." He said that if McGeehan's
action was upheld, it would effectively "muzzle" university teachers on topics
not directly connected with their specialties of instruction.

Dewey asserted that the following question had never been investigated, much less settled: "What has Mr. Russell actually said and in what spirit has he said it?" In Dewey's opinion, Russell had successfully discussed the need for "a new sexual ethic," and "the spirit" that Russell emphasized was "important." Dewey attempted to protect academic freedom, the freedom of speech and expression and the autonomy of educational institutions. He admitted that he disagreed with some of Russell's philosophy, especially that expressing "a logic more appropriate to mathematical than to social and moral subjects." Nevertheless, he noted that "such difference in conclusions" gives "no reason for penalizing one who discusses in a serious spirit the issues involved." According to Dewey's statement, the difference in conclusions should not be excluded but be "publicly discussed." He believed that "the only thing ruled out is the dogmatism and intolerance that would forbid discussion."[16]

In 1941, Dewey, Kallen, Barnes, Hook and others published *The Bertrand Russell Case*. According to Dewey's "Introduction," Barnes drew up the plans for publishing the book about the Russell incident. Dewey had first introduced Russell to Barnes, and Russell had been employed as a lecturer in Western Philosophy at the Barnes Foundation in Merion. Regarding the Russell case, Barnes was not satisfied with acting on behalf of "religious toleration and intellectual freedom," but felt that "the social importance of the case" should be published as "a public record of the issue." Dewey wrote that though "this book is a result of his [Barnes'] suggestion," the authors of the essays were selected not by Barnes but by a group representing the Committee for Cultural Freedom. Barnes did not make any suggestions, much less give instruction about the content, but accepted "different philosophical and social standpoints." Dewey evaluated Barnes' attitude positively, because the intention of the publication was to foster "the democratic method of discussion" by "the method of intelligence, the scientific method" as "the alternative" to "some aspect and degree of totalitarianism."[17]

In the "Foreword" to the book, Barnes wrote that the aim of the publication was not to build up "a vindication" of Russell nor to argue in favour of "academic freedom," but to present "the record of an inquiry into the facts of the case." In his view, "neither Democracy nor Russell was given an opportunity to raise a voice in their defence" and hence the court's decision proved to be "a parody of wisdom, justice, and public welfare." Barnes insisted that "the stake is the lifeblood of Democracy, the right of every individual to be free from the tyrannical acts of dictators."[18] Likewise, Dewey thought that "the social importance" of the incident transcended "the injustice done to Mr. Russell personally" and "the question of the merits or demerits of the particular views he set forth," but "the issue underlying it is no more settled than the Dred Scott case settled the slavery issue." Dewey announced his "belief in the social importance of public discussion of moral problems" that is associated with "scientific method" and "a sense of public responsibility," a belief that would aim at "the freedom of the human spirit and the democratic way of life."[19] Dewey also wrote a chapter titled "Social Realities Versus Political Court

Fictions." What was at issue for him was not "the correctness or the wisdom of Mr. Russell's particular views," but "the wisdom or unwisdom of public discussion of sex and marriage when these topics are approached in a scientific manner and with serious, ethical interest." Dewey recognized that Justice McGeehan's judgement was made up by courtroom fictions that demonstrated insult to and contempt for Russell.[20]

In an essay entitled "Behind the Bertrand Russell Case," Kallen observed the religious background of the judgement, that is, that "the case grew out of churchman's assault." He criticized the stratagem of the court as having been composed by church persons including Justice McGeehan and Jean Kay. For Kallen, in the schools and colleges "the new idea can be studied freely, and with a minimum of social risk and a maximum of social advantage," and "it can be scrutinized closely, freely compared with its alternatives, and judged impartially without that clash of vested practical interests which occurs in the extra-mural world."[21] Dewey and Barnes aimed to determine social fact from the perspective of academic truth, rather than applying a dogmatic and coercive interpretation to the Russell incident. Barnes' intention to reconstruct the style of education that had been practised in the 1920s and 1930s in Philadelphia developed into a comprehensive form of democratic education involving the Russell incident in 1940. In later years, Russell recollected his life in the US with despair, but recollected his employment at the Barnes Foundation as follows.

> Many liberal-minded professors protested, but they all supposed that as I was an earl I must have ancestral estates and be very well off. Only one man did anything practical, and that was Dr Barnes, the inventor of Argyrol, and the creator of the Barnes Foundation near Philadelphia. He gave me a five-year appointment to lecture on philosophy at his Foundation. This relieved me of a very great anxiety. Until he gave me this appointment, I had seen no way out of my troubles. I could not get money out of England; it was impossible to return to England; I certainly did not wish my three children to go back into the blitz, even if I could have got a passage for them which would certainly have been impossible for a long time to come. It seemed as if it would be necessary to take John and Kate away from the University, and to live as cheaply as possible on the charity of kind friends. From this bleak prospect I was saved by Dr Barnes.[22]

Dewey and Barnes acted in cooperation during the Russell incident. Russell's views about love, marriage and divorce were treated as inappropriate and abominable since they were seen as breaking the implicit norms at that time connected with the morality of academics, and were burdened with the stigma of threatening the stability of citizens' social lives. The attack on Russell was the by-product of citizens' smouldering anxieties and unease in the face of the growing tension in international society. As a result, Russell's appointment to the college was blocked. Dewey, Barnes, Kallen, Hook and others continued their assertion of the court's injustice. They were apprehensive that when citizens were governed by fear, this would result in the loss of their critical thinking and judgement whereby injustice and unfairness would spread throughout society. In turn, this implied that others could be dissolved into a homogeneous space wherein heterogeneous views and opinions were removed because of the inability to think and judge. On the other hand, Dewey supported Russell in terms of respecting democratic education and the public sphere, which are open to the politics and ethics of communication.

Educational Censorship and the Oppression of Rights

The tendency to assault and oppress school education was increasing, and the boundary partitioned by the barbed wire of this oppression was about to engulf the most far-flung corners of the educational environment. Although Dewey's practices involving public education were directed at the collapse of such boundaries, the sparks that ignited disputes were seen across the US.

In "Investigating Education" published in *The New York Times* and *The New York Herald Tribune* on 6 May 1940, Dewey wrote that "the veiled assault on public education" that was conducted in the form of "investigations" must arouse progressive educators to "renewed vigilance." In his view, the censorship against school education had been strengthened; for instance, in New York, Governor Lehman approved a resolution to appropriate $30,000 for "a legislative investigation" into the public school system, and in Washington, Martin Dies, Chairman of the House Committee to Investigate Un-American Activities, promised "an investigation into the political and social affiliations of textbook writers." Nevertheless, Dewey did not necessarily regard "investigation" itself as the useless aspect of this case. He said that regardless of whether the investigation was focused on schools or or textbook writers, he had "no objection" as long as it supported "the best educational practice" and had "a clear-cut objective" that was pursued "without prejudice or favor." He added that in a democracy, any elected body of representatives had "the right to look into the methods and practices" of schools supported by public taxation, and "a scrutiny of the writers of textbooks used in those schools" should not be regarded as "an unwarranted invasion of rights."

Notwithstanding, the institutionalization of "investigation" at that time aimed at "a different purpose." According to Dewey, "the quest today is for 'subversive' activities and 'subversive' textbooks; and the problem becomes one of determining what is 'subversive' and what is not," since the textbooks that presented "the theories of state and revolution" by Marx, Lenin or Trotsky were seen as "ipso facto 'subversive.'" He concluded that such assaults under the name of "investigation" would "reduce the educational system of America to the condition of bondage which exists in the totalitarian states of Italy, Germany and Soviet Russia."[23]

Dewey's anxiety materialized into actual incidents. The suppression of social studies textbooks written by Harold Rugg of the Teachers College, Columbia

University, broke the ice. The target of this suppression was 14 volumes of the textbooks *Man and His Changing Society* for grades 3 to 12.[24] Between 1929 and 1939, Rugg's social studies textbook series sold 1,317,960 copies and over 2,687,000 workbooks. However, the crackdown on Rugg's textbooks was strengthened and his description of "advertisement" as inducing "an economic waste" was criticized by the advertising industry.[25] Thereafter, Rugg's social studies series was stigmatized by the business world as "subversive" and its use was prohibited in Binghamton, New York State, in April 1940.

Dewey was firmly opposed to the prohibition of Rugg's textbooks. According to Dewey, the action of removing Rugg's textbooks "climaxed agitation that has for years been inspired by groups in other communities to silence Mr. Rugg by forcing his books out of the schools." He considered that the campaign of excluding books regarded as "subversive" from the public schools had spread across the country, and "Carl L. Becker, David Saville Muzzey, Roy Hatch and the late DeForest Stull were victims of similar persecution." Dewey asserted that he welcomed "any investigation" that has "as its goal the development of thoughtful, intelligent, critical-minded students and citizens," but that he would oppose "those who would pervert a free educational system by opening it to the exploitation of prejudice, bigotry and unenlightenment" and would resist attempts by "pressure groups to gain control of the public schools."[26]

Furthermore, Dewey wrote "Censorship Not Wanted" in *The New York Times* of 11 May 1940. In that piece he stressed that "the discussion of a wide variety of opinion, unorthodox and orthodox, with an intelligent teacher in the classroom, is the best protection the schools can afford against our students being later misled by unscrupulous propagandists of one doctrine or another." It was more advantageous for young people to "face controversial issues in the open atmosphere of the schoolroom" than to "seek out what is forbidden in some dark, unwholesome corner." Dewey insisted: "No thought is so dangerous as a forbidden thought." It was not approved for him to silence any opinion regarded as "unorthodox." He criticized the way in which a clear boundary had been created between "orthodox" and "unorthodox," and that the exclusion and suppression of the "unorthodox" minorities were performed confidentially while promoting the inclusion of "orthodox."[27] In regard to the Rugg and Russell incidents, Dewey advocated that "the dogmatism and intolerance that would forbid discussion" should be "the only thing ruled out." From this perspective, Dewey appealed the injustice of the assault on Rugg.

In the 1930s, Dewey promoted the construction of democratic education and the public sphere in terms of criticizing and redefining traditional liberalism. He regarded the interactive relations of face-to-face communication, which had been eroded by the expansion of marketization and standardized nationalization, as "liberalism in a vacuum." Instead, he aimed to create the public sphere on the basis of people's trust and interaction and to build "a renascent liberalism" as "radicalism" open to democratic deliberation and participation. He defined democracy as "a way of living together" or "a way of life, social and individual." For him, aesthetic experience lay at the very core of the public sphere because "art" is "the most universal and freest form of communication" that constitutes "the common qualities of the public world." Dewey's involvement in education through the Barnes Foundation, the Russell incident and the controversy over Rugg had been prepared for by his pursuing a strategy to defend democratic education based on dialogue and the politics and ethics of the public sphere.

However, Dewey's challenges did not move forward in a linear way and he encountered various difficulties. His critical concerns were directed at the exclusive movements against education that were governed by the dominance of uniform values and observance of norms through inspections and censorship, and by the infringement of educational freedom and diversity. These practices were meant to dissolve the heterogeneous view into the encircling space of homogeneity and extinguish the existence of the others. The censorship control during the Russell incident and regarding school textbooks projected the fear and unease of citizens in face of the increasingly strained situation in international society. Individuals' fears led to assaults on educational institutions, and confined educational freedom and autonomy. The prejudices that regarded Russell and Rugg as "subversive" expanded throughout society, and they both came under heavy criticism by the general public.

Dewey explored the prospects for releasing and collapsing the exclusive region of the narrow, closed-minded view which had been triggered by the loss of critical thinking and judgement. For him, creating justice by encouraging open communication and dialogue without hindrance, and defending educational freedom in democracy, were public matters. His vision of democratic education pointed to the practical direction that would shield an "articulate public" from "the eclipse of the public" and open the avenue to creating "a way of living together." Dewey's conception of bridging aesthetic experience and the public sphere would be actualized in connection with democratic processes and the practices of art education. The democratic education and politics developed by Dewey led the way to educational reform in the form of "radicalism" and became historical proof of creating "democracy as a way of living" through the potentiality of art.

Notes

1 John Dewey, "A Liberal Speaks Out for Liberalism," op. cit., pp.282–287.
2 Ibid., p.287.
3 Ibid., pp.287–288.
4 John Dewey, "The Meaning of Liberalism," op. cit., pp.364–367.
5 John Dewey, "Liberalism and Equality," op. cit., pp.368–371.
6 John Dewey, "Liberalism and Civil Liberties," op. cit., pp.372–375.
7 John Dewey, "The Challenge of Democracy to Education," *The Later Works*, vol.11, pp.181–190.
8 John Dewey, "Democracy and Education in the World of Today." *The Later Works*, vol.13, p.294.

9 Nel Noddings, *The Challenge to Care in Schools: An Alternative Approach to Education*, New York: Teachers College Press, 1992.

10 John Dewey, "Democracy and Education in the World of Today," op. cit., pp.294–303.

11 Bertrand Russell, *Principles of Social Reconstruction*, London: George Allen and Unwin, 1916.

12 Bertrand Russell, *Marriage and Morals*, New York: Liveright, 1929.

13 Bertrand Russell, *The Conquest of Happiness*, London: Unwin Books, 1961.

14 Ikki Hidaka, *Bertrand Russell: Love and Marriage*, Kashutsu Shobō Shinsha, 1974, pp.23–25.

15 "Decision of Justice McGeehan," *The Bertrand Russell Case*, John Dewey, Horace M. Kallen (eds), New York: Da Capo Press, 1972, pp.213–225.

16 John Dewey, "The Case for Bertrand Russell," *The Later Works*, vol.14, pp.231–234.

17 John Dewey, "Introduction," *The Bertrand Russell Case*, op. cit., pp.7–8.

18 Albert C. Barnes, "Foreword," *The Bertrand Russell Case*, op. cit., pp.11–12.

19 John Dewey, "Introduction," *The Bertrand Russell Case*, op. cit., pp.8–10.

20 John Dewey, "Social Realities Versus Political Court Fictions," *The Bertrand Russell Case*, op. cit., pp.55–73.

21 Horace M. Kallen, "Behind the Bertrand Russell Case," *The Bertrand Russell Case*, op. cit., pp.13–53.

22 Bertrand Russell, *The Autobiography of Bertrand Russell 1914–1944*, Oxford: Routledge, 2000, pp.461–462.

23 John Dewey, "Investigating Education," *The Later Works*, vol.14, pp.370–371.

24 Harold Rugg, *Man and His Changing Society*, Boston: Gin and Co, 1929–1939, 14 vols.

25 Elmer Winters, "Man and His Changing Society," *History of Education Quarterly*, no.7, 1967, p.510.

26 John Dewey, "Investigating Education," op. cit., pp.371–372.

27 John Dewey, "Censorship Not Wanted," *The Later Works*, vol.14, p.373.

Epilogue

Democratic Education and the Public Sphere: Towards Dewey's Theory of Aesthetic Experience

The Criticality of Liberalism and Its Reconstruction in Education

There is an increasing demand to explore the question of how we can create democratic education and the public sphere in the era of globalization of the twenty-first century. Since the 1980s, the dominant ideology of education has been formed by the sense of neoliberalism that glorified the crushing victory of the autonomy of the global market economy, and free and unregulated competition inherited from nineteenth-century liberalism. Criticizing the liberal democracy that was promoted after the New Deal of the 1930s, the neoliberal ethos swept through the educational reforms of privatization and liberalization and attempted to introduce the market mechanism into schools.

The reason why advocates of neoliberalism criticized liberal democracy was that they had assumed that its theory of building a welfare state would result in the bureaucratization and systematization of school control. The educational reforms proposed by Friedman, Chubb and Moe represented neoliberalism that urged the delegation of authority from the government to the market by praising the laissez-faire liberalism of the nineteenth century. The marketization of the school system, that is the introduction of choices, services and competition, constitutes the dominant concept of educational reform and prescribes the standards for the present-day educational environment.

On the other hand, the global economic depression triggered by the monetary crisis in 2008 exposed the limitations of neoliberalism. In the present situation, a quarter of a century having passed since the end of the Cold War, the neoliberal strain that seemed to achieve supremacy in global society is trapped in deadlock. While the reorganization of the social economic system advances, re-evaluation of the New Deal liberalism of the Roosevelt Administration is spreading and urges government intervention in the field of economics. New concerns regarding the construction of education and the public sphere have spread under the diverging circumstances of the different political spectra between neoliberalism and the welfare state.

However, Dewey presented an educational vision that differed from mainstream liberalism during the era of transition from laissez-faire to the New

Deal, around the time of the Great Depression in 1929. He adopted an innovative strategy for constructing democratic education and the public sphere by releasing democratic ideals from the lure of the dominant liberalism. For him, laissez-faire and the New Deal were, so to speak, a reversed mirror image based on the same principle. Dewey criticized both laissez-faire and the New Deal, and specified his conception of democratic education that was extended to include the notions of community and association. Dewey's vision of education and the public sphere was formed at the crossroads where various motifs of liberalism competed with each other, and during the transition phase of marketization to welfare state that was rushed onto the new stage of the public sphere. For him, the public sphere was not an exclusive region filled with homogeneous values and concerns, but aimed at open and multiple networks of communities built by social and cooperative activities. Dewey attempted to create an educational system that was connected with the idea of democracy and to build the public sphere based on aesthetic experience. He promoted art education projects as Director of Education at the Barnes Foundation, through which Dewey and Barnes were engaged in the reform of democracy-led art education in Philadelphia.

The Reconstruction of Education and the Public Sphere in the 1920s and 1930s

In this book, I have described Dewey's theory and practice in the 1920s and 1930s of democratic education and the public sphere that are concerned with aesthetic experience. Specifically, I have clarified his view of bridging the democratic politics of the public sphere and art education at the Barnes Foundation. The conclusions reached in each chapter can be summarized as follows.

In the 1920s, Dewey criticized traditional liberalism and proposed the idea of educational reform based on democratic processes and practices. In *The Public and Its Problems*, he defined the relationship between "the public" and "the private" not by hypothetical causes of action, but from the view of their functional consequences. Dewey's theory differed from traditional liberalism; he denied the theory that substantiated the distinction of "the public" and "the private" into the a priori and pre-established boundaries of the normative realm, such as a state or a market, and reinterpreted it from the continuous point of view constituted by plural and multilayer spaces. The public sphere that Dewey proposed would be constructed by collaborative communities and associations that were based on interactive and face-to-face communication. Dewey's conception of the public sphere was a regional and spatial concept, as well as a temporal and diachronic concept of construction and reconstruction. Through this, Dewey tried to reorient the social space of impersonal and anonymous relationships, brought about by the expansion of the market realm and industrialism, into a democratic community created by the politics and ethics of dialogical communication. He criticized Lippmann's elitism, which urged bureaucratic control of society, and advocated the restoration of an "articulate public" from "the eclipse of the public." According to Dewey's theory, the public sphere was not a conception superior to and encompassing the private sphere, nor was it spaces that emerge naturally and spontaneously; rather, it was the political and ethical arena that generates communication and aims at solutions to the problems at risk of being forgotten if the articulate public disappears and dialogical relationships are lost.

Dewey cemented his vision of democratic education and the public sphere in his articles published in *The New Republic*, *The New York Times* and others. While the economic prosperity of consumer society expanded and laissez-faire policy continued to reign in the Republican Party administrations of Harding, Coolidge and Hoover, exclusive movements occurred in the 1920s such as the enactment of the Johnson Quota Act and the Immigration Act, the Scopes trial and the execution of Sacco and Vanzetti. Dewey placed an emphasis on the positive role that education played in reviving a democracy and pursued a strategy for building schools as dialogical and cooperative communities. For him, "dialogue" that produced a "participator" was distinct from a "soliloquy" led by a "spectator" of broken and imperfect thought. Dewey's democratic education fostered "dialogue" that furnishes "social intelligence" by "hearing." Dewey rejected religious and racial "bigotry and intolerance" that led to indiscriminate prejudice and ignorance, and impeached "nationalism" as "the religion of multitudes" that caused an inability to think and judge. Dewey highlighted educating "the public mind" for forming critical and cooperative thinking and communication in schools. Dewey insisted that the school was "the shuttle" that would intertwine "threads" of various cultures, traditions, languages and religions, and bring together "exceedingly heterogeneous elements of our population." Besides, Dewey understood "educational science" from the perspective of qualitative processes and results, rather than quantitative measurement. For him, "education is by its nature an endless circle or spiral" and "is an activity which includes science within itself."

In the 1930s, Dewey enunciated in Liberalism and Social Action that "the first object of a renascent liberalism is education," by reconstructing ideas of traditional liberalism such as Locke's political theory, laissez-faire economics and the New Deal type of welfare state. He defined "democracy" as "a way of living together" or "a way of life, social and individual" that organized social action and intelligence. Dewey's theory of a democratic community grew out of the "faith in the possibilities of human nature" and the "belief in the Common Man." He made a point of the importance of participation in community and associations, saying that "the very fact of exclusion from participation is a subtle form of suppression." He explored "participation" and "dialogue" that were opposed to "exclusion" and "suppression." Dewey's theory of democratic politics was formed in response to the political, economic and social situation of the 1930s. He promoted the establishment of a new party through the League for Independent Political Action and the People's Lobby. Dewey advocated the necessity of taking radical measures for coping with the Great Depression, criticizing the New Deal under the Roosevelt Administration. He sought education to ensure the freedom and equality of citizens who participate in a democratic community.

The rapid social changes following the Great Depression made conspicuous the discussion regarding the social function of the school. In educational studies, the Teachers College of Columbia University took an initiative in undertaking research. Kilpatrick, Rugg, Counts, Childs and Newlon, who were influenced by Dewey's philosophy and played leading roles in the Progressive Education Association in the 1920s, came to change their positions from child-centred education to social reconstructionism in the 1930s. In October 1934 they published a new journal, *The Social Frontier*, in order to encourage schools to perform social reconstruction towards collectivism. Although Dewey agreed with the mainstream ideology of *The Social Frontier* that asserted the limitation of laissez-faire individualism and associated education with political and economic connections, he refused to link education with solving political issues or guiding social changes directly. Rather, he emphasized the importance of creating active and cooperative learning in a democratic community. For him, "learning" was not "an accumulated and transmitted body of knowledge" but "the acts of apprehending, understanding, and retaining . . . for subsequent use," which were inspired by the "constant development of cross references, of interdependencies and interrelations." In other words, he believed that "learning is learning to think" and "reflective thinking" must be "an educational aim." Dewey introduced "methods of inquiry and mutual consultation and discussion" rather than imposition and inculcation in the classrooms, and suggested a vision for school of "educational agencies" that were constructed by "social action" and "public action" on the basis of "educational freedom" and "autonomy in education."

Art Education and the Public Sphere

One of the characteristics of Dewey's educational theory was that it attempted to release the potentialities of art at the base of community experiences, and to bridge aesthetic experience and the public sphere in democratic politics. He believed that aesthetic experience lay at the depth of the public sphere, and expected that art education would be extended to include democratic processes and practices. In *Art as Experience*, Dewey interpreted aesthetic experience as being concerned with mediating communication that would offer fuller and richer meanings of life. The concept of art for him was understood by the communication of experience in everyday lives and communities. He criticized the rise of nationalism and imperialism that had separated art from ordinary life; the expansion of marketization that had caused "the impersonality of a world market;" the appearance of industrialization and mechanization that had brought about "'impersonalization' of the human soul" and the "quantification of life;" and the totalitarian state that had functioned as "propaganda" for the sake of maintaining dictatorships. On the other hand, Dewey pursued art as an experience of mediating communication in the democratic politics of mass culture. He considered that art is "the cultural bases of democracy" rather than "adornments of culture."

Dewey's vision of bridging aesthetic experience and the public sphere was practised in the art education project of the Barnes Foundation. The Barnes Foundation, whose purpose was stated as the "advancement of education and the appreciation of the fine arts," was founded in Merion, a suburb of Philadelphia, in December 1922. Barnes not only collected works of art by Renoir, Cézanne, Manet, Degas, Monet, van Gogh, Matisse, Picasso, Modigliani, and others, but also published books such as *The Art in Painting*, *The French Primitives and Their Forms*, *The Art of Henri Matisse*, *The Art of Renoir* and *The Art of Cézanne*. Dewey deepened his theory of art through exchanging ideas with Barnes. The friendship between Dewey and Barnes started when Barnes attended Dewey's seminar at Columbia University in 1917. Barnes showed an interest in Dewey's theories of democracy, experience and education.

Dewey was inaugurated as the first Director of Education of the Barnes Foundation, since the purpose of the Foundation was to promote art education. Dewey was expected to develop art education from the perspective of democratic ideals. Buermeyer, Munro and Mullen served as Associate Directors of Education for the Foundation. At the opening ceremony of the new building of the Barnes Foundation held on 19 March 1925, Dewey emphasized the significance of the Foundation as an educational institution in response to Barnes' request that he do so. According to the former, art was not "something apart, not something for the few" but "something which should give the final touch of meaning, of consummation, to all the activities of life." Art for him was related with the "most common, most fundamental, most demanding public recognition."

The Barnes Foundation initiated an innovative art education project based on Dewey's theory of democratic education. Barnes conceived of a plan to reconstruct art education in Philadelphia in cooperation with the School of Fine Arts at the University of Pennsylvania. Barnes made contact with Penniman, President of the University of Pennsylvania, and Laird, Dean of the School of Fine Arts, and reached an agreement with the university in May 1924. Buermeyer and Munro were supposed to conduct art courses at the university. Barnes also expected that the works of art owned by the Foundation would be effectively used in Philadelphia public schools. Furthermore, the Barnes Foundation approached the Pennsylvania Academy of the Fine Arts, the oldest art school in the US. On affairs such as these, Barnes frequently consulted with Dewey.

However, Barnes' art education projects met with frustration and he was obliged to adapt them throughout their development, facing criticism and difficulties in the negotiating processes with the universities and city officials. For this, the Foundation criticized Theodore Dillaway, who had contributed to the advancement of art education as Director of Art Education in Philadelphia public schools, and Samuel Fleisher, who had founded the Graphic Sketch

Club. Barnes often sent letters to Dewey to ask for his advice. Dewey told Barnes that what was needed for the Foundation was not "the policy of negative criticism" by "controversial methods," but an "intelligent method" to build an "effective cooperation" with the university and city, and to strengthen the "connections." However, the cooperative alliance between the Barnes Foundation and the University of Pennsylvania terminated in 1926. Besides this, the Foundation's intention to build collaboration with the Pennsylvania Academy of the Fine Arts, the Philadelphia public schools and the Philadelphia Museum of Art fell by the wayside. Barnes' desire to construct an art education centre that would lead to innovative education research and practices in Philadelphia was not fulfilled, in spite of Dewey's conciliatory proposal towards "cooperation."

Dewey discussed the potentialities of art that lay at the root of the public sphere through his involvement in the art education project of the Barnes Foundation. Even though Dewey and Barnes were not discouraged by repeated failures, it was not at all easy for them to build collaborative networks with academia, which in the 1920s and 1930s held great influence in the traditional sense. In the 1930s, the Friends of Art and Education was organized to promote art and education in Philadelphia, in which Dewey served as the Honorary President and Barnes as President. The Friends of Art and Education criticized the Federal Art Project (FAP) of the Works Progress Administration (WPA) initiated by President Roosevelt as part of the New Deal in 1935. The FAP, introduced as one of the projects of Federal Project Number One, provided governmental financial support by employing 5,000 to 10,000 artists who had lost their jobs as a result of the Great Depression, and offered opportunities for ordinary citizens to enjoy the arts in their everyday experiences of life through the siting of mural paintings, posters, pictures and sculptures in public spaces such as walls, public schools, public offices, stations, libraries, post offices and hospitals. The FAP, which was considered to be one of the roots of public art, significantly changed the mode of art.

In Philadelphia, the Pennsylvania FAP was inaugurated with the support of the Philadelphia Museum of Art. The Friends of Art and Education attacked the Pennsylvania FAP as "a hindrance to a genuine art movement" and a "fraud" against citizens. Dewey supported Barnes' action as Honorary President of the Friends of Art and Education. Nevertheless, attempts to reform education by the Barnes Foundation had never been welcomed by artists, educators and policy makers in Philadelphia. From the beginning, Dewey's theory of bridging aesthetic experience and the public sphere was not suggested in an explicit way, but could only be understood through his connection with the educational projects at the Foundation. The various difficulties that Dewey and Barnes encountered characterized their unaccomplished project of art education based on democratic processes and practices. Dewey's educational activities in the Barnes Foundation indicated how difficult it was to practice democratic education that was associated with aesthetic experience.

In the 1930s, Dewey remarked that "the relation between democracy and education is a reciprocal one, a mutual one, and vitally so," and that "democracy is itself an educational principle, an educational measure and policy." In his view, "the idea of democracy" should not be comprehended as "something fixed" but had to "be continually explored afresh" and "constantly discovered, and rediscovered, remade and reorganized." In addition, he placed aesthetic experience at the heart of the public sphere. Dewey insisted that "works of art are the only media of complete and unhindered communication between man and man that can occur in a world full of gulfs and walls that limit community of experience."[1] Dewey's theory of aesthetic experience was founded on his belief that art was "the most universal and freest form of communication" that constructed "the common qualities of the public world." Art was seen as the undercurrent of the interactive and cooperative experience of communication in everyday life.

Barnes wrote "The Educational Philosophy of John Dewey" in *The Humanist* in 1946. He pointed out that Dewey's philosophy of education "rests on the axiom that the indispensable elements of the democratic way of life – scientific method as intelligence in operation, art, education – are all bound together in a single organic whole." In Barnes' understanding, "morality, science, art, all alike, are forms of communication, possible only through the sharing of experience which constitutes civilized living," and "education includes all of them; but only if education is conceived, not in the conventional sense, as preparation for life, but as living itself." Barnes concluded that to have a developed philosophy of education was thus "the supreme achievement of John Dewey – an achievement rarely paralleled in scope in the entire history of education."[2] Russell, who had been employed as a lecturer at the Barnes Foundation, published *A History of Western Philosophy* (1946), expressing the view that "this book owes its existence to Dr. Albert C. Barnes, having been originally designed and partly delivered as lectures at the Barnes Foundation in Pennsylvania." Russell introduced a chapter on "John Dewey" and showed his "respect and admiration" for the latter.[3] The art education project of the Barnes Foundation was promoted on the basis of Dewey's theory of democratic education that built a bridge between aesthetic experience and the public sphere.

A Vision of Democratic Education and the Public Sphere

In this book, I have considered Dewey's theory and practice of democratic education and the public sphere from the perspective of reconstructing traditional liberalism around the concept of aesthetic experience in the 1920s and 1930s. Historically, liberalism had never been a monolithic thought or movement developed by a linear principle, but rather contained plural genealogies that included mutual strains, disagreements and competitions. The period in which Dewey articulated his theory of democracy and art education corresponded to the era that saw a watershed of liberalism, which shifted from laissez-faire to a welfare state. Meanwhile, Dewey's liberalism formed a strain that cannot necessarily be said to have been mainstream. It was because the theory of civil society advocated by liberalism had concentrated on a philosophy involving the concept of nature, characterized by individualism at its core, that an alternative value that would replace its tradition had not fully matured. Therefore, it is not an overstatement to regard Dewey's ideas, which aimed to conquer an individualistic tradition of civil society and enrich the aesthetic experience of community and association, as unorthodox in terms of mainstream liberalism. Indeed, Dewey experienced various difficulties and frustrations, including the affairs of the establishment of a third party, New Deal criticism, challenges to social reconstructionism, the art education project at the Barnes Foundation and the Bertrand Russell incident. Generally speaking, Dewey's practices displayed an aspect of the "defeat" of its "radicalism," as Lagemann's study clarifies. On the other hand, his ideas also led to positive effects and practices in democratic education and served as a driving force for supporting progressive education and art education at the Barnes Foundation.

Dewey was involved in educational reform based on democracy and the public sphere, stating that "the first object of a renascent liberalism is education." Dewey's "radicalism" was composed of his theory that understood "a vacuum" of liberalism in the relational domain of interaction generated by networks of face-to-face communication, which he sealed by defining democracy as "a way of living together." While laissez-faire and the New Deal borrowed the term "liberal" and gained influential power, they resulted in eroding the domain of association where people interacted with each other. Dewey adopted a strategy for interpreting the distinction between the public and private spheres continuously, immanently criticizing diluted relationships and the normative realm that were caused by the expansion of marketization and standardized control. It is important to see his idea of the public sphere as simultaneously a regional and spatial concept, and a temporal and diachronic concept, which differed from the principle of civil society that traditional liberalism had advocated. Dewey sought an innovative vision of democratic education exceeding laissez-faire marketization and the New Deal welfare state. His theory of the public sphere was extended to the political and ethical dimensions formed by networks of trust and dialogue that emerge from cooperative activities and interactions in the community and through associations, and was inspired by the prospect of creating "democracy as a way of life." Dewey explored the potentialities of art that were at the depth of the public sphere, which allowed him to play a key role in the art education project at the Barnes Foundation. Promoting democratic education by bridging aesthetic experience and the public sphere was at the heart of Dewey's educational theory in the 1920s and 1930s. In Dewey's view, democratic education was the guiding thread concerned with the creation of art education and the public sphere.

Notes

1 John Dewey, *Art as Experience*, op. cit., p.110.
2 Albert C. Barnes, "The Educational Philosophy of John Dewey," *The Humanist*, Winter, 1946, pp.160–162.
3 Bertrand Russell, *A History of Western Philosophy, and Its Connection with Political and Social Circumstances from the Earliest Times to the Present Day*, London: G. Allen & Unwin, 1946.

References

Abe, Kiyoshi, *Public Sphere and Communication: A New Horizon of Critical Research*, Kyoto: Minerva Shobo, 1998.

Adorno, Theodor W., *Minima Moralia: Reflexionen aus dem beschädigten Leben*, Frankfurt am Main: Suhrkamp, 1962.

Alexander, Thomas M., *John Dewey's Theory of Art, Experience & Nature: The Horizon of Feeling*, Albany, NY: State University of New York, 1987.

Anderson, John, *Art Held Hostage: The Battle over the Barnes Collection*, New York: W. W. Norton, 2003.

Appleby, Joyce, *Liberalism and Republicanism in the Historical Imagination*, Cambridge, MA: Harvard University Press, 1992.

Arendt, Hannah, *The Human Condition*, Chicago, IL: The University of Chicago Press, 1958.

Arendt, Hannah, *Eichmann in Jerusalem: A Report on the Banality of Evil*, New York: The Viking Press, 1963.

Barnes, Albert C., "Cubism: Requiescat in Pace," *Arts & Decoration*, vol.6, January, 1916.

Barnes, Albert C., "The Barnes Foundation," *The New Republic*, vol.34, no.432, 14 March 1923.

Barnes, Albert C., "The Shame in the Public School of Philadelphia," *Journal of the Barnes Foundation*, vol.1, no.1, April 1925.

Barnes, Albert C., "Art Teaching that Obstacles Education," *Journal of the Barnes Foundation*, vol.1, no.2, May 1925.

Barnes, Albert C., "Art Teaching that Obstacles Education," *Journal of the Barnes Foundation*, vol.1, no.3, October, 1925.

Barnes, Albert C., "Educational Disorder at the Metropolitan Museum," *Journal of the Barnes Foundation*, vol.2, no.1, January, 1926.

Barnes, Albert C., "Day-Dreaming in Art Education," *Journal of the Barnes Foundation*, vol.2, no.2, April, 1926.

Barnes, Albert C., *A Disgrace to Philadelphia*, Philadelphia, PA: Friends of Art and Education, 1938.

Barnes, Albert C., "Art as Experience," *The Educational Frontier*, no.13, 1939.

Barnes, Albert C., "Method in Aesthetics," *The Philosophy of The Common Man: Essays in Honor of John Dewey to Celebrate His Eightieth Birthday*, New York: G. P. Putnam's Sons, 1940.

Barnes, Albert C., "The Educational Philosophy of John Dewey," *The Humanist*, Winter, 1946.

Barnes, Albert C., *The Art in Painting*, Merion, PA: The Barnes Foundation Press, 2000.

Barnes, Albert C. and de Mazia, Violette, *The French Primitives and Their Forms: From Their Origin to the End of the Fifteenth Century*, Marion, PA: The Barnes Foundation Press, 1931.

Barnes, Albert C. and de Mazia, Violette, *The Art of Henri Matisse*, New York: Charles Scribner's Sons, 1933.

Barnes, Albert C. and de Mazia, Violette, *The Art of Renoir*, New York: Minton, Balch, 1935.

Barnes, Albert C. and de Mazia, Violette, *The Art of Cézanne*, Marion, PA: The Barnes Foundation Press, 1939.

Becker, Carl, L., *The Declaration of Independence: A Study in the History of Political Ideas*, New York: Alfred A. Knopf, 1942.

Bell, Daniel, "Adjusting Men to Machines: Social Scientists Explore the World of the Factory," *Commentary*, vol.3, no.1, January, 1947.

Benjamin, Walter, *Das Kunstwerk im Zeitalter seiner technischen Reproduzierbarkeit*, Berlin: Suhrkamp, 2013.

Bernstein, Richard J., *The Restructuring of Social and Political Theory*, Philadelphia, PA: University of Pennsylvania Press, 1978.

Bernstein, Richard J., *Beyond Objectivism and Relativism: Science, Hermeneutics, and Praxis*, Oxford: B. Blackwell, 1983.

Bernstein, Richard J., *The New Constellation: The Ethical-Political Horizons of Modernity/ Postmodernity*, Cambridge, UK: Polity Press, 1991.

Bingham, Alfred M., "Books," *Common Sense*, vol.4, 1935.

Bowers, C. A., *The Progressive Educator and the Depression: The Radical Years*, New York: Random House, 1969.

Buehrer, Edwin T., "In Defense of Liberalism," *The Christian Century*, vol.52, no.1210, 25 September 1935.

Buermeyer, Laurence, "An Experiment in Education," *The Nation*, vol.120, no.3119, 15 April 1925.

Buermeyer, Laurence, "The Graphic Sketch Club and Art Education," *Journal of the Barnes Foundation*, vol.1, no.1, April, 1925.

Buermeyer, Laurence, "Art and the Ivory Tower," *Journal of the Barnes Foundation*, vol.1, no.2, May, 1925.

Buermeyer, Laurence, "Art and Day-Dreaming," *Journal of the Barnes Foundation*, vol.1, no.2, May, 1925.

Buermeyer, Laurence, *The Aesthetic Experience*, Merion, PA: The Barnes Foundation Press, 1929.

Burke, Kenneth, "Liberalism's Family Tree," *The New Republic*, vol.86, no.1109, 4 March 1936.

Cahill, Holger, *New Horizons in American Art*, New York: The Museum of Modern Art, 1936.

Cahn, Steven M. (ed.), *New Studies in the Philosophy of John Dewey*, Hanover, NH: University Press of New England, 1977.

Chamberlain, John, "The World in Books," *Current History*, vol.43, 1935.

Chubb, John E. and Moe, Terry M., *Politics, Markets, and America's Schools*, Washington, DC: The Brookings Institution, 1990.

Cohen, Nancy, *The Reconstruction of American Liberalism, 1865–1914*, Chapel Hill, NC; London: The University of North Carolina Press, 2002.

Cohen, Sol, *Progressives and Urban School Reform: The Public Education Association of New York City 1895–1954*, New York: Bureau of Publications, 1964.

Columbia Associates in Philosophy, *An Introduction to Reflective Thinking*, Boston, MA: Houghton Mifflin, 1923.

Counts, George S., *Dare the School Build a New Social Order?*, New York: Arno Press & The New York Times, 1969.

Cremin, Lawrence A. *The Transformation of the School: Progressivism in American Education 1876–1957*, New York: Vintage Books, 1964.

Croce, Benedett, "On the Aesthetics of Dewey," *The Journal of Aesthetics & Art Criticism*, vol.6, March, 1948.

Czitrom, Daniel J., *Media and the American Mind: From Morse to McLuhan*, Chapel Hill, NC: University of North Carolina Press, 1982.

Danto, Arthur, "Every Straw Was the Last," *New York Times Book Review*, 22 November 1987.

Darling-Hammond, Linda, *Powerful Teacher Education: Lessons from Exemplary Programs*, San Francisco, CA: Jossey-Bass, 2006.

de Selincourt, O., "New Books: The Public and Its Problems," *Mind: A Quarterly Review of Psychology and Philosophy*, vol.37, 1928.

Dewey, John, *Democracy and Education*, New York: Macmillan, 1916.

Dewey, John, *Reconstruction in Philosophy*, New York: Henry Holt, 1920.

Dewey, John, "Dedication Address," *Journal of the Barnes Foundation*, vol.1, no.2, May, 1925.

Dewey, John, "Experience, Nature and Art," *Journal of the Barnes Foundation*, vol.1, no.3, October, 1925.

Dewey, John, "Individuality and Experience," *Journal of the Barnes Foundation*, vol.2, no.1, January, 1926.

Dewey, John, "Affective Thought in Logic and Painting," *Journal of the Barnes Foundation*, vol.2, no.2, April, 1926.

Dewey John, *The Public and Its Problems*, Denver, CO: Alan Swallow, 1927.

Dewey, John, "In Response," *John Dewey: The Man and His Philosophy, Address Delivered in New York in Celebration of His Seventieth Birthday*, Cambridge, MA: Harvard University Press, 1930.

Dewey, John, *How We Think: A Restatement of the Relation of Reflective Thinking to the Educational Process*, Boston, MA: D. C. Heath, 1933.

Dewey, John, *Experience and Education*, New York: Macmillan, 1938.

Dewey, John, *Education Today*, New York: G.P. Putnam's Sons, 1940.

Dewey, John, *Problems of Men*, New York: Philosophical Library, 1946.

Dewey, John, "A Comment on the Foregoing Criticism," *The Journal of Aesthetics & Art Criticism*, vol.6, March, 1948.

Dewey, John, *Experience and Education*, translated by Harada, Minoru, Tokyo: Shunju-sha, 1950.

Dewey, John, *Philosophy of Education, Problems of Men*, Totowa, NJ: Littlefield, Adams, 1958.

Dewey, John, *The Early Works of John Dewey, 1882–1898*, 5 vols, Boydston, Jo Ann (ed.), Carbondale, IL: Southern Illinois University Press, 1967–1972.

Dewey, John, *Education Today*, translated by Sugiura, Hiroshi, Ishida, Satoru, Tokyo: Meiji Tokyo Shuppan, 1974.

Dewey, John, *Problems of Men*, translated by Sugiura, Hiroshi, Taura, Takeo, Tokyo: Meiji Tokyo Shuppan, 1976.

Dewey, John, *The Middle Works of John Dewey, 1899–1924*, 15 vols, Boydston, Jo Ann (ed.), Carbondale, IL: Southern Illinois University Press, 1976–1983.

Dewey, John, *The Later Works of John Dewey, 1925–1953*, 17 vols, Boydston, Jo Ann (ed.), Carbondale, IL: Southern Illinois University Press, 1981–1991.

Dewey, John, *The School and Society, The Child and the Curriculum*, Chicago, IL: The University of Chicago Press, 1990.

Dewey, John, *The Correspondence of John Dewey, 1871–1952*, Hickman, Larry A. (ed.), InteLex, 2005.

Dewey, John, Barnes, Albert C., Buermeyer, Laurence, Mullen, Mary and de Mazia, Violette, *Art and Education*, Merion, PA.: The Barnes Foundation Press, 1954.

Dewey, John and Kallen, Horace M. (eds.), *The Bertrand Russell Case*, New York: Da Capo Press, 1972.

Du Bois, W. E. B., *The Souls of Black Folk*, Oxford: Oxford University Press, 2007.

Du Bois, W. E. B., *Darkwater: Voices from within the Veil*, Oxford: Oxford University Press, 2007.

Dykhuizen, George, *The Life and Mind of John Dewey*, Boydston, Jo Ann (ed.), Carbondale, IL: Southern Illinois University Press, 1973.

Edman, Irwin, "Art as Intelligence," *The Nation*, vol.120, no.3112, 25 February 1925.

Fott, David, *John Dewey: America's Philosopher of Democracy*, Lanham, MD: Rowman & Littlefield, 1998.

Friedman, Milton & Rose, *Free to Choose: A Personal Statement*, New York: Harcourt Brace Jovanovich, 1980.

Friends of Art and Education, "Program of Friends of Art and Education," 1212, vol.2, no.2, The Artists' Union 1212 Walnut St., Philadelphia, PA, March, 1938.

Fuiman, Harry, *The Progressive Decay of the Pennsylvania Museum of Art*, Philadelphia, PA: Friends of Art and Education, 1938.

Galbraith, John, Kenneth, *The Great Crash 1929*, Boston, MA; New York: Houghton Mifflin, 1997.

Garrison, Jim (ed.), *The New Scholarship on Dewey*, Dordrecht; Boston, MA: Kluwer Academic, 1995.

Geuss, Raymond, *Public Goods, Private Goods*, Princeton, NJ: Princeton University Press, 2001.

Giroux, Henry A., *Border Crossings, Cultural Workers and the Politics of Education*, New York; London: Routledge, 1993.

Greenfeld, Howard, *The Devil and Dr. Barnes: Portrait of an American Art Collector*, New York: Penguin Books, 1989.

Habermas, Jürgen, *Theorie des kommunikativen Handelns*, Frankfurt am Main: Suhrkamp, 1981.

Habermas, Jürgen, *Strukturwandel der Öffentlichkeit*, Frankfurt am Main: Suhrkamp, 1990.

Habermas, Jürgen, *Erläuterungen zur Diskursethik*, Frankfurt am Main: Suhrkamp, 1991.

Habermas, Jürgen, *Faktizität und Geltung: Beiträge zur Diskurstheorie des Rechts und des demokratischen Rechtsstaats*, Frankfurt am Main: Suhrkamp, 1998.

Hart, Henry, *Philadelphia's Shame: An Analysis of Un-American Administration of the Federal Art Project in Philadelphia*, Philadelphia, PA: Friends of Art and Education, 1938.

Hartman, Gertrude, *The Child and His World: An Interpretation of Elementary Education as a Social Process*, New York: E. P. Dutton, 1922.

Hartz, Louis, *The Liberal Tradition in America: An Interpretation of American Political Thought Since the Revolution*, New York: Harcourt, Brace, 1955.

Hazlitt, Henry, "John Dewey's History and Analysis of 'Liberalism,'" *New York Times Book Review*, 1 September 1935.

Hickman, Larry H. (ed.), *Reading Dewey: Interpretations for a Postmodern Generation*, Bloomington, IN: Indiana University Press, 1998.

Hidaka, Ikki, *Bertrand Russell: Love and Marriage*, Kashutsu Shobo Shinsha, 1974.

Hirsch, E. D. Jr, *Cultural Literacy: What Every American Needs to Know*, Boston, MA: Houghton Mifflin, 1987.

Honneth, Axel, *Das Andere der Gerechtigkeit: Aufsätze zur praktischen Philosophie*, Frankfurt am Main: Suhrkamp, 2000.

Hook, Sidney, *Pragmatism and the Tragic Sense of Life*, New York: Basic Books, 1974.

Horkheimer, Max and Adorno, Theodor W., *Dialektik der Aufklärung: Philosophische Fragmente*, Amsterdam: Querido Verlag, 1947.

Hoy, Terry, *The Political Philosophy of John Dewey: Towards a Constructive Renewal*, Westport, CT: Praeger, 1998.

Jackson, Philip W., *John Dewey and the Lessons of Art*, New Haven, CT: Yale University Press, 1998.

Kallen, Horace M., "Salvation by Intelligence," *Saturday Review of Literature*, 13 December 1935.

Kilpatrick, William Heard (ed.), *The Educational Frontier*, New York: D. Appleton-Century, 1933.

Kilpatrick, William H., "Launching The Social Frontier," *The Social Frontier: A Journal of Educational Criticism and Reconstruction*, vol.1, no.1, October, 1934.

Knight, Frank H., "Pragmatism and Social Action," *The International Journal of Ethics: A Quarterly Devoted to the Advancement of Ethical Knowledge and Practices*, vol.46, January, 1936.

Krugman, Paul, *The Conscience of a Liberal*, New York: W. W. Norton, 2007.

Kudo, Yasuyo, *The Public Art Policy: The Transformation of the Publicness of Art and Cultural Policy in America*, Tokyo: Keiso Shobo, 2008.

Lagemann, Ellen C. *An Elusive Science: The Troubling History of Education Research*, Chicago, IL: The University of Chicago Press, 2000.

Lamprecht, Sterling P., "Philosophy Put in Touch With Affairs," *New York Herald Tribune Books*, 27 November 1927.

Lewis, David Levering, *W. E. B. Du Bois: The Fight for Equality and the American Century 1919–1963*, New York: Henry Holt, 2000.

Lippmann, Walter, *Public Opinion*, New York: Macmillan, 1922.

Lippmann, Walter, *An Inquiry into the Principles of the Good Society*, Westport, CT: Greenwood Press, 1973.

Lippmann, Walter, *The Phantom Public*, New Brunswick, NJ: Transaction, 1993.

Locke, John, *Two Treaties of Government*, London: Cambridge University Press, 1970.

Lovett, Robert Morss, "A Real Public," *The New Republic*, vol.52, no.664, 24 August 1927.

Malherbe, Ernst Gideon (ed.), *Educational Adaptations in a Changing Society*, Cape Town; Johannesburg: Juta, 1937.

Meyers, Mary Ann, *Art, Education, and African-American Culture: Albert Barnes and the Science of Philanthropy*, New Brunswick, NJ: Transaction, 2004.

Mitchell, Lucy Sprague, *Two Lives: The Story of Wesley Clair Mitchell and Myself*, New York: Simon and Schuster, 1953.

Mizoguchi, Yuzo, "The Public and Private in Chinese History of Thought," Sasaki, Takeshi, Kim, Tea-Chang (eds), *The History of Thought of the Public and Private: Public Philosophy*, vol.I, Tokyo: University of Tokyo Press, 2001.

Mizubayashi, Takeshi, "The Prototype and Development of the Japanese-style 'Public-Private' Distinction," Sasaki, Takeshi, Kim, Tea-Chang (eds), *The Public and Private in Japan: Public Philosophy*, vol.III, Tokyo: University of Tokyo Press, 2002,

Mullen, Mary, *An Approach to Art*, Merion, PA: The Barnes Foundation Press, 1923.

Mullen, Mary, "The Barnes Foundation: An Experiment in Education," *Journal of the Barnes Foundation*, vol.1, no.1, April, 1925.

Mullen, Mary, "A First Requisite in Art Education," *Journal of the Barnes Foundation*, vol.1, no.2, May, 1925.

Mullen, Mary, "An Experience in Studying Paintings," *Journal of the Barnes Foundation*, vol.1, no.3, October, 1925.

Mullen, Mary, "Learn to See," *Journal of the Barnes Foundation*, vol.2, no.1, January, 1926.

Mumford, Lewis, *The Myth of the Machine: Technics and Human Development*, New York: Harcourt, 1967.

Munro, Thomas, "A Constructive Program for Teaching Art," *Journal of the Barnes Foundation*, vol.1, no.1, April, 1925.

Munro, Thomas, "College Art Instruction: Its Failure and a Remedy," *Journal of the Barnes Foundation*, vol.1, no.2, May, 1925.

Munro, Thomas, "Franz Cizek and the Free Expression Method," *Journal of the Barnes Foundation*, vol.1, no.3, October, 1925.

Munro, Thomas, "The Dow Method and Public School Art," *Journal of the Barnes Foundation*, vol.2, no.1, January, 1926.

Munro, Thomas, "The Art Academies and Modern Education," *Journal of the Barnes Foundation*, vol.2, no.2, April, 1926.

New York Times, "Dr. Dewey Praises Russia's Schools," 6 December 1928.

New York Times, "Socialist Candidates," 4 November 1932.

New York Times, "Dr. Dewey Regulates Judges. But Not Children," 23 February 1937.

New York Times, "New Group Fights Any Freedom Curb," 15 May 1939.

New York Times, "Philosophy of Americanism," 20 October 1939.

Niebuhr, Reinhold, "The Pathos of Liberalism," *The Nation*, vol.141, no.3662, 11 September 1935.

Noddings, Nel, *The Challenge to Care in Schools: An Alternative Approach to Education*, New York: Teachers College Press, 1992.

North American, "Art Critics Flay Barnes Foundation," 20 May 1924.

Palyi, Melchior, "Book Reviews," *The American Journal of Sociology*, vol.44, no.3, November, 1938.

Paringer, William A., *The Paradox of Liberal Reform: A Critique of Deweyan Praxis*, Ann Arbor, MI: UMI, 1989.

Park, Robert E., "Book Reviews: The Public and Its Problems," *The American Journal of Sociology*, vol.34, 1928.

Parker, Walter C., *Teaching Democracy: Unity and Diversity in Public Life*, New York: Teachers College Press, 2003.

People's Lobby Bulletin, "Liberalism and Social Action," vol.5, no.10, February, 1936.

Pepper, Stephen, "Book Reviews: The Public and Its Problems," *The International Journal of Ethics: A Quarterly Devoted to the Advancement of Ethical Knowledge and Practice*, vol.38, 1927–1928.

Pepper, Stephen, "The Development of Contextualisitic Aesthetics," *Antioch Review*, vol.28, 1968.

Philadelphia Inquirer, "Foundation Fights Tax; A. C. Barnes Protests City Levy on Property in Suit," 1 October 1930.

Progressive Education Association, *Progressive Education Advances: Report on a Program to Educate American Youth for Present-Day Living*, New York, London: D. Appleton-Century, 1938.

Progressive Education Association, *Frontiers of Democracy*, vol.10, New York, 1943.

Public Ledger, "Dr. Barnes Gives $6,000,000 for Art Museum in Merion," 13 January 1923.

Public Ledger, "African Art Work for Merion Museum is Most Comprehensive in the World," 5 February 1923.

Putnam, Hilary, *Reason, Truth and History*, Cambridge, MA: Cambridge University Press, 1981.

Putnam, Hilary, *Realism and Reason*, Cambridge, MA: Cambridge University Press, 1983.

Putnam, Hilary, *The Collapse of the Fact/Value Dichotomy and Other Essays*, Cambridge, MA; London: Harvard University Press, 2002.

Putnam, Hilary, *Ethics without Ontology*, Cambridge, MA: Harvard University Press, 2004.

Ravitch, Diane, *Left Back: A Century of Battles over School Reform*, New York: Simon & Schuster, 2000.

Read, Herbert, *Education Through Art*, London: Faber and Faber, 1943.

Rockefeller, Steven C., *John Dewey: Religious Faith and Democratic Humanism*, New York: Columbia University Press, 1991.

Rorty, Richard, *Philosophy and the Mirror of Nature*, Princeton, NJ: Princeton University Press, 1979.

Rorty, Richard, *Contingency, Irony, and Solidarity*, Cambridge; New York: Cambridge University Press, 1989.

Rorty, Richard, *Objectivity, Relativism, and Truth*, Cambridge; New York: Cambridge University Press, 1991.

Rorty, Richard, *Philosophy and Social Hope*, London: Penguin Books, 1999.

Rugg Harold, *Man and His Changing Society*, Boston, MA: Gin, 1929–1939, 14 vols.

Russell, Bertrand, *Principles of Social Reconstruction*, London: George Allen and Unwin, 1916.

Russell, Bertrand, *Marriage and Morals*, New York: Liveright, 1929.

Russell, Bertrand, *A History of Western Philosophy, and Its Connection with Political and Social Circumstances from the Earliest Times to the Present Day*, London: G. Allen & Unwin, 1946.

Russell, Bertrand, *The Conquest of Happiness*, London: Unwin Books, 1961.

Russell, Bertrand, *The Autobiography of Bertrand Russell 1914–1944*, Oxford: Routledge, 2000.

Ryan, Alan, *John Dewey and the High Tide of American Liberalism*, New York: W. W. Norton, 1995.

Schack, William, *Art and Argyrol: The Life and Career of Dr. Albert C. Barnes*, New York: Yoseloff, 1960.

Schilpp, Paul Arthur (ed.), *The Philosophy of John Dewey*, Chicago, IL: Northwestern University Press, 1939.

School Management, "Dewey Favors Federal Department of Education," vol.3, no.4, April, 1934.

School Management, "John Dewey Asks Rotarians to Cooperate with Schools in Character Development," vol.4, no.1, October, 1934.

Sennett, Richard, *The Fall of Public Man*, Cambridge: Cambridge University Press, 1977.

Shaw, A. H., "De Medici in Merion," *The New Yorker*, 22 September 1928.

Shusterman, Richard, *Pragmatist Aesthetics: Living Beauty, Rethinking Art*, Oxford; Cambridge, MA: B. Blackwell, 1992.

Smith, Adam, *Wealth of Nations*, Buffalo, NY: Prometheus Books, 1991.

Steel, Ronald, *Walter Lippmann and the American Century*, Boston, MA: Little, Brown, 1980.

Temin, Peter, *Lessons from the Great Depression: The Lionel Robbins Lectures for 1989*, Cambridge, MA: MIT, 1989.

The Barnes Foundation, "The Educational Program of the Barnes Foundation," *Journal of the Barnes Foundation*, vol.1, no.1, April, 1925.

The Barnes Foundation, "Notes and Comments," *Journal of the Barnes Foundation*, vol.1, no.1, April, 1925.

The Committee for Cultural Freedom, "Manifesto," *The Nation*, vol.148, no.22, 27 May 1939.

The Committee of the Progressive Education Association on Social and Economic Problems, *A Call to the Teachers of the Nation*, New York: John Day, 1933.

The John Dewey Society, *The Teacher and Society, First Yearbook of the John Dewey Society*, New York, London: D. Appleton-Century, 1937.

The John Dewey Society, *Educational Freedom and Democracy, Second Yearbook of the John Dewey Society*, New York, London: D. Appleton-Century, 1938.

The John Dewey Society, *Democracy and the Curriculum: The Life and Program of The American School, Third Yearbook of the John Dewey Society*, New York, London: D. Appleton-Century, 1939.

The John Dewey Society, *Teachers for Democracy, Fourth Yearbook of the John Dewey Society*, New York, London: D. Appleton-Century, 1940.

The New Republic, "Liberty and Common Sense," vol.99, no.1278, 31 May 1939.

The Preliminary Commission of Inquiry, *The Case of Leon Trotsky: Report of Hearings on the Charges Made against Him in the Moscow Trials*, New York; London: Harper & Brothers, 1937.

The President's Research Committee on Social Trends, *Recent Social Trends in the United States*, McGraw-Hill, 1933.

The Social Frontier, "Editorials," *The Social Frontier: A Journal of Educational Criticism and Reconstruction*, vol.1, no.1, October, 1934.

Thorndike, Edward L., *Educational Psychology*, New York: Arno Press, 1969.

Thorndike, Edward L., *The Measurement of Intelligence*, New York: Arno Press, 1973.

Time, "Art," 14 February 1938,

Tocqueville, Charles Alexis Henri Maurice Clerel de, *Democracy in America*, New York: A. A. Knopf, 1987.

Tsurumi, Shunsuke, "The Outline of the Development of Pragmatism," *Iwanami Lectures on Modern Thought, vol.6: People and Freedom*, Tokyo: Iwanami Shoten, 1952.

Tsurumi, Shunsuke, *Studies of Marginal Art*, Tokyo: Chikuma Shobo, 1999.

Tyack, David, *Seeking Common Ground: Public Schools in a Diverse Society*, Cambridge, MA: Harvard University Press, 2003.

Wallace, Graham, *The Great Society*, New York: Macmillan, 1914.

Wallace, Graham, *Human Nature in Politics*, New Brunswick, NJ: Transaction Books, 1981.

Washington Post, "John Dewey, Great American Liberal, Denounces Russian Dictatorship," 19 December 1937.

Watson, John B., *Psychology: From the Standpoint of a Behaviorist*, Philadelphia, PA: Lippincott, 1919.

Westbrook, Robert B., *John Dewey and American Democracy*, Ithaca, NY: Cornell University Press, 1991.

Whitehead, Alfred North, *Science and the Modern World*, Cambridge: Cambridge University Press, 1925.

Winters, Elmer, "Man and His Changing Society," *History of Education Quarterly*, no.7, 1967.

Yamawaki, Naoshi, *Glocal Public Philosophy: A Vision of Good Societies in the 21st Century*, Tokyo: University of Tokyo Press, 2008.

Index